CHSP
HUNGARIAN STUDIES SERIES
NO. 27

EDITORS
Peter Pastor
Ivan Sanders

Attila Seres

HUNGARIAN-SOVIET ECONOMIC RELATIONS, 1920–1941

Translated from the Hungarian by
THOMAS J. AND HELEN D. DEKORNFELD

Social Science Monographs, Boulder, Colorado

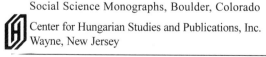 Center for Hungarian Studies and Publications, Inc.
Wayne, New Jersey

Distributed by Columbia University Press, New York
2012

EAST EUROPEAN MONOGRAPHS
NO. DCCLXXXIX

Originally published as *Magyar-szovjet gazdasági kapcsolatok 1920–1941*
© 2010 Attila Seres

© 2012 Attila Seres
© 2012 Center for Hungarian Studies and
Publications, Inc.
47 Cecilia Drive, Wayne, New Jersey
07470–4649
E-mail: pastorp@mail.montclair.edu

Library of Congress Control Number 2012931115
ISBN 978–0–88033–692–5

Printed in the United States of America

CONTENTS

ACKNOWLEDGMENTS

It has been more than half a decade since the history of the political and economic relations between the Soviet Union and Hungary, a problem area handled quite ambivalently by Hungarian historiography prior to that time, became the focal point of my scholarly interest. Right at the beginning of my studies I felt that the reexamination of this historical problem, because of the fragmentation of its source materials, its international complexities and the linguistic competency essential for the study, made this a much greater challenge than the study of a strictly national or of a local historical problem. In these areas the researcher could work with relatively readily circumscribed sources which could usually be found in the local, urban, or provincial archives. The research difficulties were due not so much to the problems of arranging the various trips to Russia, but to the problems in overcoming the bureaucratic and administrative barriers which characterize the Russian archives and which created highly unfavorable working conditions, unknown to most Hungarian scholars and difficult for them to comprehend.

I would certainly not have been able to engage in productive research activities if I did not have individuals standing behind me and providing me regularly with professional advice and personal encouragement. First and foremost I wish to thank the members of my family, my wife Szilvi, my mother and my sister for the endless patience and understanding they have shown during many years and long absences. When I was writing my book they were my principal support. The essential institutional framework, the professional support, the existential background and confidence necessary for my studies, as well as the important relaxed working environment was provided for me by the Institute of History of the Hungarian Academy of Sciences and supported by its director, Ferenc Glatz. I am truly grateful for his assistance. I would also like to extend my thanks to Péter Sipos who drew my attention to the research opportunities inherent in this area and who later became my doctoral dissertation advisor. My work then became the basis for this book. Thanks are also due to Tibor Hajdu and Pál Pritz for having reviewed the manuscript of my dissertation from a scholarly perspective and contributed to the proper nuances of its content, its completeness, and its style. A very special acknowledgment is due to Éva Mária Varga, the head of the Institute of Hungarian Archives in Moscow and to the Russian historians Olga V. Khavanova and Aleksandr S. Stikhalin, who have all made inestimable contributions to my studies during my trips to Russia as well as assisting me in the arrangement of the administrative problems related to my research work. The same is true for Attila Kolontári who most generously made the Russian documents he discovered during his studies available to me. It would be most improper if I would not mention the historians, considerably wiser and more experienced than I, who have followed my activities with interest and support over a number of years. They include Lajos Gecsényi, Emil Palotás, Emil Niederhauser, István Vida, Peter Pastor, Béla Zseliczky and Tamás Krausz.

Attila Seres

TABLES

INTRODUCTION

During the two decades between the end of World War I and the beginning of World War II the Hungarian economy was repeatedly in serious difficulties and even, occasionally, in crisis. Such a critical situation arose after the end of World War I and the signing of the Trianon Peace Treaty when the costs of the war and, primarily, the loss of huge areas brought the economy of the country to the verge of collapse. Another critical period was between 1929 and 1933 when the Great Depression sweeping over Europe caused a severe recession in Hungary. At the time of the outbreak of World War II Hungary had to struggle with such serious shortages in raw materials that the security and continuity of productivity of the national economy was in serious jeopardy. At the time of the economic upheavals one of the ways in which productivity could be kept in balance and even started on a pathway toward growth was to improve the country's balance of payments and strengthening the country's international economic position thereby attracting foreign capital into the country. This in turn would improve and increase industrial and agricultural investments. Another approach was the support of export oriented production via the discovery of new markets and other economic measures.

It was at the time of the above mentioned crises that economists and the responsible government officials increasingly came to the conclusion that it was a desirable option for Hungary if, in addition to its traditional commercial partners such as the successor states of the Austro-Hungarian Monarchy, particularly Austria and Czechoslovakia, it could open a market with the Soviet Union which controlled practically a whole continent and had apparently inexhaustible sources of raw materials. In addition to the significant geographic and economic parameters of the Soviet state it was also an important factor that in contrast to Hungary, which by its geographic position and size was forced to adapt itself to the world's economic system, the Soviet economy, while not entirely independent from global trends, showed a number of unique features in its structural base and management principles and was thus less exposed to international effects. This type of "uniqueness" was one of the reasons why at the time of the Great Depression the Soviet economy remained intact and even underwent advances in heavy industry and infrastructure, which were made possible by the coerced "Great Breakthrough" at a cost of significant sacrifices.

To date an unprejudiced primary source-centered historical analysis of Hungarian-Soviet economic relations between the two World Wars, has not been undertaken. The need for a modern monograph focusing on this topic in detail is indicated not only by a lacuna in the professional literature but also because the study of the Hungarian system of economic relations in a broader context makes it possible to draw valid conclusions about Hungary's economic scope of action and foreign trade orientation.

We believe that in the "freedom of choice versus predetermined course of action" debate Hungarian historians did not pay sufficient attention to economic perspectives and arguments. Their inclusion in the historical discourse, however, would make it possible to interpret the foreign policy alternatives of the Horthy era, particularly during the second half of the 1930s, in a much clearer framework.

The goal of my work, therefore, is to describe and analyze the evolution of Hungarian-Soviet economic relations between 1920 and 1941, based on Hungarian and Russian primary sources. I also wish to identify the factors which shaped and determined Hungary's external economic activity and how these were adapted to the Soviet markets as parts of the possible basis for the export of Hungarian industrial and agricultural products and for the import of industrial raw materials.

I also consider it to be important to understand to what extent the ideological barriers built by the Hungarians and the Soviets were determinant factors in the economic cooperation between the two countries. This question could be studied within a more general theoretical framework because it is a natural consideration to what extent the economic policies and economic orientation of two totally different hostile political systems, with widely different internal structures, could be reconciled. This clearly is an unavoidable question because in my view in the Hungarian historical literature of the 1950s and 1960s the aversion toward Bolshevism and its principal site, the Soviet Union, by the interwar Hungarian political elite and Hungarian society was overemphasized. Because of the rigid ideological framework, it was impossible to delineate accurately to what extent the memories of the 133 days of the Hungarian Soviet Republic determined the reflexes and the alternatives of Hungarian diplomacy vis-à-vis the Soviet Union and to what extent these memories influenced the evolution of the country's pre-World War II range of activities.

Beyond economic and political relations there is another theoretical economic problem which makes a significant contribution to the assessment of the Hungarian-Soviet relations, particularly those which during 1940 and 1941, were crowned with partial success. The potential place of the state in marketing activities became one of the widely debated themes of economic theory and policy between the two World Wars. This question had been analyzed by representatives of classical school of economics as early as the nineteenth century mainly within the framework of theories based on economic freedom and competition. The most important debates, however, were triggered between the two World Wars, by World War I itself and by the major economic upheavals produced by the Great Depression of 1929–1933 and their effects on the national economy of a number of countries.[1] In the history of the development of Hungarian-Soviet economic relations the 1939–1941 period could be used as a case study of the way the Hungarian state, claiming the pressing interests of the national economy, interfered with free market activities by legislation and by various other methods. A glaring example of government pressure becomes evident to us when we follow the history of the trade treaty made with the Soviet Union and its fate after June 27, 1941.

Chapter One

SOURCES AND LITERATURE

Problems of Researching the Archival Sources

The authors of historical monographs, published prior to regime change, had only limited research opportunities and suffered from restricted access to Soviet archival sources. The opening of the primary Russian sources and their use in the reconstruction of Hungarian-Soviet economic relations between the two World Wars was an important task for two reasons: these sources were either not available for scholarly work at all or only to a very limited extent and also because when placed alongside the much more readily available Hungarian documents it was possible to avoid the danger of offering a one-sided interpretation of the course of the events.

During the first half of the 1990s collections of documents became available in the Russian archives which, prior to that period, were considered to be secret and were hidden from scholarly investigation. The same cannot be said for the specialized archives which are beyond the control of the Russian Federal Archives Service (ROSSARKHIV) such as those in the various ministries. One of these is the Foreign Policy Archive of the Russian Federation (AVP RF) in the Ministry of Foreign Affairs, which contains material essential for the study of economic history.[1] One of the critical sources for the study of Hungarian-Soviet economic and political relations was this archive because the most important segment of the decision-making mechanism of foreign relations of the Soviet Union between 1917 and 1945 was the People's Commissariat for Foreign Affairs, known after 1945 as the Ministry of Foreign Affairs. In this collection of documents we could find the reports from the envoys which provide the most reliable information about the conditions of the Hungarian-Soviet relations. The collection also include the submissions of the board, called "kollegiia" (Kollegiia NKID), the most important section of the Commissariat for Foreign Affairs, which prepared the materials for the decision makers of the Party and state organs. These documents also include the letters and telegrams of the high-ranking foreign affairs officials (commissars, deputy commissars, section heads, etc.), as well as the expert notes and analyses prepared for internal use. Within the administrative hierarchy of the Commissariat for Foreign Affairs, between 1917 and 1945, there was an independent administrative unit which had the responsibility of coordinating the foreign policy with foreign trade policies of the Soviet Union with the other economic administrative authorities, primarily the Commissariat for Foreign Trade. During the 1920s this task was the responsibility of the Economic and Legal Divisions but after the reorganizations, at the beginning of the 1930s, also involving the Commissariat for Foreign Affairs, it became the responsibility of the Economic Division.[2]

Unfortunately the regulations of the Foreign Policy Archives, which determine the rules of access to the documents, are not in conformance with the wide-range international scholarly interest and with the needs of the researchers. The major barrier is that the researchers are not given access to the archival inventories, the so called "opisi," which are essential for their work in unearthing important documents. The documents are selected by the staff of the archives on the basis of the themes submitted to them. The documents are selected arbitrarily. Thus, some documents crucial for the accurate reconstruction of the events, or for the nuances of the complete picture, never come to the researcher's attention. Even though in the archives of the Economics Department of the Commissariat for Foreign Affairs an independent archival collection was established its material is not available for review. In other document collections, such as the reports of the commissars of the Commissariat for Foreign Affairs, and in the one collection, entitled "Hungarian Special Department," consisting of the reports of the Soviet envoys in Hungary, we have found numerous notes, reports and transcripts which allow a closer look at Hungarian-Russian economic relations and of their Soviet interpretation. The administratively imposed research barriers in the Foreign Policy Archive are partially counterbalanced by the documents available from other sources, such as Russian

State Economic Archive (RGAE), which are very helpful in reconstructing the history of Hungarian-Soviet economic relations. It is in this archive that the documents of the highest governmental agency, the Commissariat for Foreign Trade, are preserved. It is in this collection that we can find the correspondence and telegrams between the foreign trade apparatus in Moscow and its tightly controlled trade delegations in other countries.

Copies of the minutes taken at the meetings of the Politburo of the Central Committee of the Russian Communist (Bolshevik) Party, the highest decision making body of the Soviet party-state, can now be found at the Russian State Archive of Social and Political History (RGASPI), which is the successor to the Central Party Archive (Tsentral'nyi Partiinyi Arkhiv) of the Marx-Engels-Lenin Institute (IMEL). The most important decisions affecting international trade relations, the appointment of leaders of the Soviet trade missions in other countries, foreign trade measures and directives to the People's Commissariat for Foreign Trade were made by the Politburo on the basis of submissions from the People's Commissariat for Foreign Affairs and from the People's Commissariat for Foreign Trade.[3] The laconic text of the minutes does not have much informative value because it contains only the essence of the submission and the decisions made on that basis. Occasionally the reason for the decision is included but the background material for the decision making, including the various views expressed in the debate, was usually omitted from the minutes. Yet this material is essential to determine the weight assigned to Hungarian-Soviet economic relations by the Soviet leadership and the level of the administrative apparatus to which it rose.

During the 1920s and 1930s in Hungary the principal administrative structure for foreign economic relations was the Ministry of Commerce. Unfortunately the most important collection of documents in its archives as well as those of its successor, the Ministry of Commerce and Communication was destroyed during the siege of Budapest in 1944–1945.[4] Thus the relatively intact document collection of the Division of Economic Policy of the Ministry of Foreign Affairs became the principal source of material for Hungarian-Soviet economic relations, particularly because in matters of international trade the Ministry of Commerce worked in cooperation with the Ministry of

Foreign Affairs. I did find documents in this collection which originated in the Ministry of Commerce but which did not survive there when that building was destroyed.

In the National Archives of Hungary a separate fond was established for the documents of the Hungarian Legation in Moscow albeit this collection consists primarily of documents dealing with administrative problems of the legation, personnel matters and the architectural problems of the building. Not every report from the ministers, from 1934 to 1941, was present in the archives of the Ministry of Foreign Affairs and some of these missing reports were found scattered through other material in the archives of the Policy Division and of the Economic Policy Division, labeled "general" or "reserved." Fortunately the large majority of the political and economic reports did not vanish. Copies, originally sent from Moscow to the Hungarian legation in Berne survived the war and eventually were taken by emigrants to the US where they were deposited at the Institute on East Central Europe of Columbia University. Later microfilm copies were returned to the National Archives of Hungary.[5]

Our knowledge of Hungarian-Soviet economic relations would not be complete without the sources derived from the Business Document Collection, Section Z, of the National Archives of Hungary. Of principal interest were the documents originating from the organizations interested in the Soviet market, such as The Anglo-Hungarian Bank, The Pest Hungarian Bank of Commerce, the Manfréd Weiss Works, Hungarian State Railway and Machine Industries (MÁVAG), the Ganz Works, etc. These documents throw a light on the business and financial background of Hungarian-Soviet economic relations and contain much data which complement the perspective that can be drawn from the sources in the Ministry of Foreign Affairs.

In studying this area one must not omit paying particular attention to the personal papers of Mihály Jungerth-Arnóthy, the first person to be appointed Hungarian minister in Moscow who played a key role in Hungarian-Soviet relations between the two World Wars. These papers include his autograph diary entries (1920–1944) and the typed recollections of varying length—based on the diary entries which he prepared during World War II. There is probably no other member of the Hungarian diplomatic service during the interwar period who had been studied as extensively in Hungarian historiography.[6] Mihály Jungerth, born in 1883, joined the Ministry of Foreign Affairs in 1919 where he became the head of the Prisoner of War Division until 1923. During 1921 and 1922 he represented Hungary at the negotiations in Denmark and the Baltic States about the return of the Hungarian prisoners of war who were still in Russia. During these negotiations Jungerth acquired considerable information about the political and economic issues of the Soviet republics and was henceforth considered a "Russian expert" at the Ministry of Foreign Affairs. This became a significant factor in his future diplomatic career. After 1923 he was the head of the Talinn (Reval) mission and was accredited during the same year in Latvia, Lithuania and Finland. In 1928 the legation was transferred to Helsinki and until 1933 it was from there that he represented Hungarian interests in the Baltic States. In 1933 he was appointed minister in Ankara in order to prepare the normalization of Hungarian-Soviet relations from there.[7] This seems very likely because from Ankara he was transferred to Rome to represent Hungary in the Hungarian-Soviet negotiations. On March 31, 1934, he was appointed Hungarian minister in Moscow, initially with a dual appointment, preserving his Ankara position.[8] In 1935 he was appointed solely to head the Moscow legation and he remained in this position until 1939.

His personal papers were deposited at the end of the 1940s or the beginning of the 1950s in the Archives of the Labor Movement. Presently this material is in the successor of the above organization: the Archives of Political History and of Trade Unions (PSZL). According to the entries his diary survived only in a fragmentary fashion but it does accurately reflect the most important turning points in Hungarian-Soviet relations, namely the preparations for the 1924 Berlin negotiations, the discussions at the 1934 Rome negotiations and the suspension of the diplomatic relations between the two countries in 1939. Reading the diaries and the memoirs we find that, in comparison to the other material presented above, such as the documents in the Ministry of Foreign Affairs and those related to the Moscow legation, in many instances he recorded events which took place behind the scenes and of which no official report, notes or minutes survive. These include notes of audiences with the regent, Miklós Horthy, the conferences at the Ministry of Foreign Affairs prior to the 1924 and 1934 Hungarian-

Soviet negotiations, and consultations with leading Hungarian diplomats, such as the head of the Political Division, the permanent deputy minister of foreign affairs, etc.

Contradictions in the Literature

In Soviet and Hungarian historiography there were systematic collections of interwar documents published on foreign affairs, some of which were economically relevant. On the Soviet side the most important such source was the series on diplomatic history, the *Documents of the Foreign Policy of the Soviet Union*, and published by an editorial committee made illustrious by the name of Andrei Gromyko, the minister of foreign affairs. The twenty-one volumes covering Soviet foreign policy, between the 1917 October Revolution and 1938, were published between 1957 and 1977. Neither the content of, nor the methodology, measured up to the standards of modern document collections. So far as content was concerned these volumes were assembled in order to show the concept that the efforts of the Soviet Union to create "world peace" were consistent and ongoing. In fact, the volumes endeavored to create a historical precedent for the foreign policy clichés of the Soviet Union characteristic of the post-World War II period. The information available to us today makes it evident that the material was selected accordingly and thus it does not provide us with information about the major directions of Soviet foreign policy. The changes in these directions and the major change from the revolutionary diplomacy of the years after the 1917 October Revolution to the Soviet great power foreign policy of the late 1930s and 1940s focused on the strict protection of national interests. So far as the methodological deficiencies are concerned, it is sufficient to mention that the archival identification of the published documents was not given, making it impossible to use them as guides for additional research. In several of the volumes of this monumental series documents relating to Hungary were published but only those which were politically relevant. These documents were taken from their original context and ignored the most basic rules of source material publication by omitting all those reports, telegrams and instructions which might have complemented the contents of the documents or which might also have placed them in a different light. The editorial board of the volume, consisting of prominent people, even forty years after the fact, failed to publish the minutes and the confidential exchange of letters which preceded the February 6, 1934, exchange of notes between Hungary and the Soviet Union and that was officially backdated to have been issued on February 4.[9] Obviously the editors engaged in a cover up as the unpublished documents indicated that the Soviet Union had suffered a minor loss of prestige.

On the Hungarian side an example of "cover up" and insufficiently careful editing is provided by the five-volume collection of documents, *Iratok az ellenforradalom történetéhez* (Documents for the History of the Counterrevolution), edited by Dezső Nemes and Elek Karsai, and published between 1953 and 1967. When the editors selected the material for these volumes they left out critically important and logically interdependent documents. From the memorandum of the Gyáriparosok Országos Szövetsége (GYOSZ) [National Alliance of Manufacturers], addressed to the government in 1924, they omitted the introductory part which provides a list of the Hungarian-owned industrial and commercial properties nationalized in Russia and of the Hungarian balances still outstanding. The editors gave no reason for this omission which was a dubious practice since this information was not available from any other source. They also omitted the secret correspondence about the limits placed on the staffs of the foreign missions which was an important addendum to the diplomatic agreement of September 5, 1924, and to the September 12 agreement regulating the nature of the diplomatic and economic relations.[10]

The history of the commercial relations between Hungary and the Soviet Union between the two World Wars until 1938 was first studied by József Buzás and published in an essay in 1955.[11] Because of the limited research facilities of the time, the author was unable to discuss essential and decisive problems related to the economic relations of the two countries during the 1920s and 1930s. These problems included such things as the concessions Hungary was given in Soviet agriculture and industry, the establishment of mixed Soviet-Hungarian commercial companies, the extension of the Danubian water transport system, etc. From the perspective of the first half of the 1950s the historical period he chose to investigate was still too recent and he not only had no access to the relevant Soviet archival sources but he was even denied access to the admittedly unorganized material from the recently nationalized private Hungarian companies and commercial banks which was assembled in the Central Economic Archives. This forced him to rely exclusively on the material in the Economic Policy Section of the Ministry of Foreign Affairs. It must be the lack of adequate sources that made him consider the establishment of the Russian-Hungarian Trade Corporation in 1923 as a proven fact.[12] Sources that became available for study at a later date, such as the archives of the Anglo-Hungarian Bank or the documents of the Court of Registration, clearly show that the Hungarian Royal Court, acting as a Court of Registration, refused to grant permission for the formal registration of the new company and thus the company was not included in the registry of companies and was not allowed, under the effective legislation, to engage in any form of commercial activity.[13]

Buzás followed the history of the economic relations between the two countries until 1941 in a monograph co-authored by András Nagy. In the carefully composed volume the authors placed this issue in the artificial context of the antagonism between the Horthy system and the Bolshevik regime.[14] It was easy to demonstrate that the leaders of the counterrevolution, imbued with national-Christian sentiments, had strongly negative sentiments vis-à-vis Communism, particularly after the fall of the Hungarian Soviet Republic in 1919 and the genesis of the successful counterrevolutionary government. The ideological antagonism of the two fundamentally different systems could be clearly followed until the very end of the era. At the same time it was difficult to interpret the other obvious historical fact that the government of the Hungarian counterrevolutionary system, identifying itself as a strong opponent of the collective system, later established political and economic relations with the Soviet Union, which was referred to as the "principal nest of Bolshevism." Finding a solution for this glaring contradiction would have required a much more differentiated and rational approach. In spite of this it must be said that, from the second half of the 1940s until the 1970s, the majority of the Hungarian authors approached these topics on an ideological basis. They attempted to throw light on the political-economic relations between the two countries from the perspective of Soviet foreign affairs by applying post-

1945 clichés to the pre-1941 conditions. From the scholarly works of those years the only thing that becomes apparent is the dichotomy between a major power, "endeavoring to maintain peace in Europe" and tolerant toward the small countries on one side and a deceptive political leadership focusing on the exploitation of the economic resources of the Soviet state while engaging in aggressive anti-Soviet activities on the other.[15]

Changes appear only in the scholarly works of the authors in the 1980s who used the available source material more circumspectly and discussed the relations between the countries more objectively. By that time there was a change in the context of the historical studies of the era because after the 1970s the effects of the scholarly debate about the nature of the counterrevolutionary system became apparent. These debates resulted in a more nuanced analysis of not only to the organizational structure and functions of the system but also of its foreign policy and economic policy.[16] The short monograph of György Ránki, published in 1981, must be given recognition. In this study he discussed the earlier processes of international relations in a new way, namely in the context of economic freedom of movement and of foreign economic activities. He also studied the interdependence of foreign and economic policies and the effects of the regional economic endeavors of the great powers on their foreign policy.[17] In 1986 György Kövér published an objective review on the Hungarian-Soviet economic relations between the two World Wars which emphasized the central problems of the issue.[18]

Studies in Hungarian economic history could now rely on a number of syntheses published after 1989. These, however, are summaries which study Hungary's global and regional foreign economic activities and the related foreign trade orientation only in general terms.[19] We do not have a contemporary monograph that had the goal of showing every aspect of Hungary's 1918–1941 foreign trade policy and within this a detailed discussion of the existing commercial relations with the neighboring countries and the major European powers, like the Soviet Union. In discussing international trade activity the authors of the surveys focus almost exclusively on the existing bilateral economic agreements between Hungary and its historically and politically traditional economic partners, namely the successor states: Austria, Czechoslovakia,

Romania, and Yugoslavia and, even more so, Germany and Italy. This leaves open the question of why the economic rapprochement between Hungary and the Soviet Union really got under way in 1939. Were the motives based on the general economic situation which made the Hungarian government increasingly anxious to reach an economic agreement with the Soviet Union? In the Hungarian academic literature on economics we find only suggestive comments about the cost of the upturn in Hungarian economy, based on the 1938 Győr program, and the authors generally fail to mention that this economic boom had to be maintained while there was a drastic reduction in the availability of raw materials needed for the increased production. It is true that János Honvári and Béla Csikós-Nagy suggested that after the start of the war and the establishment of the maritime blockade between Germany and Great Britain and after Italy's entry into the war the Hungarian options for obtaining raw materials from abroad were significantly curtailed. This had a strong negative effect on some branches of industry.[20]

In preparing my statistical tables I took the *Magyar Statisztikai Közlemények* (Hungarian Statistical Reports) series, issued by the Royal Hungarian Central Statistical Office, as my source. On the basis of the data in the series it was possible to learn not only about the intensity of the commercial activities, their volume and their balance, but also about the composition of the merchandise and about the production profiles. The only "blemish" of the series is that it does not contain data about the 1920–1924 Hungarian-Soviet trade activities because at that time no data were assembled in Hungary about the Soviet Union. Publication of the new series of foreign trade data in *Magyar Statisztikai Közlemények* began in 1929 and it was at this time that data for the 1922–1926 foreign trade activities were produced retroactively. Soviet statistics are also available. A Soviet collection of foreign trade data was published in 1939 and a later collection, published in 1960, both contain only an anemic analysis of the 1922–1924 foreign trade activities. One of the difficulties in analyzing the Soviet data is that in conformity with the Soviet economic reporting system, the fiscal year began on July 1 and ended on June 30 of the following year. It was only in January 1929 that the Soviet statistics began to follow the system of reporting economic statistical data traditional in the rest of Europe. Prior to 1929 therefore the Soviet data and the Hungarian ones do not overlap and make comparisons difficult. In the Soviet volumes I frequently found incomplete series of data and internally contradictory information. As an example: the 1939 Soviet collection does not include the composition of the goods exported to or imported from various countries.[21] It is of interest that the editors of the *Magyar Statisztikai Szemle* (Hungarian Statistical Review) published an issue which had as its principal goal a description of the demographic and economic geography of the Soviet Union. This was the first attempt to summarize the results of the research of the Hungarian statistical sciences relative to the Soviet Union and for this reason the issue of the review, produced in a sound and scholarly fashion, can be viewed as the catalog of all of the information available about the Soviet Union. In this issue László Pap published a study about the foreign trade of the Soviet Union which makes it possible to some extent to research and check the Hungarian data in a retrospective fashion.[22]

Chapter Two

ATTEMPTS AT CAPTURING THE SOVIET MARKET AFTER THE TRIANON PEACE TREATY

Conditions for Hungarian-Soviet Economic Relations

Other than the significant loss in territory and population one of the most serious consequences of the peace treaties after World War I was the drastic reduction in the country's potential for economic productivity. This was due to the collapse of the unified economic structure of the Austro-Hungarian Monarchy. According to the 1920 census there were nearly eight million people living on the 93,000 square kilometer territory that was left for Hungary after the final settlement of its borders. The Trianon Peace Treaty made Hungary lose more than 70 percent of its territory and nearly 60 percent of its former population. The situation was further aggravated by the serious losses in manpower including the death of almost one million soldiers which caused considerable harm to the productive forces. Of the various branches of the economy the most serious loss was suffered by agriculture the income from which was reduced by almost 60 percent. Industries that suffered the least damage still lost more than 50 percent of their former income.[1]

The economy of the post-Trianon country was relatively more heavily industrialized than that of historic Hungary because the branches of the economy requiring raw materials or semi-finished goods remained in higher concentration within the new borders. Economic conditions thus favored industrialization. The economy, harboring a potentially dynamic development, required essential imports and these could be financed only from exports. Consequently the improvement of the international balance of payments, namely the income from abroad, or derived from economic ties with foreign countries, such as foreign trade, influx of foreign investments and tourism, became determinant factors for the shaping of economic policy. Within the above, there was a need for the strengthening of Hungary's bargaining position and for a positive balance of foreign trade.[2] This was the reason for the Bethlen government, in power throughout most of the 1920s, to concentrate on the promotion of foreign trade and on the establishment of bilateral international agreements. Following the economic recovery and financial stabilization, in 1924, the gradually improving heavy industry (machinery), light industry (textiles and food) and chemical industry had ameliorated export opportunities and in the 1920s a significant percentage of the national income was derived from foreign trade.[3] During the second half of the decade this component of the national income rose to 40 percent.[4] It should be noted that the peculiar economic structure of the country demanded this direction for development. Economic output was still dominated by agriculture and the massive employment in agriculture consistently demanded new markets.

After the war it seemed that the successor states of the Austro-Hungarian Monarchy would constitute obvious partners in the economic cooperation. The many decades-old economic structure of the Dualist state and the commercial networks established among the several regions strongly suggested that the economic unity of the Danube Basin would sooner or later be reestablished. The traditional economic interdependence of Hungary and the various other components of the Monarchy was based, at the end of the nineteenth century, on having a significant part of Hungary's agricultural output shipped to Austria, Bohemia, and Galicia in return for industrial products.[5] Following the dissolution, the Hungarian government reached a commercial agreement with every one of the successor states. On February 11, 1922, a compensatory, reciprocal trade agreement was signed with Czechoslovakia. An agreement was signed with Austria on February 8, 1922, with Yugoslavia on March 22, 1924, and, a most favored nation trade agreement, with Romania on April 16, 1924.[6] During the 1920s Austria and Czechoslovakia were Hungary's most important trading partners and the system established between these countries at the time of the Monarchy remained unchanged after 1920. Hungary was still exporting agricultural products to Austria and to Czechoslovakia and was importing industrial goods and raw materials from both countries. The foreign trade orientation toward the successor states was not without serious hazards. After the Trianon Peace Treaty came into effect the governments of these countries were led by political considerations and endeavored to integrate economically the huge new acquisitions into their territorial assemblage by new investments and new customs policies. These attempts to establish an autarchic, complex national economy presented the grave danger of depriving Hungarian economic production, partially or completely, of its previous sources of raw materials and of its traditional markets. The functioning of Hungarian economic infrastructure was thus at the mercy of the political whims of the Little Entente—Czechoslovakia, Romania, and Yugoslavia.[7]

This servile position induced the Hungarian government to establish economic partnerships with countries which could supply significant quantities of raw material and thus were able to meet the demands of the Hungarian industry. These countries were also larger in size and populations which enabled them to accommodate the products of Hungarian industry and agriculture on their markets. In this way Hungary could make its industry independent of mineral resources that were mined in the former Hungarian territories now under the sovereignty of Czechoslovakia and Romania. Because of geographic proximity, territorial characteristics, the import-export needs, and the traditions of earlier economic ties made two countries especially appealing. These were Germany, whose economy kept improving under the 1924 Dawes Plan, and Soviet Russia which established the New Economic Policy (NEP) and which now offered considerable preferential opportunities to Western countries.

With Germany Hungary had established a temporary economic agreement on June 1, 1920.[8] Although Germany became Hungary's third most important economic partner during this decade, the attempts to base the advances in Hungary's economic productivity on German market acceptance and to orient Hungarian foreign trade toward Germany became difficult due to the peculiarities of the Hungarian economy. As we have seen, Hungarian agricultural products were readily accepted by the more industrialized but agriculturally less favored western and central European countries. Meanwhile Hungarian industry, strongly supported by the Bethlen government, could find markets for its products only in the less developed eastern European and Balkan countries.[9] The USSR had a continent-sized market and apparently inexhaustible supplies of raw materials in addition to outstanding economic parameters. According to the 1926 census the Soviet Union had a population of 147 million living in an area of 17 million square kilometers.[10] It is true, however, that just as Hungary Russia, which was governed by a Soviet Communist regime, emerged from World War I with extremely unfavorable economic and social conditions. Almost all of the areas of the former tsarist Russia were devastated by the Civil War and by international intervention. It is characteristic of the decline in production capacity that the data for 1920, the year when the Civil War and international intervention came to an end, show that the industrial production was only 18 percent when compared to 1913, i.e. the last year of peace. The volume of agricultural production dropped to 40 percent. The depredations of the Civil War completely destroyed the economic infrastructure and caused enormous losses in the forces of production. From the beginning of 1918 to the end of 1920 the population of the country decreased by 8.3 million. In 1920 the productivity was only 27.1 percent of that of 1913. The railway system and roads were largely destroyed and in 1920 the transportation capacity was a mere one third of that in 1917.[11]

The economic policies, based on War Communism of the Civil War period was replaced in 1921 by the NEP which legalized the freedom of internal trade, permitted the establishment of small private enterprises, and made it possible to privatize enterprises employing less than twenty workers. The composite economic structure, combining state properties, cooperative properties and small agricultural and manufacturing properties, contributed not only the basis for internal evolution but also created a political-economic environment far superior to the previous one, for the reestablishment of economic relations between the Soviet Union and the West.[12] According to some data the ordinances promulgated in 1921–1922 resulted in approximately ten thousand enterprises returning to private hands.[13]

At the same time the return of Soviet Russia to the mainstream of European commerce was made difficult by the model of economic control that differed widely from free market capitalism. The Council of Commissars, functioning as the governing body, issued a decree on April 22, 1918, which nationalized foreign trade and introduced a total state monopoly.[14] This meant that in practice all foreign trade transactions were managed by commercial organizations owned by the state. Even though NEP broke the dominance of the state in industry and commerce and made it possible to attract private capital, it did not affect the foreign trade monopoly.

Consequently, signing a bilateral intergovernmental economic agreement became essential for the establishment of systematic and effective commercial traffic between the Western nations and the Soviet Union. This agreement defined the basic principles of the commercial transactions with the Soviet state-owned export and import companies and also regulated the method of payment after the goods had been delivered. The Western capitalist countries also came to the end of the war with a substantial economic deficit and hoped to meet their needs for raw materials, at least partially, by purchases from the Soviet market. These countries therefore had a real interest in reaching an agreement with the Soviet state and thus in 1921–1922 several of them signed an interim commercial agreement with the Soviet Russia. Great Britain signed a treaty on March 16, 1921, Germany on May 6, Austria on December 7, and Italy on December 26. For the Hungarian economic leadership a sharp signal was given by the fact that on July 5, 1922, a Czechoslovak-Soviet trade agreement was signed which opened the path for the Czech agricultural machinery manufacturers, Škoda and Bächer, to the Soviet markets.[15] The principal and profound changes in the system of European commercial liaisons came with the Rapallo trade agreement between Germany and the Soviet Union signed on April 16, 1922. This agreement represented great strength and produced a massive economic upturn that could be taken advantage of by Hungarian economic policies.[16] The agreement with the Western countries made it possible for the Soviet government to open a trade mission in the capital of each country. The Russian representatives enjoyed diplomatic immunity and after a while the offices of the commercial representations were granted extraterritorial rights. The leaders of Soviet foreign affairs regarded these missions as the de facto official legations of the Soviet Union.[17]

Parallel to the opening of the trade missions abroad, the foreign trade structure and network of the Soviet Union's economy came into being. Soviet governmental export and import companies could open offices within the existing Soviet commercial missions. Some of these corporations with specializations were of great interest to Hungary. For lumber exports, Exportles; for textile raw materials, Exportlen; for industrial raw material exports, Promexport; the oil export deliveries, Soyuznefteexport; and the import organization for heavy industry products and partial products, Mashinoimport. These organizations were under the control of the Commissariat for Foreign Trade and thus, indirectly, under the government. This meant that for every business transaction they had to ask permission from their legal supervising body. This made them in effect segments of the state's economic policies and represented the state monopoly on foreign trade.[18]

It should be noted that the Soviet type state presence and the monopoly which extended over almost every phase of the national economy was viewed by Hungary, and indeed by the entire capitalist world, with distaste and rejection. This made clear what was meant in the Hungarian sources of the 1920s and 1930s by the term "one hand system" when referring to the administration of the Soviet economic system and, particularly, to the Soviet foreign commerce organization. It would be more accurate, however, to refer to it as "an economic policy directed by one hand."[19]

The evolution of the economic relations between Hungary and the Soviet Union was made easier by the fact that there were no such problems as the issue of debts and of the nationalized enterprises which weighed heavily on the economic and political relations of other Western powers and the Soviet Union. The postwar economic conditions in the Soviet Union were greatly aggravated by the enormous indebtedness of the country. According to 1924 data, the loans taken on by the tsarist government and, after 1917, by the Provisional Government, primarily for military purposes, amounted to 15.4 billion gold rubles.[20] These debts were not regarded as binding on itself by the Soviet government. The collective governing body, the Federal Central Executive Committee (VTsIK), had promulgated a decree on February 3, 1918, to consider all foreign debts null and void. In the confrontation between the Entente powers and the Soviet Union another economically driven problem was the nationalization of the economic units, industrial and agricultural organizations, banks, etc. that were partially owned by Western capitalist interests. Nationalization of partly foreign-owned properties in Russia produced a total of more than two billion gold rubles for the Soviet Union.[21] The demands for restitutions by the Western countries, particularly by the most heavily involved: Great Britain and France, were rejected by the Soviet government. All of this heavily impacted British-Soviet and French-Soviet relations.

The extent of the Hungarian demands for compensation can be learned from a summary statement, prepared by the National Alliance of Industrialists (GYOSZ) probably in August of 1924, which the association submitted to the government just prior to the Hungarian-Soviet negotiations in Berlin. According to this document the number of Hungarian assets nationalized in the territories of the Soviet states after the October 1917 Revolution and outstanding debts did not represent a significant amount. The largest demand could have been made for the assets of Vielwert-Dedina manufacturing company in Kiev, which manufactured railway equipment and which was at one time part of the Hungarian MÁVAG Corporation. It employed about three hundred workers and, prior to the war, its director was Bertalan Bálint, a Hungarian citizen. The plant survived the Civil War with relatively minimal damage and, according to the GYOSZ data, at the time of nationalization its outstanding balance amounted to four million gold crowns and its fixed assets were worth approximately one million rubles. The remainder of the Hungarian demands consisted of the unpaid bills for materials and goods exported prior to the war. The Ganz Electric Company (Ganz Villamossági Rt.) was owed two hundred thousand rubles, The Hungarian Metal and Lighting Goods Factory (Fém- és Lámpaáru Gyár) one hundred thousand gold crowns, The Pest Hungarian Bank of Commerce (Pesti Magyar Kereskedelmi Bank), thirty-five thousand rubles.[22] A later document, submitted by the Ministry of Finance to the Ministry of Foreign Affairs, revealed that of all the companies and individuals who had suffered losses only the lumber company, owned by the Egressi family, submitted an official report about its loss and stated that its compensatory demands were for one hundred million crowns.[23] This amount was negligible compared to the British and French loans made to the tsarist governments and to the

Provisional Government and to the value of the nationalized British and French properties. The situation was made complicated by the compensation agreement included in the Brest-Litovsk Peace Treaty signed on March 1918 by the Austro-Hungarian Monarchy and Soviet Russia. This agreement, however, referred only to the bilateral waiver of compensation for the military expenditures and for wartime damages. It did not pertain to the prewar loans or to the assets nationalized after the war. During the first half of the 1920s Hungarian and Soviet diplomats were nevertheless bothered by the absence of any arrangement for the settlement of the reparation issue. One of the reasons for this was that in reacting to the revolutions in Germany and Hungary, the VTsIK on November 13, 1918, annulled the Brest-Litovsk Peace Treaty. The same was done by Paragraph 72 of the Trianon Peace Treaty.[24] Paragraph 193 of the Trianon Peace Treaty specifically ordered that Hungary give up all benefits assured to it by the Brest-Litovsk Peace Treaty and by the international agreements complementing that treaty.[25]

Official and Unofficial Ties

Contacts on the highest level between Hungary and Soviet Russia took place for the first time at the International Economic Conference organized by the Entente powers in Genoa on April 10, 1922. Following the Paris Peace Conference, the Genoa meeting was the first large-scale international economic conference where a good number of Europe's victorious and defeated great powers and small states were represented. The official goal of the spectacular meeting was the reestablishment of prewar economic relations but, in fact, the Entente powers were trying to get the Soviet government to repay the loans made to the pre-Soviet governments and to return to the foreign owners the production facilities nationalized after the 1917 October Revolution. They also wanted the Soviet government to compensate the foreign investors who had suffered losses.[26] In order to neutralize the compensation demands of the Entente powers the Council of People's Commissars had established a committee to assess the internal losses caused by the war. This group filed its report with the government on

November 23, 1921, and the report was to serve as a working document for the Soviet delegation getting ready to go to Genoa. The committee estimated that the damages to the national economy caused by the foreign intervention amounted to 107 billion gold rubles and it was this figure that was used by the Soviet delegation at the Genoa Conference.[27] The conference gave an opportunity for the establishment of both official and unofficial relations. The Hungarian delegation was led initially by Prime Minister István Bethlen and after his departure by Miklós Bánffy, the Minister of Foreign Affairs. Under his management the delegation wanted to use the opportunity for political maneuvering and for gaining the acceptance of certain economic proposals. The principal European political and economic issues were discussed at the conference by four separate committees [28] Hungary, however, did not have the opportunity to exert any significant influence in resolving economic problems because it was not a member of the Economic Committee and thus could indicate its views only in writing.[29]

In this political atmosphere it was a given that Germany and Russia would find each other and that the two "outlaw" states of Europe would get closer to each other. It was on April 16, while the conference was in session that in Rapallo, close to Genoa, Germany and Soviet Russia reached an agreement for the resumption of diplomatic relations. In this agreement the Soviet Union relinquished its demands for German reparations and Germany abandoned its request that the properties nationalized in Russia be returned to their German owners. The paragraph, most damaging to the economic interest of the Western great powers, stated that Germany had to fulfill its obligations specified in the agreement only if the Soviet Union did not meet the demands for reparations presented by other countries. The political significance of the agreement was that it freed both countries from their previous state of isolation and that it resulted in a fruitful economic cooperation until the first half of the 1930s.[30]

The Soviet delegation negotiated not only with the Germans but also with the representatives of the Little Entente countries. After the Soviet-German agreement had been reached, the Little Entente representatives became more accommodating because they were concerned that Hungary might also reach an agreement with the Soviets. Therefore, on Czechoslovak initiative, they conducted negotiations with the Soviet

Commissar for Foreign Affairs Georgi V. Chicherin. Of the representatives of the Little Entente only Eduard Beneš, the Czechoslovak minister of foreign affairs and Momčilo Ninčiś, the Yugoslav one, participated in the discussions held for the purpose of normalizing economic relations. Soon, however, not only the Romanians but the Kingdom of the Serbs, Croats and Slovenes also turned against the Czechoslovak proposals and thus the Czech delegation was forced to abandon all plans for an agreement. The negotiations with the Little Entente resulted in a complete failure and an agreement with the great powers also became unlikely.[31] The Soviet delegation did not believe that an agreement could be reached with the forces endeavoring to maintain the status quo but still considered it to be of great importance that the Soviet Union be granted the widest possible international recognition.

It seems likely that the failure of the negotiations with the Little Entente countries encouraged the shapers of Soviet foreign policy to emphasize and utilize Soviet Russia's identity of interest with the defeated countries in a rejection of the Paris area peace treaties. In doing so the Soviets were encouraged to find a modus vivendi with Hungary and Bulgaria. During the conference the commissar for foreign affairs met with the Hungarian minister of foreign affairs. The notes of the latter reveal that they had met on April 24 and May 2 to conduct meaningful behind the scenes discussions. The principal matter of discussion between Chicherin and Bánffy was the normalization of relations between the two countries and the creation of a framework for political cooperation. As a consequence Hungary would recognize Soviet Russia which would possibly provide political and even military cooperation against Romania. In the discussions between the two ministers there was no mention of economic issues even though the bases for a rapprochement could have been not only a joint platform against the Versailles system but, more importantly, the matter of mutual trade interests.[32]

This is surprising because, according to the data available to us, the Hungarian government wanted to discuss at the conference the matter of reestablishing economic relations between the Soviet Russia and the small states in central Europe. The National Archives of Hungary holds a draft of a memorandum, in French, that the Hungarian delegation was going to introduce at the Genoa Conference and which contained a proposal for the reestablishment of economic relations with Soviet Russia.

The proposal was going to ask the great powers, present at the conference, that the successor states of the Austro-Hungarian Monarchy, including Hungary, be treated as equals in the discussions relative to the reestablishment of economic relations with Soviet Russia and that these small countries share equally in the benefits provided by the trade agreements with Soviet Russia. The submission claimed that the Hungarian recommendation was justified by the fact that the economic recession in Europe was largely due to the Soviet federation being excluded from European activities even though it represented a major economic potential for Europe by its size and by its wealth of raw materials. The document also stated that the economic revival of the small central European countries depended, to a large extent, on the resumption of economic relations with the Soviet Russia because their economic life was upset by the World War which deprived them from their source of raw materials and from their markets. This was also justified by the geographic position of the successor states. Three of them, Hungary, Austria, and Czechoslovakia lacked direct access to the sea which deprived them of the advantages of maritime trade. Thus continental commerce became a matter of the greatest importance for them.[33]

Thus Bánffy did not take the opportunity offered by personal contact with Chicherin to discuss economic problems and to gain economic advantages from a Soviet partner. Bethlen, returning from Genoa, also seemed to be quite reticent about economic matters. In his press conference the prime minister stated that the German-Soviet agreement would not have any major significance as long as the Communists were in power in Russia because this made it unlikely that any foreign private capital would be used in the rebuilding of the country. Reacting to a news item in the American press he denied that there had been a Hungarian-Soviet behind the scene discussion. He said, "In this matter the Hungarian delegation took the position that, compared to the great powers, Hungary had only minor interests vis-à-vis Russia but that Hungary would join in any agreement that the great powers might eventually reach with Russia. Hungary would definitely not take the initiative in this area. If the great powers were willing to reach an agreement under certain conditions Hungary would participate but if no such agreement was reached Hungary would not do so on its own."[34] Further research is needed to answer the question of what happened to change the

Hungarian position between the time the memorandum on cooperation with Soviet Russia was written and Bethlen's reserved public statement. The position taken by the Hungarian prime minister showed that in total opposition to the text of the memorandum's proposals, the Hungarian delegation refused to take any initiative in trying to have Russia under the Communists reenter into the mainstream of European economics.

The representatives of the Hungarian business community, manufacturers and bankers, wished to exploit the possibilities existing in the Soviet markets in spite of the unfavorable political background. The first reliable data about a start of economic relations between Hungarian entrepreneurs and the Soviet state organizations came from early 1922. On February 27, Miksa Fenyő, the managing director of GYOSZ, went to see the Soviet-Russian Trade Mission in Berlin and there had discussions with First Secretary Stefan Brodovskii. According to Fenyő, he went to Berlin not only as the representative of the manufacturers but also as the official delegate of the Hungarian government in order to negotiate about the start of economic relations. The Soviet official advised him that the establishment of economic relations between the two countries, in whatever form, was contingent upon the recognition of the Soviet regime and upon the signing of an agreement between the two countries.[35] This matter was raised by Deputy Commissar for Foreign Affairs Maxim Litvinov at the March 8, 1922, meeting of the Politburo, but the laconic nature of the minutes of this meeting does not allow us to form an accurate picture of what Litvinov had recommended.[36] The decision of the Politburo can be deduced, however, from a later document, signed by Litvinov, and sent to the counselor of the Soviet-Russian mission in Berlin on March 17. The directive did not raise any objections in principle to the establishment of contact with the Hungarian government in Berlin but emphasized that in order for this to happen the two states had to recognize each other, at least de facto, meaning that a temporary trade agreement had to be made which made it possible to establish reciprocally their trade missions.[37]

From the perspective of the Soviet government direct or indirect economic benefits were outweighed, during the first part of the 1920s, by the potential political returns of opening their markets. By granting concessions the Soviet government wanted not only to return to the European commercial mainstream but also hoped for diplomatic recognition. This explains why, until 1924, Soviet Russia made the de facto recognition as a condition for cementing trade relations and of the opening of its markets. This also meant that the signing of a bilateral trade treaty with a particular country could not be carried out until the Soviet state was not recognized de jure and formal diplomatic relationships had been established.

Soon after the end of the Genoa Conference, between June 7, and July 17, 1922, the Hungarian General Bank of Credit (Magyar Általános Hitelbank Rt.) [MÁH], supervising the strategic corporations, sent a professional delegation to the Baltic States to study the economic situation of the Soviet federation and the possibility of establishing trade relations for the export of Hungarian industrial products and the importation of Soviet raw materials. Members of this delegation included Count Iván Csekonics, the former envoy to Warsaw and Rezső Kállay, the deputy director of MÁH, and an engineer at the Ganz Factory, one of the bank's properties. With the assistance of Mihály Jungerth, the Hungarian minister in Reval (Tallinn), the members of the delegation met with the commercial attaché of the Soviet Trade Mission. Following the discussions the Hungarian experts decided that they would recommend to the MÁH managers that in parallel with the consolidation of the Russian economy and finances, trade relations be established with Soviet Russia. In his reports describing the discussion, the Hungarian minister added that, "…in addition to the Bank of Credit, the Anglo-Hungarian Bank was also interested in the local economic situation. This bank has a permanent representative in Riga."[38]

The Problem of Financing Hungarian Exports

In starting a Hungarian-Soviet exchange of goods attention had to be paid to those items which were available for export and those for which there was an import need. The greatest attention had to be paid, however, to those goods which, if exchanged, would contribute to the increase in output on both sides. It was the Soviet Union's natural endowments, such as huge forests and enormous mineral resources that made it a desirable trade partner for Hungary while Hungary, as an exporter of industrial and agricultural products, could achieve appreciable results in the Soviet market. In 1920 and 1921 a shortage of oil seriously endangered the functioning of the entire Hungarian economic infrastructure. This shortage was due to the exhaustion of wartime productivity, to the paralysis of former commercial relations and, primarily to the interference with, or cancellation of, Romanian and Polish deliveries.[39] To overcome the chronic shortage, Károly Koffler, the secretary of GYOSZ, made a deal on September 18, 1922, in Berlin with the representative of the Neftesindikat's local office for the delivery of 4,000 tons, i.e. more than 400 tank-car loads of oil.[40] According to Koffler's recollections, for the next two years the Hungarian crude oil refining industry obtained its supplies almost entirely from the Soviet Union. Thus, after 1922, the shortages caused by the war and its consequences could be remedied and the continuity of domestic processing was assured.[41] The importation of crude oil, primarily from the Grozny fields, was managed and supervised in 1923 and 1924 by members of a tightly knit family-business lobby, István Freund, Oszkár Szirmai, György Mayer, etc., who controlled the crude oil business and importation activities under the auspices of the Association of Hungarian Crude Oil Refiners, Inc. (Magyar Ásványolaj-finomítók Egyesülése Rt.), and the Central Crude Oil Industry, Inc. (Központi Ásványolaj-ipari Rt.).[42] According to some sources the Central Crude Oil Industry, Inc. negotiated in 1923 with the Berlin office of Neftesindikat about a contract for refining crude oil imported from the Soviets in Hungary and then moving it on to the European markets.[43] This suggests that the national demands had been largely met and that the domestic refining industry could consider accepting orders beyond the domestic requirements. In addition to crude oil, Hungary also had the opportunity to import from the Soviet Union such items as a variety of metals (iron, manganese, copper, zinc and lead), high quality anthracite, and different kinds of lumber and asbestos used primarily in the building industry.

Even during the years prior to World War I Russia constituted a major market for the various products of Hungarian industry, particularly for agricultural machinery. On the 1913 list of exports to Russia the first place is occupied by a variety of machines constituting almost 20 percent of the entire export.[44] The agricultural machinery was used primarily in the fertile southern areas of the huge empire, the Ukraine and south Russia. After Trianon more than 80 percent of Hungarian industrial capacity remained within the new borders of the country and thus, after 1921, machinery exports exceeded the imports.[45] The Soviet government considered the increase in agricultural production and the expansion of arable areas a priority even though they lacked one of the basic elements of modernization. In the Soviet agricultural areas use of machinery was well below the desired level, the available equipment was largely obsolete and domestic production was unable to meet the increasing demands of the expanding domestic market. According to data from the beginning of 1924 Russian agriculture had to struggle with a 57 percent shortage of sowing and planting machines and a 90 percent shortage of reaping machines.[46]

Hungarian animal husbandry, particularly horse breeding was in a relatively more favorable position. The war led to a significant decrease in the number of horses in Hungary because, according to some estimates, more than 50 percent of the former stocks of horses came under the control of the successor states. In spite of this an appropriate breeding stock remained. In the spring of 1920 the number of horses in Hungary was determined to be approximately 717,000. Prior to the outbreak of World War I Russian horse-breeding was of European importance but the war caused enormous losses. Prior to the war there were 8,850 state and private stud farms raising about 800 thousand animals but by the end of the Civil War there were only 149 stud farms with 8,500 breeding stock. Because of their experiences during the Civil War the Red Army insisted of increasing the cavalry forces but had great difficulties in securing an adequate number of horses.[47] Even after the Trianon Peace Treaty Hungary was able to export about 27,000 horses annually and in the second half of the 1920s it became one of the most important animal exporters to the Soviet Union.[48] According to the statistical data of the 1920s, in addition to agricultural machinery and horses, Hungary exported to the Soviet Union products of the electrical industry, such as lamps and switches, diesel motors, and agricultural products including seeds and fodder plants.

There were, however, some products, particularly grains and, quite particularly, wheat that were considered major export products for both countries which led to frictions between Hungary and the Soviet Union when they were trying to sell them on the international market. The Soviet grain export was targeted toward the same countries, Germany,

Austria, and Italy, which were considered the traditional grain markets for Hungarian exports. The competitive situation created by the Soviet grain export could not be ignored because their higher costs of long distance transportation was offset by their asking less than the world market prices for their products. The situation became particularly worrisome in Austria. Austria had to import about 600,000 tons of grain each year and during the first half of the 1920s about 40 percent of this was provided by the annually increasing Hungarian exports. During the summer of 1923 the Hungarian Embassy in Vienna reported several times that Austrian business executives wanted to sign a contract with the Soviet Trade Mission in Vienna for the importation of large amounts of grain.[49] Had the Austro-Soviet agreement come into being, it would have severely affected Hungarian exports to Austria because that country was one of Hungary's most important foreign markets. This agreement would have firmly introduced Soviet agricultural products to Austria and later the Soviet Union could have agreed to cover Austria's entire need for foreign grain. According to Soviet foreign trade statistics grain exports to Austria began only in 1925–26 and were even then, with approximately 6,800 tons, considerably below the Hungarian exports.[50] Yet, in the first half of the 1920s the Soviets gave serious consideration to taking advantage of the fluctuations in Hungarian-German and Hungarian-Austrian economic relations and by increasing their grain exports to Austria to establish a superiority vis-à-vis Hungarian agricultural products.[51]

During the 1920s the most sensitive issue in Soviet foreign trade policies was the problem of credit. As we have seen, the recession following the end of World War I was responsible for the most serious problem, namely the lack of capital. The Soviet state import enterprises, and thus, indirectly, the Commissariat of Foreign Trade as the representative of the Soviet Union, agreed only in the rarest of instances to make immediate payment for goods imported into the Soviet Union. Thus the Western exporters could expect a successful action only if they were able to assure some form of credit to the Soviet state budget agencies for the compensation of the cost of the merchandise.

One of the forms of credit used was the "consignment." This meant that payment for the purchased products, or for the outstanding part of it, had to be made only after the stored merchandise had been sold on the domestic market. The time for payment in most cases usually amounted to six to nine months after the merchandise had been sold and thus payments were made from the income of the domestic sales or from the profits made on these sales. If the due date for payment could not be met the merchandise in use had to be returned to the original seller. This form of credit held substantial risks for the seller because in the case of expensive and delicate machinery, which were most frequently the subjects for consignment, there was almost always some damage or depreciation within six months of use.[52]

For this reason the most popular form of credit in the 1920s was the "simple merchandise credit." In this case the Soviet importer, on receipt of the merchandise, issued a six to twenty-four months letter of exchange that the foreign exporter had to have discounted at a relatively high rate of interest. In addition, the Soviet import organizations favored those offers which, after the sale, assured them of long-term credit arrangement.[53] According to the 1932–1933 data, the market interest rate for discounting Soviet letters of exchange was between 16–25 percent.[54] In a significant number of the capitalist countries the state provided a substantial warranty for the Soviet letters of exchange even though these were only a percentage of the total value of the goods to be sold. Thus, for instance, Czechoslovakia guaranteed 50 percent of the credit granted to the Soviet Union, Poland 60 percent, Italy and France 70–75 percent, and Austria and Germany 70–80 percent.[55] This meant that the Western companies could be compensated to this extent for the losses suffered by the discounting of the Soviet letters of exchange.[56] In the absence of a state guarantee those companies could not include this projected loss in the cost of their products.

The Hungarian state did not want to, and could not afford to, assume even a part of the risks associated with the granting of credits. The reason for this was not ideological or political but was due to the pressure imposed by the economic situation suffering from a lack of capital. The need for capital is shown by the Bethlen government applying for a League of Nations loan of 600–700 million gold crowns. Hungary actually received a loan of 250 million gold crowns but in 20 years it had to repay more than 600 million gold crowns and also had to agree to pay 170 million gold crowns as wartime reparations.[57] This was the major financial problem for Hungarian-Soviet economic relations.

It obviously was not a matter of the Hungarian government providing no assistance to Hungarian exports and exporters and between the two World Wars it did provide a number of such benefits in the economic-political arena. A frequent method of supporting the export business was the "surcharge system." In this case the exporters received a certain surcharge, in addition to the sum calculated at the official exchange rate. This made it possible for them to sell their goods abroad at a lower price while receiving the full cost or even more than that. Another form of export business support was the so-called "foreign exchange compensation." Through a bank, participating in the foreign exchange compensation program, the Hungarian companies exporting goods to foreign markets could sell the foreign currency including the surcharges to Hungarian importers who were granted permission by the Hungarian National Bank. In addition the Hungarian government also endeavored to grant export credits. Compared to other countries, however, this was done in a peculiar fashion because the government did not have its own ways of doing it. For this reason it tried to help the exporters by letting them participate in the foreign loans it was negotiating.[58]

Under these conditions Hungarian exports to the Soviet Union had a very slow start and the Hungarian machine manufacturers could achieve a breakthrough only on May 7, 1924. This was the day when the first machinery export contract was signed with the Soviet Union. The Soviet Trade Mission in Berlin signed a consignment contract with the Hofherr-Schrantz-Clayton-Shuttleworth Hungarian Machine Manufacturing Inc. (Hofherr-Schrantz) for ten threshing machines worth approximately 50,000 US dollars.[59] Encouraged by the success of Hofherr-Schrantz, MÁVAG also signed a consignment contract, presumably still in May, for a much larger sum than its competitor.[60] These orders did not mean that the above mentioned position of the Commissariat for Foreign Affairs, which tied any large-scale commercial activity to the resumption of an official relationship between the two countries, had been substantially modified. The deals with the two Hungarian companies were presumably the result of an incident which led to troubles in the formerly smooth Soviet-German relationship. On May 3, 1924, the German police, on official instructions and seeking a German Communist, entered the offices of the Soviet Trade Mission and thoroughly searched the premises. The German authorities, by doing this, clearly violated the extraterritorial rights granted by the Rapallo agreement. The trade mission's offices were closed on the day of the incident, the personnel was reduced on orders from the higher Party organizations in Moscow, negotiations under way with German companies were halted, and the purchases in effect were halted completely until July 29 when the conflict was finally resolved.[61] It was primarily for this reason that the attention of the Soviet foreign commerce organizations turned toward the Hungarian agricultural machinery industry. The cyclical nature of agriculture demanded that there be no hitch in purchases and that the machines be delivered before harvesting had to begin. Relative to the Hofherr-Schrantz contract it was the urgency of the matter that was used as an excuse by the Commissariat of Foreign Trade.[62]

Attempts to Gain Hungarian Concessions in the Soviet Economy

Knowing the disarranged state of the Soviet economic infrastructure it was clear to the Soviet leadership that the short-range economic growth, essential for long-range development, was beyond its capacity. So long as the Western powers maintained their demands for repayment of the loans made to the tsarist state and to the Provisional Government and compensation for the foreign-owned real estate and other property nationalized by the Bolshevik regime, there was no chance of getting additional foreign loans or attracting investors to the Soviet Union.

In order to attract foreign capital the Soviet government chose a solution which, in these constraints, was viewed even by foreign investors as a compromise. It was on November 23, 1920, that the Council of Commissars, acting as the executive branch of government, issued the decree about the general economic and legal conditions for granting concessions which made it possible to attract foreign capital for the Soviet economy. Under the various time-span concessions foreign private capital acquired the right to temporarily operate industrial, agricultural and railway enterprises, exploit forests and crude oil resources and to repatriate some of the profits. In exchange it was obliged, using its own resources, to renovate and make functional the industrial and agricultural enterprises, taken over by the statc at the time of the revolutions and Civil War, for which they were given a concession. The foreign investors were also obliged to grant additional credit for the restoration of the Soviet economy. The decree mandated that the huge forests in the areas of the western Siberian and European Russian administrations (gubernias) be part of the concessions and that the oil fields of Baku and Grozny be leased out.[63] The Soviets hoped that with the investment of new funds the concessions would assist them not only in reorganizing industrial plants and improve the efficiency of extractive industries but also would introduce modern Western technology. The Soviet government expected that by permitting the concessions there would be not only direct and indirect economic advantages but also political benefits. The concession policies proved to be most useful in the Soviet endeavor to escape from its political isolation. Because they permitted the former owners of the nationalized properties to lease their previously owned companies, this suggested that if political arrangement could be made the Western countries would receive at least partial compensations. While under the concession agreement the Western entrepreneurs could not become the owners of their property but were only renters or operators of the enterprise or mine for a specified period of time, they could take part of their profits out of the country, were entitled to use the roads, railroads, ports and telegraph facilities and were even allowed to use foreign labor. The agreement provided a commitment that the capital invested in the production facility and the profits gained from the investments would not be confiscated by the state again.[64]

The contents of the concession agreements are shown clearly in the mining concession of the American businessman Armand Hammer and in the agricultural concession of the Krupp Works, the gigantic German steel corporation. The second concession agreement was made with Hammer on October 29, 1921, and allowed him to rent the rich asbestos mines in the southern Ural area. In exchange he was obligated to hire 1,200 local workers and to restart production in the mines, closed since the Civil War, with local labor and by using modern mining equipment. In addition Hammer was to import thirty-six million pounds of food products one tenth of which was to go to Petrograd and the rest was to be distributed in the southern Ural area. Ten percent of the asbestos mined and 50 percent of the net profits went to the American investor.[65] In the agreement signed on March 16, 1923, the Krupp Company agreed that it would, over twelve years, convert the 27,000 acres of steppe, south of Rostov, into arable land. To organize the storing, refining and selling of the products, the German consortium established a huge agricultural combine under the name of Gigant (Giant). Twenty percent of the harvested products belonged to the investor. This became one of the largest agricultural concessions in the Soviet Union.[66]

It had been unknown to Hungarian historiography that there had been an instance when a Hungarian commercial interest attempted to obtain a concession in Soviet industrial production and thus participate in a country with a huge market capacity. This is documented in the report of the Soviet Trade Mission in Berlin on February 2, 1923. The report, addressed to the Main Concession Committee (Glavkontseskom-GKK), an organization attached to the Council of Commissars and responsible for the awarding and supervising of concessions, stated that they had been approached with a request for a concession by a business conglomerate consisting of influential Hungarian capitalists having government support. The report mentioned that the conglomerate included Government Counselor Ödön Diósy, the head of a division in the Ministry of Commerce, Sándor László, the CEO of Hofherr-Schrantz, Gyula Klein, the managing director of MÁH and Miksa Fenyő, the managing director of GYOSZ.[67]

The relationship between the three businessmen is easy to trace. Klein, the managing director of MÁH was also a vice president of the Hofherr-Schrantz company's Hungarian subsidiary and was also a member of the Board of Directors of the economically influential Ganz-Danubius Machine, Wagon and Ship Building Corporation (Ganz-Danubius Gép-, Vagon- és Hajógyár Rt.). It is also significant that the Hungarian affiliate of Hofherr-Schrantz and Ganz-Danubius were affiliated with MÁH and with other important companies such as the Ganz Electrical Company (Ganz Villamossági Rt.), the Rifle and Machine Company (Fegyver- és Gépgyár Rt.), the Láng Machine Company (Láng Gépgyár) and the Ericsson Hungarian Electrical Company (Ericsson Magyar Villamossági Rt.).[68] The above mentioned report indicated that Fenyő owned shares in both Ganz companies. As mentioned earlier, among the Hungarian capitalists Fenyő was the strongest supporter of an economic rapprochement with the Soviet Union. The businessmen were trying to find out under what conditions they could participate in the activation and use of the two shipbuilding companies (Russud and Naval), located in the southern part of the Ukraine in the estuary of the Southern Bug River, in the city of Nikolaev (Mykolaiv), namely how could they get a concession for the operation of the two companies? At the time of the tsarist regime there were three major shipyards in Nikolaev. The first one, Naval, was building primarily freighters, the second one, Russud, was building surface warships, and the third one, Baltika, was specializing in submarine construction. The three shipyards together constituted Europe's largest shipbuilding facility covering over an area of one million square meters. The construction and assembly plants branched off from a huge central shed. Before the war the three shipyards employed over 18,000 workers. Hungarian archival documents reveal why the Hungarian businessmen chose the Nikolaev shipbuilding industries. During World War I the German authorities, occupying the Ukraine, took over these strategic industries and began to make an inventory of technical supplies and equipment. Sándor László visited the site during the summer of 1918 as a MÁH representative in order to ascertain whether the MÁH and its affiliated organizations had the opportunity to take over one or more of these shipyards before the German syndicates could do so.[69]

The GKK consulted several high administrative groups about the concession offer including the Supreme Economic Council (VSNKh), the Commissariat for Foreign Affairs and the Commissariat for Naval Affairs. In reaching its decision on April 5, the VSNKh referred to the political and security-based recommendations of these three agencies when it turned down the application for the concession.[70] On behalf of the Commissariat for Foreign Affairs, Deputy Commissar Maxim Litvinov made it a condition of negotiating and contracting with Hungarian corporations that the Hungarian government formally recognized the Soviet Communist regime.[71] The Commissariat for Naval Affairs also considered the offer unacceptable because all of the Soviet Union's Black Sea fleet was built in these shipyards and therefore their being handed over to a foreign capitalist group endangered the reliability of warship construction.[72] The same views were expressed by the Supreme Economic Council which felt that the Nikolaev shipyards had an important role in the defenses of the country.[73] Referring to these recommendations the GKK rejected the offer. The principal reason for the rejection was political. The practice of granting concessions was influenced to a large extent by international political trends. The Soviet government endeavored to accept the concession requests from the citizens of those countries which had well balanced, if not great, relationships with the Soviet Union. A de facto recognition of the Soviet regime and the existence of at least some commercial agreements was a precondition for the assurance of an economic investment and thus the achievement of some economic preferences in the Soviet markets. It was not a coincidence that the Rapallo agreement gave concession discussions a boost and during the year after the agreement there was an upsurge in the offers for concessions. The same was also true in reverse. According to the explanation given by recent Russian historiography the first "wave of acceptances" was the cause of the sudden decline and stagnation in 1924 and 1925 because the Western capitalist corporations took a wait and see stance hoping that they would get at least a partial compensation in exchange for their nationalized properties.[74]

The second reason was a security consideration. In order for the presence of the capitalist interests, functioning on a market economy principle, to cause the least possible trouble between the Soviet government and the foreign capitalists the Soviet government, in investigating the concession offers and signing agreements, was particularly careful so that no production facility should get into foreign hands which could create a monopolistic situation for the foreigners in certain economic areas. Industries and mines in some areas, e.g. in the vicinity of the borders were not handed over as concessions and the foreign investor could not acquire a lease for strategic industries such as rifle or precision instrument manufactories. The same principle applied to manufactories which survived the Civil War relatively unscathed and the productivity of which could be restarted with internal resources.[75] The Nikolaev shipyards fell into this category not only because of their strategic nature but also because they survived the major national cataclysm following the 1917 revolutions with relatively minor damage, so much so that by the turn of 1923–1924 they could begin to match the prewar orders.[76]

Consequently the GKK did not even investigate the financial references of the Hungarian consortium making the offer, its position in the market place or the investments it would be able to make to improve the productivity of the shipyards, should it be awarded the concession. Yet the size of its capital and the credit available to the corporation or consortium making the offer were considered to be important considerations because after its installation it was expected to grant additional credit or make financial contributions to the reorganization of the Soviet economy and to the demands of certain social needs. Yet, it can be seen from the response of the Supreme Economic Council that in addition to the political and security issues there might have been a third reason, of an economic-financial nature, for the rejection of the application. The Soviet administrative agency believed that in case of a competition for concessions the Hungarian group would not be able to compete successfully with their powerful German or American rivals. Between 1922 and 1927, a total of 163 concessions were awarded of which Germany received 37, Great Britain received 22, and the USA received 19.[77]

Hungarian Attempts to Establish a Joint-Stock Company Trade Enterprise

In addition to consignments and simple merchandise credit there was a third form of credit which offered a solution for the financing of the exports to the Soviet Union. The Commissariat for Foreign Trade and the Soviet trade missions abroad under its supervision were able to create joint-stock company trade enterprises with individual companies or with groups of companies in the host countries. Occasionally these were linked to the trade concession agreements. For the large Western corporations, corporate groups and concerns that owned half the stocks this had the benefit that they could gain an exclusive position for the export and import of certain merchandise and that they could finance the very promising export activities directed toward the Soviet Union. The British, German, and Austrian interests forming these joint-stock companies were frequently accused by their domestic competitors that they were monopolizing trade with the Soviet Union. The other half of the shares was owned by the Commissariat for Foreign

Trade and thus, indirectly, by the Soviet Union. From the perspective of Moscow participation in the joint-stock company trade enterprises was advantageous not only because in this way it could keep foreign trade in supervised channels but also because it could obtain substantial credits from its partner companies and from the banks in their orbit. In the West the joint-stock corporations frequently included financial institutions which were able and willing to assume some of the risks of the credits they provided.

For the Hungarian commercial circles the example for the joint-stock company trade enterprises was provided by those established in Germany and Austria. The first one of them was established in Berlin on October 20, 1922, under the name of Rusgertorg (Russko-Germanskoe Torgovoe AO) and with a capital of thirty thousand British pounds. It was owned jointly by the Commissariat for Foreign Trade and the German conglomerate trademarked under the name of the German industrial magnate Otto Wolf. Its principal activity was the export of metal products to Soviet Russia and the import of various raw materials from there.[78] This huge undertaking also came to the attention of Hungarian diplomacy. In his report of December 8, 1922, György Ghika, the consul in Hamburg, informed Prime Minister Bethlen that the Wolf group provided a credit of 750,000 British pounds to the joint-stock trade company, many times its basic capital.[79] In Austria two joint trade enterprises were established, RATAO and Rusavtorg. Of these RATAO (Russko-Avstriskoe Torgovoe AO) was established on August 23, 1923, with a base capital of 300,000 rubles. Half of the shares were owned by the Commissariat for Foreign Trade and the other half by an Austrian organization called Arsenal which was a corporate group composed of a number of small and medium-sized industries and associated with two banks.[80] The company exported textile-making machinery, agricultural equipment, electro-technical tools and chemicals to the Soviet Union from where it imported to Austria a variety of industrial raw materials, agricultural products as well as furs and hides.[81]

In order to establish a Hungarian-Soviet joint-stock company trade enterprise the Anglo-Hungarian Bank (Angol-Magyar Bank) [AMB], and the corporations allied with it, lobbied vigorously with both the Hungarian and Soviet governments. It is easy to see that the market plans of the AMB were affected adversely by the large-scale investment plans of the MÁH in the Soviet Union because it was the AMB which had previously represented the interests of the MÁVAG which, in turn, was considered one of the principal competitors of Hofherr-Schrantz in the production of agricultural machinery and in the enormously lucrative export of industrial machinery. In the management of the AMB and in the planning of its business policies its president, Count Imre Károlyi and Vice President Simon Krausz were the dominant figures. Károlyi was respected as an expert and was also the brother of Count Gyula Károlyi, the prime minister of the Szeged counterrevolutionary government in 1919. Károlyi had served as president of the bank since 1913 but unwilling to limit his economic expertise to banking, he also became involved on his rural estates in agricultural research on improving the productivity of cereal grains. Krausz, known at the time of the Dual Monarchy as a stock market "shark," established at the beginning of the 1920s the group of companies that became associated with his name. They included the OFA Lumber, Inc. and a transportation company, Nova Transportation and Industry, Inc.[82]

The leaders representing the AMB started negotiations on March 1, 1923, in Berlin with the head of the Soviet Trade Mission, Boris Stomoniakov. Károlyi and Krausz wanted to assemble a number of companies, already affiliated with the bank, as part of the Hungarian parity, under the aegis of a joint-stock company Hungarian-Soviet enterprise. These Hungarian companies would be considered as potential importers in the Soviet market. The production and marketing by cooperating Hungarian companies and Soviet enterprises would have functioned as the branches of the controlling holding company. At the negotiations the Soviet group recommended to the leaders of the Hungarian financial institution that it would be better if they participated in the establishment of agricultural machinery repair facilities, or in the creation of model estates for the improvement of the cereal grains or for the setting up of stud farms. Another suggestion was to follow the example set by the Krupp Company and contract for agricultural and forestry concessions. The Soviet diplomat told the Hungarian businessmen that their companies could count on preferential treatment leading to a greatly advantageous situation only if the company to be established delivered industrial products, primarily agricultural machinery, to the Soviet collectives on credit and also assisted in the reconstruction of

Soviet agriculture and industry with credits, new investments, and the introduction of technical know-how.[83]

The March 2, report of the Soviet Trade Mission in Berlin about the discussions with Károlyi and Krausz rapidly reached the desk of Georgii Piatakov, who as chairman of the GKK was in charge of all of the concession issues. Piatakov forwarded the report to the Supreme Economic Council and to the Commissariat for Agriculture with the request for a ruling on the matter of the agricultural production concessions discussed in the report.[84] The former agreed in principle that the discussions continue with the Hungarian capitalist group but considered it to be important that the favored group make its suggestions about the way its investments would be made in the Soviet Union in more concrete terms.[85] A positive response was received from the Commissariat for Agriculture as well. It considered it to be desirable that Hungarian capital was going to be invested in the improvement of Soviet agriculture in the form of concessions or joint-stock companies, but considered the Hungarian offer to be so vague in form that it did not make any positive counter-proposal. "The possibilities for agricultural and forestry concessions are well known...therefore if the Main Concessions Committee and the Commissariat for Foreign Affairs had no other political considerations it was all right to engage in negotiations with the Hungarian companies" was the conclusion of the organization most involved in the matter.[86]

The GKK agreed with these views and the Soviet Trade Mission in Berlin, referring to them, sent a letter on May 5 to the AMB in which it indicated that it was willing to continue negotiations on awarding concessions on agricultural and forest management, on the establishment of agricultural machinery repair facilities and on creating a joint export-import enterprise. It insisted, however, that the basic condition for reaching an agreement was that the general conditions pertaining to the normalization of the relationship between the countries be met.[87] This favorable response is the explanation why Károlyi endeavored to place before the leaders of the Hungarian commercial experts and before the Soviet partners a completed deal and why he summoned a statutory meeting of the Russian-Hungarian Trade Corporation for June 28, 1923. The bylaws of the joint-stock company had been completed a few days earlier by Róbert Ország, a director of AMB, and were going to be submitted to the statutory meeting for approval.

The bylaws stated that, "The goal of the joint-stock company was the export of a variety of merchandise and raw materials from Russia and the export of a variety of merchandise and, primarily, industrial products from Hungary to Russia with the trading of all of this merchandise being done on its own account and as consignments. Additional goals included the setting up and operation of industrial, commercial, and agricultural establishments, particularly in Russia." The headquarters of the company would be located in Budapest but it was also stated that branches, local offices and agencies might be set up both within the two countries and abroad. The statutes also specified that for the time being the initial capital of the corporation would be 200 million crowns,[88] consisting of 200,000 fully paid-up shares of a face value of 1,000 crowns and held anonymously.[89]

There were eight subscribers present at the initial meeting of the company who unanimously voted to accept the proposed bylaws. The shares were divided so that the large majority was held by the AMB. Imre Károlyi and Róbert Ország each held 500 shares. The remaining 1,000 shares were bought by senior officials of the bank, Alfréd Halász, Gyula Vass, Dezső Wolf, Artur Fényes, and Gyula Radó with each holding 200 shares. For the first three years the Board of Directors included, in addition to Károlyi, who also served as the president of the Board and Ország, the following members: Virgil Pósfay, an official of the Ministry of Foreign Affairs and the head of the Division of Social Policies who later became the director of the International Danubian Transportation Division, Hubert Dvorák, a counselor of the Ministry of Commerce and a director of MÁVAG, and Tivadar Kőnig, state secretary of finance.[90]

On the same day the Board of Directors submitted, for the purpose of formal registration, to the Royal Court in Budapest, three copies of the bylaws, the minutes of the initial meeting, the signature sheets showing the deposition of the basic capital and the entry in the account of the bank showing the deposit of the basic capital. The latter document was certified by a notary public. The official of the Court of Registration, reviewing the application for incorporation, raised a number of concerns about the submitted documents both as to form and content. He criticized the petitioners about the accuracy of the transliteration of the name and description of the foreign companies into

Hungarian as well as the fact that in the Russian name of the company the term "corporation" appeared only as initials (Russko-Vengerskoe Tovarnoe A. D.). Relative to the title the reviewer found a more serious concern about the content, namely, the term "Russian" was impermissible without convincing evidence that the company had, in fact, established an appropriate business connection with Russia. The reviewer added that the name of the company, "…considering the smallness of the initial capital relative to the goals of the company and to the foreign exchange conditions of the day, was too highfaluting with all the addenda." He also drew the applicants' attention to the fact that there were additional formalistic deficiencies, such as the insufficient precision in the definition of the company's endeavors and the need for additional textual amplifications and additions.[91]

The negative stand taken by the Court of Registration came as a surprise to the leadership of the AMB which, in order to assure the success of the incorporation of the new company, used even the tools of political lobbying by appointing influential ministerial officials to the Board of Directors of the joint enterprise. In order to comply with the arguments of the Court of Registration two additional members were added to the Board of Directors. At as special meeting held on September 19 Simon Krausz and Stephen Alley were elected to the Board of Directors. Alley was the president of the Marconi Wireless Telegraph, Ltd. of London which was an associated shareholding partner of the AMB.[92] The leaders at the head of the financial institution referred to the representation of the state on the Board of Directors in a letter written on September 21, to Géza Daruváry, the minister of foreign affairs. In this letter they explained that the personality of the leaders and of the representatives of the Hungarian government had enough weight socially and economically to guarantee that the enterprise engaged in by the bank was serious and that the bank would be able to perform the functions specified in the bylaws. In a veiled manner they asked the minister to exert some pressure on the Court of Registration to approve the registration. The minister was to do this in the form of a letter to the bank stating that he was in support of their project and that he believed that the registration was permissible from an economic perspective. In opposition to the stated concerns, the letter was also to state that, "The indicated goals conformed to the usual commercial practices and thus they could be considered to be adequate from a general commercial perspective and for the achievement of the goals stated at the time of incorporation."[93]

On October 17 the previously appointed members of the board met for the purpose of modifying some of the items in the bylaws in conformance with the changes requested by the Court of Registration. The group decided that in the Russian name of the company the abbreviation of the term "joint-stock company" would be replaced by the term being spelled out in full (Aktsionernoe Druzhstvo). It also agreed to submit the official translation of the foreign language components of the bylaws, prepared by the Translation Office of the Ministry of the Interior. The text of the second paragraph of the bylaws was expanded by the inclusion of the concrete definitions of the merchandise to be moved. "The goal of the company is to import crude oil, raw hides, iron ores and other raw materials from Russia and to export agricultural and industrial machinery, chemicals, and improved seed grains…from Hungary to Russia." They had decided also to prove in a credible fashion that there was a business arrangement with the Soviet Union by submitting the four letters received from the Berlin Soviet Trade Mission, including the original copy of the above mentioned May 5 letter, "…which show that the above mentioned Soviet Trade Mission, according to the oral negotiations with the founding members, not only considered the establishment of the Russian-Hungarian Trade Corporation a desirable event but also indicated that there would be a certain beneficial consideration on the part of their government."

The Board of Directors admitted that for the accomplishment of the proposed goals the initial capital of 200 million crowns was insufficient and therefore emphasized that after the company initiated its activities the founding bank would assure the provisioning of the necessary funds either by raising the initial capital or by granting appropriate credits. The board members participating in the meeting stressed that there could be no question whatever about their commitment to the establishment of the company and that the Board of Directors of the new company would include representatives from the Ministries of Foreign Affairs, Finance, and Commerce.[94]

Yet, a November 1, 1923, report of the Berlin Soviet Trade Mission unmistakably points out that the responsible Soviet officials had put the entire affair *ad acta* because their offer of May 5 was not followed by any further negotiation. Károlyi and Krausz, tied up with problems of registration, did again go to Berlin after the October 17 meeting of the board. In the German capital they informed the Soviet Union that the joint-stock company had been established in Hungary and made the recommendation that the Soviet partner take over 50 percent of the shares. The response of the Soviet diplomat was not designed to raise any hopes. As it had been stated in the report that the mission had submitted to Moscow, "We have told them at the very beginning of the negotiations that in the interim the relations of the government to the concessions had undergone a major change and that we were no longer interested in the former arrangements although a final decision has been requested from the Commissariat for Foreign Trade and from the Main Concession Committee." In his report to the two central agencies Stomoniakov raised the question whether it was worthwhile from a political perspective to continue the discussions about such a company and, if so, what demands should be made from the Hungarians.[95]

It seems certain that it was this return visit of the leaders of the AMB to Berlin that made Emil Walter, an official of the Economic Policy and Transportation Division of the Ministry of Foreign Affairs hold a discussion at about the same time with Nikolai Krestinskii, the Soviet ambassador in Berlin. Walter submitted a letter signed by the Hungarian chargé d'affairs in Berlin, Gusztáv Emich, in which the Ministry of Foreign Affairs empowered him to negotiate about the reestablishment of economic relations between Hungary and the Soviet Union. "I told Walter," wrote Krestinskii in his report about the discussions, "that from those states which are of lesser economic interest to us, including Hungary, we regularly expected a de jure recognition and the resumption of full diplomatic relationships. It was possible that, because of Hungary's serious dependence on the Entente countries, our government would be satisfied with less and would be willing to…engage in a trade agreement." Knowing this, Walter expressed his hope that the discussions between the Soviet Trade Mission in Berlin and the Hungarian business group would be based on purely commercial considerations and that an agreement would not be held up by the absence of a diplomatic relations between the two countries. Relative to this Krestinskii wrote, "This last comment reinforced our original assumption that the principal reason for his visit and charge was the desire of the Hungarian minister of foreign affairs to promote the negotiations under way here and to neutralize obstacles of a political nature."[96]

In the mean time the response of the Commissariat for Foreign Affairs and the Commissariat for Foreign Trade arrived in Berlin and provided answers to the questions raised by Stomoniakov's November 1 report. Litvinov gave a detailed response and explained that the organs for foreign affairs did not oppose the establishment of business relations with the citizens of foreign countries, which had no "formal relations" with the Soviet Union, provided that the business relations, once established, would be of great economic significance to the country or would be of great interest to the economic organizations. Hungary, however, was not of any major significance to the Soviet Union so far as foreign trade was concerned. Litvinov told the Commissariat for Foreign Trade that if it rejected the proposal of the leaders of the AMB, the reasons given should include the absence of diplomatic relations between the two countries.[97] The position taken by the Commissariat for Foreign Trade was much more emphatic. In a brief telegram it informed Stomoniakov that, "…at the present time it was not in our interest to establish a Russian-Hungarian joint enterprise and therefore the Hungarian industrial group under Count Károlyi's leadership should be given a negative answer."[98] This was presumably conveyed to the Hungarian group because the transmittal of the negative response was reported in the November 1923 monthly report of the Berlin Soviet Trade Mission with the comment that, according to Litvinov's instructions, the motives for the rejection included mention of the unsatisfactory nature of Soviet-Hungarian political relations.[99]

Thus it was decided and had become an unalterable fact that the corporation could not be set up. The final blow, however, was delivered by the Court of Registration. It is a jest of fate that it was on the same day that Royal Court in Budapest studied the changes in the bylaws and other appended material submitted by the Board of Directors of the Russian-Hungarian Trade Corporation that the Commissariat for Foreign Trade sent its telegram of rejection. Reviewing the newly submitted request for registration the official reviewer concluded that the letters of the Berlin Soviet Trade Mission, submitted by the applicants, revealed that the applicants and the Berlin mission had not decided on the criteria of the relationship. The name of a foreign country could appear in the trade name of a company newly established only if the company could demonstrate data which showed that it could maintain an organization for the continued trade relations with the foreign country. The applicants had not done so. Even the list allocation of shares showed that the Soviet capital funds were not included in the allocation of the shares. The reviewer also concluded that the definition of the proposed activities of the company was not correct because the bylaws spoke only of merchandise and, in general, about commercial and industrial enterprises with emphasis on only some of the items on the list of merchandise.[100]

The applicants were unable to prove that the term "Russian" in the name of the company represented actual commercial liaisons and a true partnership with the Soviet Trade Mission in Berlin and with the Berlin agencies of the Soviet export and import enterprises under its supervision. Consequently the Royal Court in Budapest, in a ruling handed down on April 24, 1924, instructed the members of the Board of Directors of the new company to resubmit within three weeks their application for registration with the modifications satisfying the demands made by the "second review." Otherwise the Board had to call a meeting where the shareholders unanimously decided to abandon all efforts for the establishment and registration of the proposed company.[101] The meeting demanded by the Court of Registration was called for May 9. Róbert Ország, a member of the Board of Directors presiding, recommended a single agenda item for consideration, namely that the shareholders abandon plans for incorporation.[102] On the basis of this decision the Court of Registration ruled that effective August 5, 1924, the registration application was deleted from the records.[103]

The question is: what was the legal regulatory background which the Court of Registration used to reject the application for registration? Did Károlyi and Krausz really ignore essential formal and content requirements when both were very experienced in the business world, had participated in the establishment and management of several joint-stock companies and also had strong government support? For the establishment of domestic corporations, individual firms or partnerships and joint-stock companies the legal guidelines were contained in Act 37 of 1875, the "Commerce Law," which was enacted at the time of the

Monarchy but remained in effect after World War I.[104] Reading the paragraphs of the act carefully we must conclude that the Russian-Hungarian Trade Corporation met all the requirements essential for the establishment of a new company.[105] The correction and amplification of the formalistic items criticized by the Court of Registration, the spelling out of the full name of the foreign state, the precise definition of the goals of the company, etc., served only the formal requirements of the internal documents of the court and could not have represented an insurmountable barrier. The act does not contain any passage which would suggest that in such a case, i.e. the name of a foreign country in the name of the company, it would have been necessary to document the fact of an understanding with the foreign country. Thus the action of the court must be viewed as bureaucratic nitpicking. It must have been Paragraph 149 of the act that served as the basis for the rejection because it stated that a stock company could be established only if the initial capital necessary for its functioning was assured. If any of the three requirements for registration of a new stock company, assurance of initial capital, creation of the corporate bylaws and approval by the Court of Registration were absent the company could not be registered.[106] The Court of Registration repeatedly held that the 200 million crowns initial capital was insufficient to realize such an ambitious undertaking as the supervision of an extensive commercial activity with the Soviet Union.

The Soviet documents reveal that after the autumn of 1923 the Commissariat for Foreign Trade no longer supported the establishment of new joint enterprises.[107] This can be explained by the fact that by this time the economic effects of the activities of the joint enterprises had become manifest and it became obvious that in most cases these activities benefited primarily the Western partners. Thus, for instance, Rusgertorg in its somewhat less than one year of existence, by October 1, 1923, did 2.8 million rubles business of which the great majority, 2.4 million rubles, were spent on Soviet imports with only the remaining fraction being applied to Russian exports. Later, between October 1, 1923, and June 1, 1924, Rusavtorg did 1.1 million rubles business of which 700,000 were spent on Russian imports and thus the balance of trade during this time was greatly to the benefit of the Austrian companies.[108] Stomoniakov himself could envision an agreement with the

AMB only if there was no risk for the Soviets and recommended that an attempt should be made to obtain shares gratis, meaning that the shares of the Hungarian members of the partnership would guarantee the Soviet fraction of the shares held by the Soviets or that the Soviet participation in the initial capital be covered by the future earnings of the company.[109] There was, however, another problem. As we have seen the Soviet government demanded additional credits, beyond the guarantee of the initial capital, to increase Soviet productivity. The Hungarian documents clearly show that the financial strength of the AMB was insufficient for the implementation of such a task. The grandiose infusion of Soviet capital was seen by Károlyi and Krausz to be possible only if there was an effective Hungarian government subsidy and this is why they tried to convince Lajos Walko, the minister of commerce, to grant financial commitments toward the establishment of the company. Walko, however, was unwilling to make any financial commitment on behalf of the government.[110] As indicated earlier, the reasons for this were not primarily political and the rejection was based on serious economic reasons. The Hungarian economy, struggling with a significant lack of capital, inflation and compensation obligations did not have the reserves that could be mobilized for such a money market speculation and thus was unable to assume such an obligation.

In spite of all this, however, in 1924, attempts to establish a joint trade enterprise in Hungary again appeared. The principal proponent of such an action was Gusztáv Gratz, the former minister of foreign affairs and envoy to Austria. Because of his involvement with the second attempt of the Habsburg king to return to Hungary, he was compromised and forced temporarily to withdraw from political life. Consequently he endeavored to take advantage of his outstanding business abilities and economic expertise.[111] In addition to a number of other leading positions with financial institutions he was also the director of the Biedermann financed Railway Equipment Company, Inc. (Vasútfelszerelési Rt.).[112]

The Hungarian politician and businessman contacted the Soviet foreign representatives in Vienna for the first time on May 30, 1924. This step was evidently related to the fact that on May 6, 1924, Mikhail Levitskii, the Soviet minister in Vienna, and Szilárd Masirevich, the Hungarian minister, had their first meeting under Austrian mediation at the Austrian Ministry of Foreign Affairs on the Ballhausplatz. At the conference of the two diplomats the principal topic for discussion was the initiation of diplomatic relations between Hungary and the Soviet Union. It appeared to be a promising beginning that the framework took shape within which the two countries could begin direct negotiations for the normalization of their diplomatic relations.[113]

The reawakening hopes about the establishment of a joint enterprise were probably sustained by the fact that the first export agreement with the Soviet Union was signed by the Hungarian machine industry on May 7, 1924. Knowing this, Gratz contacted the Soviet Legation even though he had no official or unofficial authority from Prime Minister Bethlen or Minister of Foreign Affairs Daruváry to meet with Vol'demar Kh. Aussem, the Soviet minister, who had replaced Levitskii during the second half of May. This is made more likely by the fact that during their first conversation Gratz asked Aussem if he would allow him to discuss the contents of the conversation with the Hungarian prime minister. Had Gratz been instructed by Bethlen to conduct such negotiations, informing the prime minister could hardly have been an issue.[114] According to Gratz's German language notes the first meeting with Aussem was arranged by Sigmund Müntz, a reporter on the staff of the political daily, the *Neue Freie Presse*, and took place in Müntz's apartment.[115] Gratz's goal at this exploratory meeting was to arrange for orders from his railway manufacturing and repair company and to revive the hopes that motivated the interests gathered around the AMB and create a joint-stock Soviet-Hungarian enterprise that would create possibilities for the implementation of Hungarian business interests. Later Gratz claimed that in Budapest he was able to obtain Bethlen's support for this endeavor.[116]

On June 26 Gratz handed the deputy head of the Soviet Trade Mission in Vienna a document, the German language "Incorporation Document" of a Soviet-Hungarian trade enterprise. The document contained the names of all of the domestic corporations which had earlier shown an interest in the Soviet market. They included Manfred Weiss, Ganz Danubius, Hofherr-Schrantz, MÁVAG and the Central Crude Oil Industry, Inc. (Központi Ásványolaj-ipari Rt.) under the leadership of Koffler. The list also included the name of Róbert Ország, the director of AMB.[117] The Commissariat for Foreign Trade, however, informed Vienna that it had categorically rejected the proposal. The document emphasized that until Hungary formally recognized the Soviet Union, the proposal would be rejected regardless how significant the Hungarian group making the proposal was.[118] Aussem attempted to present this rigid attitude in a more pliable form:

> It is not necessary to tell Gratz that commercial relations are not possible until diplomatic relations have been resumed. It can be seen on the basis of incoming information that he supported this condition both in the press and in private conversations. In view of his efforts and for an accelerated approach to the start of diplomatic relations between Hungary and the Soviet Union, as well as for an improved way of dealing with the attacks of the bourgeois press, we should say that Moscow would "in principle" consider the application but that a real study would take place only when the diplomatic relations have started.[119]

After two business transactions in May the GYOSZ again became active and endeavored to realize the Hungarian export business through Rusavtorg or RATAO. On July 22 E. Müller, the director of Rusavtorg in Austria, went to Budapest and presented a lecture at the GYOSZ headquarters building about the activities of the joint enterprise and about the commercial transactions performed by it.[120] Gratz who served between 1911 and 1917 as the managing director of GYOSZ, and who had maintained cordial relationships with the subsequent management, tried to collaborate with the industrial association but problems arose about the schedules and forms of agreement. Gratz would have preferred to establish an integrated Soviet-Hungarian joint-stock company trade enterprise which would encompass all of the export and import activities and in which, in addition to the industrial corporations, all banks would also participate. He believed that in such an arrangement the highly problematic question of credits could also be resolved. In contrast, the GYOSZ was trying to set up a "representative company" which included only certain industrial corporations. In view of the urgency of developing export activities the GYOSZ did not want to wait until the above mentioned organization could be established and wanted to transact its commercial activities in the Soviet Union through joint

Soviet-Austrian enterprises in Vienna. Gratz felt that this would have an adverse effect on his endeavors to establish an independent Soviet-Hungarian joint enterprise. Yet, at the beginning of August he reached an agreement with the representatives of GYOSZ for the industrial enterprises to sign a temporary agreement with Rusavtorg. If, however, the establishment of an independent Hungarian company became possible the "…corporations mentioned above would regain their full freedom of activity."[121]

Gratz then went with Jenő Lukács, a director of a small electrical firm of Blau and Lukács, to Vienna where, in accordance with the agreement made with GYOSZ, he held discussions with the Soviet Trade Mission. The proposals of the two Hungarian businessmen suggested that the Hungarian companies interested in Soviet exports be allowed to join Rusavtorg in Vienna or open a Rusavtorg subsidiary in Budapest. The Soviet partners did not want to engage in business in this way and they so informed Müller and Gratz. The summary report of the Soviet Trade Mission in Vienna about the discussions stated, "We have stated to Director Müller that we would not allow such a roundabout approach because the Hungarians may do business with Russia only after diplomatic relations have been renewed but we have not forbidden him (Gratz) to continue his agitation for the resumption of commercial ties because the industrialist might influence the government and thus accelerate the resolution of the problem."[122] In a memorandum addressed to the government by GYOSZ after completion of the discussions the following conclusions were reached: "These discussions convinced our associates and the Hungarian interests that a regularly organized export was possible only if all trade with Russia would be managed by the joint Russian-Hungarian enterprise which had gained this concession from the Russian government."[123]

Political and Diplomatic Barriers to the Development of the Export-Import Trade. Negotiations in Berlin in 1924

The large-scale investment plans, export endeavors and the meritorious development of commercial relations between

Hungary and the Soviet Union proposed by the Hungarian businessmen were not supported by the Commissariat for Foreign Affairs and its leaders, Commissar Georgi Tsitserin and Deputy Commissar Maxim Litvinov. It became evident at the turn of 1922–1923 that the political and diplomatic prerequisites for Hungarian investments were at least as important as the economic considerations. Hungarian capital could not become active in the Soviet markets so long as there was no state-level agreement between the two countries, meaning that the diplomatic representatives had to prepare a commercial agreement that was equivalent to a de facto recognition and that raised the relations to an official level.[124] After the Civil War Soviet diplomacy employed this principle not only vis-à-vis Hungary but towards all Western countries and used the development of commercial relations everywhere to further the development of political ones. It is important to note that Soviet diplomacy viewed the energy resources under its control in similar fashion. It viewed the various products from its wells, such as crude oil, partially refined oil, lubricating oil, etc., as sort of "political weaponry" in their political and diplomatic relations with the Western countries since none of them could do without these various sources of energy in their industrial infrastructure. It was Litvinov's view that in exchange for oil production or oil transport concessions de jure recognition could be obtained.[125]

The most recent Russian historiography unmistakably proves that the so-called, "First Wave of Recognition" had primarily economic motivations.[126] This is the way in which Russian historiography of the history of the Soviet Union describes the spectacular foreign policy changes taking place in 1924. It was at this time that several Western capitalist countries granted de jure recognition to the Soviet Union. The first was Great Britain on February 1. This started a chain reaction and, just to mention the most important ones, Britain was followed by Italy on February 7, by Austria on February 25 and by France on October 18. It should be mentioned that under the influence of the NEP the Soviet economic indicators definitely improved and in the second half of 1925 the volume of economic productivity was only a few percentage points below the level of the last year of peace prior to the outbreak of World War I.[127]

On the news of recognition by Britain and Italy the GYOSZ addressed a submission on February 18 to the Minister of Commerce

Walko in which it urged that the state establish the political and financial preconditions essential for the establishment of commercial relations. The representatives of the alliance of the leading Hungarian industrialists and manufacturers pointed out that the decision of the British and Italian governments was influenced by the economic upswing noticeable since the NEP. The GYOSZ submission emphasized that under the new conditions Moscow would not engage in extensive negotiations with the Hungarian interests and that therefore it was essential to establish diplomatic relations as soon as possible.[128] The submission was forwarded by the minister of commerce to the Minister of Foreign Affairs Daruváry, according to whom the British and Italian recognition had created a new situation and that Hungary also had to negotiate with the Soviet government.[129]

In order to establish the basic principles for the start of Hungarian-Soviet diplomatic relations an interdepartmental meeting was held on May 22 at which, among others, Minister of Foreign Affairs Daruváry, Minister of Defense István Csáky and Minister of Agriculture István Szabó Nagyatádi participated. The Ministry of Commerce was represented by State Secretary Frigyes Wimmersperg. The Ministry of Foreign Affairs was also represented by Sándor Khuen-Héderváry, the head of the Political Division. The ministers agreed that with some limitations in the composition and mobility of a Soviet legation, they would support the normalization of diplomatic relations and would prepare the plans for the basic principles of such an action. Iván Rakovszky, the minister of the interior, added his written comments to the minutes of the interministerial meeting and joined the general opinion that the freedom of activity of the Soviet legation to be established in Budapest be limited by certain personnel restrictions.[130] The Soviet-Hungarian rapprochement, its political background and significant events, have been presented reliably by Hungarian historiography and therefore this discussion will be limited to the economic aspects of the negotiations.

The negotiations took place in Berlin between August 26 and September 12. Hungarian diplomacy was represented by Kálmán Kánya, the secretary general of the Ministry of Foreign Affairs, and, as an expert, by Mihály Jungerth, the Hungarian chargé d'affaires in Reval. The Soviet Union was represented by Nikolai Krestinskii, the ambassador in Berlin and, for a while, by Deputy Commissar for Foreign Affairs Litvinov.[131]

It was presumably the effort of Gratz and of the GYOSZ that led to the joint obligation of establishing a joint enterprise to be included in the initial drafts of the agreement regulating the diplomatic and economic relations between Hungary and the Soviet Union. Article 12 of the document dealt with this matter. In discussing the articles to be deleted Krestinskii singled out Article 12 as the first one to go because, as mentioned earlier, he believed that the joint enterprises were on their way out and could be described as being "moribund."[132] Somewhat later the Soviet diplomat stated bluntly that he refused to have the paragraph about the joint enterprises included in the agreement because it was in conflict with the current trade policies of the Soviet Union. Kánya then asked for instructions from his foreign minister in a coded telegram asking whether the matter of the joint enterprises should be pursued or not? Kánya considered it likely that if the Hungarians insisted on this article an agreement with the Soviets would become impossible. He recommended that the article be deleted in order for the Hungarians to maintain some room to maneuver and to be able to obtain a guarantee for the blockage of Communist propaganda.[133] The protection of the existing political order in the country was considered to be a much more important issue than the joint enterprises and therefore Kánya's recommendation was accepted by the minister of foreign affairs without any discussion.[134]

A much thornier problem during the negotiations was the status and personnel matters of the Soviet mission in Budapest and of a trade mission under its auspices. Citing Western examples the Hungarian organs of internal affairs feared that a Soviet trade mission could easily become a hotbed of communist propaganda. It was known in Budapest that, regardless of the possible requirements for staff, there were about eight hundred people working at the Soviet Trade Mission in Berlin. The personnel of the Berlin mission included a number of Hungarian communists who fled to Germany after the collapse of the Hungarian Soviet Republic and who, during its course, had played an important role in the management of the republic's political and economic affairs. One of these men, Gyula Lengyel, the former commissar of economy of the Hungarian Soviet Republic, had become a high official in the Soviet Trade Mission in Berlin.[135] The activities of the greatly inflated Soviet Trade Missions in London, Paris, Berlin, and Vienna were viewed with considerable concern by the political elite and by various social groups of the host countries. As we have seen by the Berlin example of May 1924, the trade mission frequently became a minor or major source of confrontation between the government of the Western host country and Soviet diplomacy. For this reason the Hungarian leadership was most anxious to avoid the establishment of an oversized Soviet trade mission in Budapest.

In order to prevent communist propaganda Article 2 of the draft of seventeen articles Hungarian proposal, written in German, stipulated that the staff of the foreign mission would be limited to eight persons. Should a trade mission also be established this number could be increased by the addition of three members. The articles that followed would have limited the freedom of movement of the personnel of the Soviet mission. Thus, for instance, any travel within the country would require prior notification and the frequency and route of travel of couriers, as well as the identity of the personnel employed as diplomatic couriers, would have to be on record. At the end of the negotiations Soviet diplomacy agreed that the personnel of the legation in Budapest would be limited to no more than fourteen, but in order for this limitation not to set a precedent for other countries or lead to limitations injurious to the prestige of the Soviet Union, the agreement on this matter was the subject of a separate confidential exchange of notes.[136]

The legal consequences of the articles regulating trade relations seemed equally insurmountable. The debate centered on the definition of the "most favored nation." The earlier commercial agreements of the Soviet Union were all on the basis of most favored nation, meaning that the contracting parties guaranteed the greatest commercial advantages to each other. They declared that so far as the rights and property of their citizens, export and import, duties, shipping and harbor fees and transportation were concerned they would guarantee all of the advantages to the other party which they had granted previously to a third country. Even though the twelve articles of the Hungarian proposal were uniformly based on the principle of most favored nation, Soviet diplomacy took the position that for the "new countries" it would not grant the advantages of "most favored nation" because this was reserved originally for only three groups of nations. These were the Asiatic countries with which Russia had a common border (Turkey, Persia, Afghanistan and Mongolia), the countries which were partly or totally separated from the former Russian Empire at the end of the World War (Estonia, Latvia, Finland, and Poland), and those western European countries which had recognized the Soviet Union prior to Hungary (Germany, Great Britain, Italy, and Austria). The position of Hungarian diplomacy, however, was that Hungary had to receive the same commercial advantages that Germany and Austria enjoyed because if this was not done the Hungarian machine industry and other interested enterprises could not be competitive in the Soviet markets. The Soviet party was not willing to yield on the matter of most favored nation and therefore the Hungarians were forced to yield but, in order to maintain a semblance of balance, they included in the agreement that Hungary excluded the Soviet Union from the special advantages granted by Hungary to its neighboring countries.[137]

Resulting from the negotiations three documents were published on September 12. The first one was a document consisting of six articles concerning the resumption of diplomatic relations. This document was antedated to September 5. It was stated in Article 3 that a trade mission would be attached to the Soviet diplomatic mission with the stipulation that its membership, enjoying diplomatic privileges, would be limited to three persons until further discussions on this matter. Article 4 contained the compulsory diplomatic legal principles according to which the members of the diplomatic mission, including the commercial one, enjoyed all of the rights and privileges they were entitled to under international law. The second document, dated September 12, was an agreement consisting of twelve articles on the modalities of the diplomatic and commercial relations. Article 1 stated that immediately following the establishment of a diplomatic mission, negotiations would be initiated for the creation of a detailed trade agreement. Articles 2 and 3 were devoted to the basic principles of trade relations. Article 2 contained the principle of the most favored nation: namely that, until a final agreement was reached, the contracting parties would guarantee the mutual exchange of advantages concerning the rights of their citizens, their property, shipping and duties. It was specified in the same article that this was a temporary arrangement that did not include the advantages granted by the Soviet Union to the three groups of nations mentioned above or by Hungary to its neighbors. Article 3 referred to the personal legal protection of Soviet and Hungarian citizens traveling in each other's country on business and of the sanctity of their property in the other country. Article 4 dealt with the resumption of mail and telegraphic contacts. The remaining articles limited the mobility of the members of the missions. It specified that from each party only one courier could be dispatched each week who could carry luggage of only sixteen kilograms with all excess being subject to control. The mission was not allowed to employ present or former citizens of the country where it was located and the members of the missions and the couriers had to refrain from meddling with the internal affairs of the host country. The third document, also dated September 12, was the above mentioned confidential exchange of letters which specified the limitation of numbers of the personnel of the missions and thus, in the final analysis, showed the dominance of the Hungarian interests. According to the confidential letters the total personnel of the Soviet missions, including the three people working at the trade mission, could not exceed fourteen persons.[138]

The parties also agreed that the agreements would be enacted at the same time, but that Soviet diplomacy would initiate the process only after having been notified that the obstacles to ratification in Hungary had been eliminated. Complying with a request by the Hungarians the legal enactment was given a three months grace period. The subsequent events, however, derailed the agreements. Prime Minister István Bethlen, who had the reputation of being "an outstanding parliamentary tactician" and who had a substantial majority in parliament, while willing to oppose the negative views of the Regent Miklós Horthy, who was in supreme command and who had to approve all legislation, was still reluctant to present the international documents to the legislature. Hungarian diplomacy was successful, however, in making Moscow agree to extend the grace period for an additional four months, i.e., until April 12, 1925. Even during this extended period the agreements were not taken to parliament for approval. Consequently Budapest asked for an additional extension of six months but Moscow was willing to agree only if the agreement was modified and the article dealing with the matter of the most favored nation was removed. The Hungarian government considered this article to be of critical importance and rejected the Soviet proposal. Thus the parties considered the agreements reached on September 12, 1924, in Berlin to be "null and void."[139]

During the negotiations the Hungarian government insisted that the diplomatic relations were not to be reestablished by a simple exchange of memoranda. The government wanted the negotiations to result in an international agreement which, according to Kánya's statement, was subject to parliamentary ratification.[140] To date Hungarian historiography has not given an explicit and satisfactory answer to the question why it was necessary for the Hungarian party to obtain parliamentary ratification. The question is: what legal regulation made the government ask for parliamentary ratification because of the commercial components of the agreement? The members of the Hungarian government never specified the article in the law that would have obligated the executive branch to seek parliamentary ratification.

At his submission to the Council of Ministers on October 10, 1924, Bethlen talked about this issue only in generalities and did not discuss any concrete problems. He claimed that the Hungarian constitution required that he submit these international documents to the National Assembly for approval. Bethlen stated that, "They [i.e. the Hungarian-Soviet agreements] in part contain such decrees which, under our constitution, makes them subjects to the legislative process."[141] According to the government's interpretation it was the second agreement, regulating commercial relations, which made it necessary to obtain parliamentary ratification. Because this caused considerable misunderstanding in both the earlier and more recent Hungarian scholarly literature, it is noteworthy that there were only two points in the second agreement that dealt seriously with commercial relations. Thus, this document was not a true trade agreement.

It was an international agreement which had two points that stipulated temporary arrangements prior to a future exclusive trade agreement. Furthermore, and in contrast to the government's claim, the commercial policy ordinances did not automatically require legislative ratification. Act IV of 1924 about the reestablishment of a balanced budget, which set the legislative basis for the fiscal reforms of the Hungarian state budget, enacted subsequent to receiving the League of Nations loan, was known in popular language as the "Financial Rescue Act" and contained legal instructions subject to a diametrically opposed interpretation. Paragraph 3 of the act stipulated that the government was to do everything in its power to make commercial agreements possible, principally with the neighboring countries, in order to eliminate the obstacles facing the development of Hungarian foreign trade. Paragraph 4 stated that the government would "submit a legislative proposal to the National Assembly that provided for all future governments a wide-ranging power to implement the indicated program, without requiring further approval from the National Assembly." This clearly included the signing of bilateral, international commercial agreements.[142] The so-called Financial Rescue Act thus did not only entitle the government to make international trade agreements in its own right, without parliamentary approval, but actually urged it to do so referring to the anomalous economic situation and to the stringent economic interests of the country. Representative Tibor Eckhardt referred to the Financial Rescue Act and claimed that this was what the government wanted to use to escape having the National Assembly, the highest political forum, debate the agreements.[143]

There was also an earlier precedent for the government not having an economic agreement ratified. It was the Hungarian-Romanian economic agreement signed on April 16, 1924, which included the principle of the most favored nation. The most favored nation economic agreement between Hungary and Yugoslavia, initialed on March 22, 1924, was instituted by the government three and one half months after signing it on the basis of a special parliamentary approval but without formal ratification.[144] In view of all this it appears to be an obvious conclusion that in the final analysis the government wished to submit to the highest political decision-making body the legitimization of a diplomatic action that was likely to run into substantial societal opposition.

Hungarian historiography clearly blames domestic and external politics for this diplomatic fiasco and cites three basic motives for it. The strong resistance of Regent Horthy and the associated vigorous protests of a significant part of public opinion. The government's hesitation and eventual withdrawal was presumably also due to the sudden cooling off of British-Soviet relations in October 1924 which made the recognition of Soviet Russia a risky step from a Hungarian foreign policy perspective. The first two of these reasons were primarily political in nature the third one deserves further comment because it had trade policy features.

The progress of events in Great Britain was eerily similar to the Hungarian one. The conservative British government, taking over on October 29, did not submit to Parliament for ratification the commercial agreement made with the Soviet Union by its Labour Party predecessor in August. It also did not submit it to the king with a recommendation for ratification. A forthcoming change in British politics became obvious earlier when on October 8, the Labour government lost a vote in the House of Commons.[145] It will take additional research to discover whether there was immediate pressure from the conservative British government circles on the Hungarian leadership, which was oriented toward Britain, to nullify the Berlin agreements. It is certainly apparent that in deciding this matter a major role was played by the comportment and desire of the British government which supported Hungary in the matter of the League of Nations loan. The views of György Barcza, the former Hungarian minister in London, as recorded in the diary of Jungerth, are important. He wrote, "England supports us in every way. We paddle entirely in their waters. In view of this we can do nothing at this time in the Russian matter."[146]

The Nature of Trade Relations during the Second Half of the 1920s

After the failure of establishing trade relations on an industry-wide basis the Hungarian enterprises were forced to seek a variety of solutions to compensate themselves for the losses ensuing from the discounts on the Soviet bills of exchange. The case of the Manfred Weiss Company is a good illustration. In the autumn of 1925 this company received a substantial order for the delivery of plows and harrows to the Soviet Union. The raw material necessary for the making of this equipment, iron rods, hoop iron, iron plates and wires, were produced by the Rimamurány-Salgótarján Iron Works Inc. (Rimamurány-Salgótarján Vasmű, Rt.) and were delivered to the Manfred Weiss Company. In order to reduce the losses originating from the financing of the project the two companies reached an agreement according to which the iron works in Ózd, in northeast Hungary, would deliver the semi-finished components below their cost of production to the

Manfred Weiss manufacturing center in Csepel, near Budapest. The companies also agreed that they would jointly appeal to the Ministry of Finance for it to waive the sales tax on the Soviet exports.[147] They explained in their letter to Minister of Finance János Bud that the Manfred Weiss Company could not assume the risks and the loss of interest associated with exports directed toward the Soviet Union by itself. The export of agricultural machinery to the Soviet Union could be profitable only if the semi-finished metal products would be relieved of the sales tax by the state. The two companies also wrote a letter to the Hungarian State Railways Company (MÁV) and asked that the transportation fee for the materials taken from Ózd to Csepel be reduced. This reduction would be limited only for those products which were ultimately destined for export to the Soviet Union. MÁV was asked to grant the same reduction in the transportation fee for the shipping of the finished products that they granted for the shipping of the semi-finished material.[148] Unfortunately the answer of the government and of MÁV cannot be found in the folder of the Manfred Weiss correspondence.

In the absence of diplomatic relations the Soviet foreign trade organizations were willing to discuss matters with Hungarian exporters and importers only when this was in the best interest of Soviet economy or of the Soviet needs for import. There is a good reference for this in a memorandum from Boris Stomoniakov, a member of the Board of the Commissariat for Foreign Affairs to Anastas Mikoyan, the Commissar for Foreign Trade. On July 9, 1929, Stomoniakov indicated that the previous position of the Commissariat for Foreign Trade had not changed. He strongly opposed any purchases from Hungary except for certain items, such as horses or agricultural machinery that the Soviet Union could buy from other countries only under more unfavorable conditions, at a higher price or of lower quality. Other than this, Stomoniakov considered all economic contacts as being harmful from a political perspective.[149]

Citing the dangers of Communist propaganda the Hungarian organs of internal affairs also raised all sorts of barriers to the realization of doing business with Soviet enterprises. It happened more than once during the 1920s that members of the Berlin or Vienna Soviet Trade Mission visited Hungary. These were generally groups of two or three people who came to Hungary to inspect the storage facilities for merchandise ordered, to check on the manufacturing processes, assess the quality of the merchandise and, occasionally, to visit trade fairs. A memorandum from the Ministry of Commerce makes it evident that all Soviet citizens entering Hungary were kept under constant surveillance by the Hungarian internal security forces. The cost of this surveillance was passed on to the private companies wishing to do business with the Soviets and who had invited the Soviet commercial experts. The costs of the surveillance had to be paid in advance and the money was deposited in the account of the Hungarian Royal State Police.[150]

In his memorandum mentioned above Stomoniakov objected to even such small groups of commercial delegates entering Hungary. He asked Mikoyan to instruct the Berlin, Prague and Vienna Trade Missions that without special permission from the Commissariat for Foreign Trade they were not allowed to establish contact with Hungarian companies and that such permission had to be submitted in each instance to the Commissariat for Foreign Affairs.[151] In order to prevent Communist agitation, Minister of Finance Sándor Wekerle, Jr. considered the surveillance of the trade delegations to be insufficient and therefore in 1930 he issued an ordinance that the import of any wood products, primarily firewood, from any country that did not have a commercial agreement with Hungary, was subject to special permit issued by the Ministry of Commerce. The purpose of the ordinance was to avoid the hiding of propaganda material in shipments which consisted of many small pieces which were difficult to examine.[152]

In summary we can state that the Hungarian companies, which on rare occasions had an opportunity to ship products to the Soviet Union, had such additional expenses imposed upon them that exports directed toward that country resulted in substantial losses. The administrative regulations, originating from both Hungary and from the Soviet Union, erected obstacles to both imports and exports resulting in an overly bureaucratic approach to commercial relations which proved unfavorable for the development of trade agreements. It should be mentioned, however, for the sake of completeness that the responsible Soviet foreign trade and foreign affairs officials frequently and uniformly took the position that the development of commercial relations was primarily in Hungary's interest.[153]

The presentation of numerical data is useful in showing how the commercial transactions between the two countries evolved. For the reasons stated above, namely the lack of Hungarian data and the time-related variations in the Soviet statistics, the results of commercial transactions between 1920 and 1924 are impossible to assess. In the period after 1929 the effects of the world economic crisis and the major changes resulting from it made these years a separate and distinct era from an economic and statistical perspective. Consequently tables 1–5 refer specifically to the period between 1925 and 1928.[154]

Table 1   Hungarian-Soviet Trade between 1925 and 1928

Year	Hungarian exports to the Soviet Union		Hungarian imports from the Soviet Union	
	Tons	in 1,000 pengős	Tons	in 1,000 pengős
1925	806.9+2,635[155]	3,681	20,350.5	3,588
1926	644.1	787	21,174.4	3,539
1927	35.6+2,947	2,250	23,345.9	2,887
1928	9.1+2,953	2,232	23,913.1	2,785

Table 2 Composition of Hungarian Export Goods to the Soviet Union between 1925 and 1928 (in 1,000 Pengős)

	1925	1926	1927	1928
Horses	2,292	–	2,188	2,215
Agricultural machines	18	193	–	–
Metalworking machines	–	40	32	16
Pumps	191	11	–	–
Electrical supplies (Light bulbs, switches, etc.)	593	122	–	–
Iron and metal goods (Pots and pans, wires) etc.)	544	421	–	1
Other (seeds, etc.)	43	–	–	–

Table 3 Composition of Soviet Export Goods to Hungary between 1925 and 1928 (in 1,000 Pengős)

	1925	1926	1927	1928
Crude Oil	2,492	2,739	2,581	2,106
Asbestos	189	347	230	511
Sodium carbonate	888	428	–	–
Iron ore	–	–	54	84
Other (paper, rubber, etc.)	19	25	22	84

Table 4 Production Profile of Hungarian Exports to the Soviet Union
between 1925 and 1928 on the Basis of Value (in Pengős)

	1925	1926	1927	1928
Industrial products	38.06%	100%	2.75%	0.76%
Agricultural products	61.94%	–	97.25%	99.24%

Table 5 Production Profile of Soviet Exports to Hungary between
1925 and 1928 on the Basis of Value (in Pengős)

	1925	1926	1927	1928
Industrial raw materials	99.35%	99.29%	99.24%	96.98%
Industrial finished products	0.85%	0.71%	0.76%	3.02%

The tables allow us to draw some conclusions. The net balance of
the trade ended with a Hungarian plus only in 1925. Starting with 1926
Soviet exports were considerably larger than Hungarian ones and thus
this period is characterized by lower Hungarian exports. Examining the
composition of the export-import goods we can conclude that the export
of horses, critically important from the perspective of Hungarian
exports, was strong, except for 1926. The export of agricultural machinery, being of relatively little value, essentially disappear beginning with
1927. So far as the nature of the trade items is concerned it is striking
that the Soviet export toward Hungary is limited almost exclusively to
industrial raw materials. The Hungarian export is considerably more
varied even though agricultural exports, with the exception of the seed
export in 1925, is limited almost entirely to horses. If we were to
remove the horses, which represented a very valuable commodity, from
the Hungarian export activities, the dominance of finished industrial
products, such as machines, electrical equipment, etc., would become

apparent. This allows us to conclude that the economic output of the two countries complemented each other very effectively by their structural proportions, import requirements and export availability. In principle Hungarian-Soviet economic relations offered considerably more opportunities than could be implemented under the unfavorable political and financial (credit) conditions.

Chapter Three

HUNGARIAN-SOVIET COMMERCIAL RELATIONS IN THE 1930S

Economic Policy Precedents to the Initiation of Diplomatic Relations

At the time of the 1929–1933 Great Depression many politicians and economists regarded the so-called "Soviet dumping" as one of the contributing factors. They blamed the Soviet Union for the precipitous fall of world grain prices, textiles, wood products, and coal, claiming that, taking advantage of its relative economic stability, it wanted to undermine the capitalist economic system. In order to block the flood of Soviet export goods a number of countries instituted protective measures, limited imports and assigned high tariffs on Soviet merchandise.[1] In France, for instance, after October 1930, an increase of 25 percent over the current official exchange rate was charged on the sale of imported Soviet goods. On February 10, 1931, the United States introduced increased "anti-dumping" tariffs on Soviet goods and completely banned the import of wood products. Initially, the Hungarian government also raised the tariffs on all merchandise imported from the Soviet Union and banned the import of certain products.[2] Regent Miklós Horthy was one of the initiators of the protest activity and composed a memorandum in October 1932 in which he invited the heads of about twenty-four countries to begin a world-wide cooperative process against the Bolshevik state threatening the existence of humanity.[3]

The surviving archival sources and the articles in the Hungarian press suggest that in the circle of the independent and authoritative economists the politically motivated demands for joining in the sanctions found little support. In fact, at the turn of 1930–1931, the economic leadership saw the regeneration of Hungarian-Soviet economic relations as one of the ways to emerge from the increasingly protracted crisis.

One of the reasons for this might have been that in 1929 it was announced that the first Five Year Plan produced significant results in the Soviet Union and increased the potential of the Soviet economy. The enormous building program beginning in that country in 1927–1928 and the evident economic mobilization following the introduction of the plan in 1929–1930 strengthened the feeling of the Bolshevik leadership that the country, standing alone, could implement the modernization of industrial production and full industrialization on its own. The system of planned economy used heavy industry as its principal moving force. It is a well-known fact that by implementing the Five Year Plan the Soviet government wanted a systemic change in the economy of the country by liquidating the multi-pillar economic structure introduced by the NEP which consisted of foreign private capital, small properties, cooperative and state properties.[4] Only a few data will be listed to illustrate the economic results of the "great breakthrough" which had required enormous sacrifices as far as human resources were concerned. In 1933, when Stalin announced the completion of the First Five Year Plan ahead of schedule, 3.5 times as much capital had been invested in industrial production as in 1929 and the number of workers in industry rose from 3.7 million to 8.5 million.

According to the Soviet economic historians taking the last year of peace, 1913, as 100 percent then the index of industrial production in 1928 was 132 percent and by 1932 it rose to 352 percent.[5] As mentioned earlier the Soviet economy demonstrated unique characteristics so far as its structural base and management control were concerned. This made it less sensitive to international influences. The autarchic arrangements arising from the "great breakthrough" was one of the reasons why the global upheaval caused by the world-wide economic crisis affected the Soviet economy, forced upswing after 1929, to a much lesser degree. The economy of the capitalist countries reacted much more sensitively to world market trends and to the changes in the conditions of the global economy.

Furthermore, it can be concluded from the findings of the most recent scholarship on the Soviet Union that the fears of the economic elite of the capitalist countries about "Soviet dumping of merchandise" were exaggerated. Soviet export toward the Western countries increased dynamically but at a steady pace from the turn of 1920–1921 until the 1930s without any spectacular increases. Actually in 1927–1928 there was a small break in the momentum of Soviet exports and in this economic period the value of foreign imports exceeded the amount of the Soviet exports. After 1931 the amount of Soviet exports dropped by almost 50 percent. This decrease might be attributed to Western tariff restrictions and to the other measures to protect the domestic markets. The nature of the Soviet export merchandise was characterized between the first half of the 1920s and 1933 by a slight relative increase in industrial raw materials. This was not due to a decrease in agricultural products but to an increase in the amount of industrial raw materials. It can be seen during the years of the economic crisis that this trend underwent a change. The total value of the agricultural products exported from the Soviet Union changed from 23 percent in 1929 to almost 29.5 percent in 1932.

At the same time there was a spectacular increase in the ratio of industrial raw materials and of semi-finished products in the Soviet imports. It rose from 65 percent in 1927–1928 to 80 percent in 1931. These two sets of data allow us to conclude that the reason for the increase in Soviet grain products in the world markets was due to the change in the structure of the Soviet production system. The "great breakthrough," requiring considerable domestic industrial investments, was based on a concentration of domestic raw materials and on the increase of the importation of foreign industrial products. The Soviet state endeavored to balance the cost of the industrial products imported from abroad by the income from the dynamic export of agricultural products.[6]

Because of the price fluctuations in the world markets, the effects of the world economic crisis were felt in Hungary primarily by agriculture even though some areas of industry were also affected. At the peak of the crisis, in 1932, industrial production had declined by 37 percent compared to 1928. The greatest drop in production occurred in those branches of industry which produced primarily production materials. These branches of industry include the iron and steel works, the machine industry, the building material industry and the lumber industry. By 1932 the combined products of the iron and steel industry, the building materials industry and the machine industry declined to 50 percent of the level of the period before the crisis. The industrial branches were affected primarily by a marked constriction of the markets where their products could be sold. Almost all of the European countries hit by the depression introduced protective ordinances resulting in Hungarian foreign commerce losing many of its foreign outlets and also resulting in a sharp decline in the inflow of foreign currencies.

While during the first half of the 1920s Austria was still definitely Hungary's principal foreign trading partner, by the turn of the 1920s and 1930s only 21 percent of Hungarian exports went to that traditional customer. In Hungarian foreign trade Germany and Italy moved into the foreground replacing the traditional Austrian markets.[7] The orientation toward the German and Italian markets was based on the Hungarian-German Trade Agreement of July 18, 1931, and on Hungary's joining the so-called "Brocchi System" in the spring and summer of 1931. This system was a preferential commercial arrangement between Italy, Austria, and Hungary. Eventually the implementation of the system proved disadvantageous for Hungary because the contingencies and preferential supports favored Italy. This meant a substantial increase in the Italian participation and the limitation of Hungarian revenues.[8]

Even though at the time of the Great Depression there were numerous articles in the Hungarian newspapers which warned public opinion of the dangers of a flood of Soviet grain and lumber imports,[9] a significant number of Hungarian business experts saw the solution of the loss of foreign markets for Hungarian industrial products in the establishment of trade relations with the Soviet Union which was less affected by the world crisis and which increased the importation of industrial products. The importance of such a move was stated by János Teleszky, the minister of finance, Sándor Kóródi, the head of the state-run Foreign Commerce Institute (Külkereskedelmi Intézet), the GYOSZ, the National Industrial Guild (Országos Ipartestület), and the leadership of numerous enterprises. Their principal argument was that the promotion and activation of trade would relieve some of the problems of disposing the products of Hungarian industry, primarily of the machine and electrical equipment manufacturers. It would also substantially increase the availability of raw materials for the domestic industries and might even improve the unemployment problems in Hungary.[10]

The program to revive Hungarian-Soviet commercial relations was first drafted for the public by Kóródi in the August 12, 1931, issue of the weekly publication *Pesti Tőzsde*. The economic expert explained that, considering the economic conditions dominating the world, the Soviet Union was the only market area that would assure the acceptance of Hungarian industrial and agricultural products. He wrote:

> Regardless how unpopular it is to promote relations with Russia, Hungary cannot isolate itself when we see that the United States and the powerful Western countries compete with each other for options to export to Russia. If Hungary does not adapt to the ways of reaching business liaisons, which had been accepted by these powerful foreign countries, the consequences of this will appear as the decrease of the utilization of our productivity, because...there would be materials to export to Russia which could be a major market for Hungarian industrial and agricultural products.[11]

The Foreign Commerce Institute considered the situation to be so pressing that in September 1931 it addressed a memorandum to Béla Kenéz, minister of commerce, in which, citing export difficulties, asked for the support of the ministry in order for the Hungarian exports to achieve a breakthrough in the Soviet markets. It was evidently on the basis of this memorandum that on October 16, 1931, a Council of Ministers decision was handed down which empowered Kóródi to go to Berlin, at the head of a delegation, and to negotiate with the Soviet Trade Mission.[12]

The negotiations began on January 4, 1932. The Soviets set two fundamental conditions, one political and one business, for the large-scale orders from Hungary. One of these was that in view of the state monopoly introduced for all foreign commerce, and similarly to commercial agreements in effect with other European countries, the Soviet Union had to be allowed to set up a trade mission in the Hungarian capital. This mission as a central government organ then could engage in direct negotiations with the Hungarian interests. Allowing this would have been essentially similar to a de facto recognition of the Soviet Union by the Hungarian government. The other condition was also in keeping with the practice of Soviet politics on trade. It required that, similarly to earlier practice, Hungarian companies wanting to export to the Soviet Union had to give a line of credit equivalent to the value of the merchandise.[13] In view of the Soviet business policy goals Kóródi recommended that it would be preferable to reach compensatory trade agreements. In this case, as compensation for the exported Hungarian merchandise or for a portion of it, the Hungarian party would have been obligated to purchase Soviet goods. On the import list the Hungarian negotiators set up were primarily raw materials, such as crude oil, asbestos, lumber, coal, and chemical goods. The Soviet partners' attention was drawn primarily to agricultural machines and other equipment, electrical industry products and agricultural products, live animals, such as cattle, horses and pigs, forage plants and seeds. The Hungarian government did not agree to the establishment of a trade mission but agreed that a three person study group could come to Hungary for six months to negotiate concrete deals.[14]

No agreement could be reached in the German capital and therefore, to continue the negotiations, two high-ranking officials of the Soviet Trade Mission in Berlin went to Budapest in May, 1932. There being no reliable sources we know nothing about the details of these discussions and have to rely on the reports in the newspapers. According to these the major differences in the business policies, such as compensation, financing and credits, could still not be overcome.[15]

The official negotiations came to an end for a considerable period but a document, dated at a much later time, reveals that the Ministry of Commerce considered the continuation of a liaison with the Soviet trade organizations sufficiently important that still in the spring of 1932 it established a one-person agency in Berlin. It was charged with supporting the Hungarian business enterprises that wanted to export to the Soviet Union and with bringing practical business matters to fruition. András Csapó was appointed to head the agency.[16]

To indicate the volume of Hungarian-Soviet merchandise trading I have selected the five year period prior to the resumption of the diplomatic relations because significant trends should have become apparent during these years. These years coincide with the worst years of the Great Depression. Table 6 shows that the yearly balance was favorable for Hungary only in 1931.[17]

Table 6 Hungarian-Soviet Trade Activity between 1929 and 1933[18]

Year	Hungarian exports		Hungarian imports	
	Tons	1,000 pengős	Tons	1,000 pengős
1929	7.0+1,108	798	16,285.1	1,904
1930	114.4	246	21,854.3	3,989
1931	13,032.1	2,424	8,345.5	154
1932	99.3	121	13,049.1	1,521
1933	125.2	178	1,195.2	366

According to László Pap's calculations Soviet participation within the Hungarian imports amounted only to 0.1 percent in 1931, to 0.5 percent in 1932 and again to 0.1 percent in 1933.[19]

The experiences of the 1920s and of the first part of the 1930s showed that the Hungarian commercial traffic was both meager and generally closed with a negative balance. Improving this commercial activity would have been to the benefit of Hungarian economy. In the autumn of 1933 István Winchkler, the director of the Foreign Commerce Institute went to Berlin to resume the negotiations which had come to a halt in May, 1932. Because I found no source material for these negotiations I had to rely on the interview that was given by the economic expert to the *Pesti Napló,* a semi-official publication of the government. In this he stated that one of the insoluble obstacles to the increase in Hungarian-Soviet trade was in the system of payments.

While the Soviet Union demanded immediate payment for its exported products it usually paid for items imported to it by voucher only. According Winchkler, the prime minister and "the others involved" would be willing to discuss the matter of the securities to be granted by the government. He did acknowledge that so far Moscow had actually met its financial obligations. He explained that by overcoming the financing problem and clarifying the government's policy on securities, Hungary could achieve a surplus of 4–5 million pengős and a positive trade balance vis-à-vis the Soviet Union. He suggested that the basis for further developments in commercial activity would be to reach a trade agreement that would reflect the legal resolution of the relationship between the two countries.[20]

When the Italian minister in Budapest told Sándor Khuen-Héderváry, the deputy minister of foreign affairs, that he had received some information about the Hungarian-Soviet trade negotiations in Berlin, Khuen-Héderváry denied that there were any political implications. The Hungarian diplomat said,

> Trade negotiations with Soviet representatives occur regularly because we have been doing business with them for years. It is possible that Winchkler talked to them about some business but I have no knowledge about this. This means nothing because there are frequently such discussions about which I am in ignorance. I pointed out the mistaken belief abroad, and also at home, that because we had no diplomatic relations with Soviet Russia we did not conduct business with them.[21]

It is apparent that Khuen-Héderváry described Winchkler's Berlin negotiations as a simple business conversation. Winchkler, in his statement, also endeavored to separate the area of trade negotiations from the matter of political recognition. Yet it was obviously a giant step forward that the Hungarian leadership even considered the possibility of providing state guarantees.

Later on the Hungarian press interpreted the economic expert's negotiations in Berlin to mean that some agreement had been reached on the compensatory payment method for the import and export transactions. According to this the Hungarian National Bank was liable to devote only 50 percent of the sum to be paid by the Soviet Union for Hungarian merchandise exported to it for compensation of the counter value of the Soviet goods imported to Hungary. This system resulted in a 1:2 compensation ratio in the trade of the two countries in Hungary's favor.[22] This meant that after 1934 the balance of trade between Hungary and the Soviet Union would have closed in Hungary's favor because Hungary could export twice as much merchandise to the Soviet Union than what it imported from there.[23] Even though I have not found any official document, text of agreement or record which would prove the fact of an agreement and would provide information about the contents of an agreement we derive information from Soviet documents of 1934–1935, that in certain commercial transactions there were compensatory ratios. This raises the question why the Soviet economic leadership made it possible that in some business transactions the compensatory mechanisms became unfavorable for them?

Hungary, dependent on foreign trade income, was forced, due to the uncertain foreign exchange conditions resulting from the world economic crisis, to engage in contractual arrangements in which trade was linked to a unique system of accounting. These were preferential agreements in which the contracting parties endeavored to reach a trade balance and provided each other a number of benefits to achieve this balance. The more favorable compensatory ratio for Hungary was evidently the result of a compromise and was designed to make up for the losses arising from discounting the Soviet bills of exchange. In addition, in the autumn of 1933 the Soviet commercial organizations evidently did not expect a significant increase in the anemic Hungarian-Soviet merchandise exchange in the presence of the unsatisfactory political relations between the two countries.

A later report from Jungerth makes it quite clear that because of the unfavorable compensatory ratios for the Soviet Union the Commissariat for Foreign Trade put Hungary on a blacklist in spite of the then existing diplomatic relations. This meant that Hungary, together with Romania and Yugoslavia, was listed among the countries from where imports had to be kept to a minimum. In the absence of a trade agreement Hungary could not appear on the annual marketing register of the planned economy and the Soviet Union could order merchandise from Hungary only if these items could not be obtained from anywhere else or if the usual supplier did not have sufficient material and thus a shortfall had to be corrected. In addition, such an order required special authorization from the Commissar for Foreign Affairs.[24] In the autumn of 1935 the Hungarian trade journals admitted that the favorable compensatory ratio, authorized only for certain individual transactions, could not be exploited by Hungary because of the general decline in trade.[25]

*Negotiations in Rome. The Establishment of
Diplomatic Relations between Hungary and
the Soviet Union*

On February 6, 1934, Hungary and the Soviet Union established diplomatic relations. The international background and the precursors of this diplomatic event and the negotiations in Rome are fully discussed in the Hungarian historical literature.[26] Consequently this discussion will be limited to the economic policy aspects of the agreement reached in the Italian capital. Even though the Ministry of Foreign Affairs was not compelled by any legal mandate to submit a commercial agreement to parliament for ratification, when the text of the agreements was being drafted Hungarian diplomacy took the position that in order to avoid the repetition of the 1924 parliamentary fiasco, the establishment and rules of diplomatic relations had to be kept separate from any commercial agreement. Mihály Arnóthy-Jungerth, the minister in Ankara, was designated to represent Hungary in the negotiations with the Soviet officials. He was ordered back to Budapest for discussions of the tactical management of the negotiations shortly after he had assumed his position in Ankara.

The diplomat returned from Ankara on January 18, 1934, and was received by Minister of Foreign Affairs Kánya that same day. This discussion was also attended by Gábor Apor the head of the Political Division of the Ministry of Foreign Affairs and by Pál Danilovics, the head of its International Legal Division. Our only information about this discussion comes from Jungerth's diary. The possibility of avoiding the process of ratification by parliament was the subject of this preparatory discussion. Looking at the 1924 agreement as a model, Jungerth wanted to exclude from it everything that would require the approval of parliament and that would have involved a legislative enactment. He argued that, "The present negotiations will be limited to the establishment of diplomatic relations and to the decisions related to it. There is no need for parliamentary ratification because the government can start diplomatic relations with any country without asking parliament." For this reason the articles concerning the temporary arrangement of commercial relations were omitted from the proposal. Referring to the economic difficulties facing the Hungarian government Jungerth had to emphasize at the forthcoming discussions the request of the government that no permanent mission be established in the two capitals. It was only thus that Horthy's approval could be obtained for raising the relations with the Soviet Union to an official level. Jungerth cited the comment of the minister of foreign affairs, well known for his sarcasm, "…Kánya emphasized that they should not send an official mission to us, nor a commercial delegation. He insisted that they should continue to do business as before. Let people come, arrange business and go away."[27]

At the preparatory discussions eventually three related documents were drafted. The first one was a diplomatic note which, in the formal language of diplomacy and in an ornate composition, declared the start of diplomatic relations. The second was a supplemental protocol consisting of eleven articles. The first article stated the Hungarian request that so long as Hungary was prevented by budgetary constraints from establishing a mission in Moscow, both governments would accredit one of their diplomats in a third country to each other's capital. The second article regulated the establishment of a Soviet trade mission in Budapest and that its personnel were to be limited to three persons. The other articles dealt with the establishment of postal and telephone contacts, etc. The last three articles took from the 1924 agreement the decisions concerning the prevention of Communist propaganda, the restriction of the courier activities and the avoidance of any interference with the domestic affairs including the ban of employing present or former Hungarian citizens at the Soviet mission. The last document was an exact copy of the letters exchanged in 1924 limiting the personnel of the Hungarian mission in Moscow to eight to ten people and the Soviet personnel in Budapest, including the trade mission to a total of fourteen.[28]

The negotiations in the Italian capital lasted from January 21 to February 4. Soviet diplomacy was represented by Vladimir Potemkin, the ambassador in Rome, while the Hungarian Ministry of Foreign Affairs was represented by Jungerth. The principal question at the negotiations concerned the delay in establishing legations, the temporary accreditation of ministers serving in another country and the drafting of the suitable documents. Just as in 1924 Soviet diplomacy considered the articles restricting the freedom of movement of the Soviet representatives to be offensive. These included the restriction of the courier services, the ban on employing former or present Hungarian citizens and the prohibition of meddling in domestic affairs.[29] Soviet diplomats kept the Italians informed about the negotiations from the very beginning and the Italians, wanting the negotiations to be successful, brought pressure to bear on the Hungarian negotiators. This went to the point that Mussolini, through Ascanio Colonna, the Italian minister in Budapest asked Prime Minister Gyula Gömbös to set up the legations as soon as possible.[30]

Jungerth argued that the government had to consider its financial difficulties and domestic policy problems such as the opposition of public opinion and of the parliamentary parties and Horthy's wishes. After lengthy discussions Moscow accepted a compromise that instead of the immediate establishment of the legations this action would be postponed until the beginning of the new fiscal year, namely July 1 and that this would be entered in Article 1 of the agreement.[31] The July 1, date was considered by the Soviet side as the ultimate concession arguing that agreeing to the Hungarian demands would set a dangerous precedent. Using this precedent other European countries could refuse in the future to send representatives to Moscow and this would endanger the smooth functioning of the Soviet diplomatic machinery. The Hungarian government was unwilling to risk the successful outcome of the negotiations and therefore Kánya authorized Jungerth to exchange memoranda and sign the agreements including the conditions demanded by the Soviets.[32] On February 6 Jungerth and Potemkin initialed the three documents and thus put an end to the ten-year long problems in the relations between the two countries.

They signed the festively composed document, antedated to February 4, about the start of diplomatic relations. The protocol, reduced to seven articles, about the regulations of the diplomatic relations remained under the date of February 6. Article 1 contained the ominous statement about the establishment of the legations. It read verbatim, "Because, for fiscal reasons, Hungary is unable to establish its legation in Moscow prior to July 1, 1934, both governments will instruct one of their diplomats in another country to represent them in the interim." Article 2 dealt with the establishment of a Soviet trade mission in Budapest and about the appointment of its three members who were given diplomatic immunity. The fourth point projected the beginning of commercial negotiations subsequent to the appointment of the diplomatic representatives. The following articles contained the already mentioned restrictive covenants about the couriers, the employment of Hungarian citizens and interference in Hungarian domestic affairs. The confidential letters, also dated February 6, were identical with the 1924 ones and confirmed that the Hungarian Legation in Moscow could have no more than ten people and that the Soviet Legation and Trade Mission in Budapest were limited to a total of fourteen people including the locally hired support staff.[33]

The key move in the preparations for the Rome negotiations was getting the support of Regent Horthy because it was well known that it was his negative stand which ultimately determined the outcome of the 1924 arguments about ratification. It was different in 1934 when Horthy's approval removed the barriers before the initiation of meritorious discussions with the Soviet diplomats.[34] Horthy's conversion to a more sensible approach was probably due mainly to Kánya who apparently told the regent about the arguments that Mussolini conveyed in his December 6 instructions which were shared by the Hungarian foreign affairs apparatus. In these arguments the foreign policy considerations played the principal role. They included that every large country and a number of small ones had already recognized the Soviet Union and that every sign suggested that the members of the Little Entente would follow suite shortly and make the relationships formal ones. Mussolini's arguments included that Communist propaganda was not influenced by the resumption of diplomatic relationships with the Soviet Union as shown by the Italian experience.[35] Horthy's attitude thus removed the principal barrier facing the beginning of the negotiations. We know from Jungerth's diary that later on it was the regent who on February 3, 1934, was instrumental in moving the agreement debate between Hungarian and Soviet diplomats toward a resolution. Kánya, seeing the unrelenting Soviet negotiation tactics, at the Crown Council meeting dealing with this issue, "presented the situation indicating that he was giving up the fight." Causing considerable astonishment, "the regent declared that if we had started the business let us finish it. This was now his view." This behind the scenes secret was revealed by Kánya to Jungerth when the latter returned from Rome.[36]

It is likely that Horthy's more elastic perspective was due to the influence of his younger son, Miklós, who at this time functioned as an economic expert. In 1928 and 1929 he worked as an official in the Anglo-Hungarian Bank (AMB) first as a deputy director and then as a director. This bank was the strongest proponent of opening the Soviet markets to Hungarian businesses. In addition to his job with the bank, young Horthy also served as the managing director of the Hungarian-Egyptian Trade Corporation, which was established in 1933 and was jointly owned by the AMB and the Pest Hungarian Bank of Commerce (Pest Magyar Kereskedelmi Bank). This company was exporting a variety of agricultural products, mainly live animals, cattle, and horses to the Near East and Middle East.[37] The company wanted to establish itself in Iran as well but because of the transport problems involved it would have been essential to have established commercial relations with the Soviet Union. In addition, the Soviet republics of Central Asia might have become importers of Hungarian live animals.

The concepts of commercial cooperation were familiar to Regent Horthy as well. He had served as the highest ranking officer of the Austro-Hungarian Monarchy's navy and distinguished himself with a number of major victories during his naval career. He was also very much interested in the fate of the Danubian flotilla. He felt that to increase Hungarian commerce toward the east, meaning the Soviet Union, the opportunities of using Danubian transportation had to be exploited. Aleksandr Bekzadian once described this saying that, "Horthy was a slave to this idée fixe."[38]

On more than one occasion Horthy was informed directly about the economic strength of the Soviet Union and about the consolidation of the Communist regime. We repeatedly find entries in Jungerth's diary mentioning private audience with the regent. On April 3, 1933, prior to the start of diplomatic relations, Jungerth had a private audience lasting for more than an hour. In addition to industrial productivity and public supplies, actual political issues such as Soviet-British and Soviet-German relations, were also discussed. Jungerth drew Horthy's attention to the fact that in 1931–1932 the Soviet government's international position had improved. Jungerth informed the regent that he [Jungerth] had frequently mentioned to Soviet diplomats the intentions of the Hungarian government to cooperate with Russia but that the memories of the Hungarian Soviet Republic made this impossible for the time being. According to the diary entry, "Horthy approved this form of managing the problem." In connection with the increasing difficulties of the Baltic States, Horthy voiced his assumption that sooner or later the Soviet would gain access to the sea. According to Jungerth, Horthy explained "with much expertise" the Soviet Union's endeavors to gain access to the sea from Vladivostok to Reval. The regent thought that this was what made a country rich and this was why he wanted to make Budapest into a seaport.[39]

Evidently there were a number of motives leading to Horthy's changing his position. The generally recognized changes in the European political constellation, the strong Italian pressure, the uniform posture of the Hungarian governmental agencies, and, presumably, his son's economic lobbying induced Horthy not to oppose the practically inevitable start of political relations with certain conditions and safeguards. Every sign seems to indicate that he recognized the commercial benefits that would ensue from it and that he considered it most important and desirable to exploit the possibilities of riverine and oceanic transport via Hungarian-Soviet cooperation.

In accordance with the agreement reached in Rome the Hungarian and Soviet governments had to appoint, by July 1, 1934, a diplomat currently serving in a third country to represent them pro temp in Moscow and Budapest. The Politburo, as early as March 5, one month after the agreement, approved the appointment of Adolf Petrovski, the Soviet minister in Vienna to serve in this position in Budapest.[40] The principal reason for this appointment was the geographic proximity of the Austrian and Hungarian capitals. In case of need one could travel from Vienna to Budapest very rapidly and at minimal expense and, furthermore, at this time, except for a commercial delegation in Prague, none of Hungary's neighbors had a Soviet diplomatic representation.[41]

Also, for some time the Soviet Legation in Vienna had been responsible for dealing with Hungary.[42] Bekzadian was appointed the regular minister to Hungary on August 5.[43] This diplomat was of Armenian descent and was born in 1879. In 1920–1921 he was one of the most influential Bolshevik politicians and the Commissar for Foreign Affairs of Soviet Armenia. As a leading official at the Berlin Soviet Trade Mission between 1922 and 1926 he gained not only political experience but most useful commercial experience as well. After 1930 he was the senior diplomat at the Soviet legation in Oslo. In 1934 he was sent from the Norwegian capital to Budapest. On March 31, 1934, Jungerth was appointed to Moscow by the Hungarian Ministry of Foreign Affairs, retaining his appointment to Ankara as well.[44] Jungerth presented his letter of credentials to Mikhail Kalinin, the chairman of the Central Executive Committee of the USSR.[45] With the establishment of the Hungarian Legation in 1935 he was designated permanent minister.

The Travel of the Trade Delegation in 1934

The start of the diplomatic relations should have contributed to an increase in the movement of goods between the two countries since this diplomatic action removed the political barriers which the Soviet leaders placed to impede the expansion of trade. Article 4 of the protocols of February 6, 1934, directed that after the appointment of the diplomatic representatives the two parties would begin negotiations about a trade agreement. Hungarian commercial interests considered it to be important that, even prior to the signing of an agreement, new commercial and investment opportunities made possible by the diplomatic relations be explored. Consequently the Hungarian government, immediately after the start of the diplomatic relations asked the Soviet side to permit a visit by a trade delegation in order for it to explore, *in situ*, the import and export possibilities.[46] Ideas about sending a trade delegation to Moscow preceded the date of the establishment of diplomatic relations. At the turn of 1933–1934 the director of the Central Motor Inspection Bureau in Moscow went to Budapest in order to reach an agreement with the Láng Machine Company and with Ganz for the purchase of diesel engines. These valuable engines had represented a significant part of Hungarian exports to the Soviet Union. In the first part of the 1930s Soviet industries repeatedly ordered high performance diesel engines to be installed in trucks and buses because these Hungarian machines did very well in comparative tests.[47] According to the information gathered by the Hungarian press it was a Soviet engineer who recommended that a Hungarian trade delegation travel to the Soviet Union to study business opportunities there. Minister of Foreign Affairs Kánya supported such a proposal and thus a decision was made for the departure of a delegation on such a trip.[48]

On February 8, two days after the diplomatic agreement, András Csató wrote a letter to the Hungarian Communist émigré, Gyula Lengyel, the head of the Commercial Policy Division of the Commissariat for Foreign Trade, suggesting the visit of a Hungarian trade delegation. In his letter Csató indicated that the goal of the delegation was for the representatives of the Hungarian economic leadership and of the business community to study the ways of improving commercial relations and the possibilities of establishing concrete export-import agreements.[49] The response from the Commissariat for Foreign Trade, dated February 15, showed that it still viewed the administrative problems as being serious. It explained that in order to understand the concepts of developing commercial activities between the two countries there had to be a delay until the first organizational steps had been taken. This meant the establishment of diplomatic missions in both countries and the appointment of the Soviet Trade Mission in Budapest. Discussion of the matter had to be postponed until the accreditation of the envoys had been confirmed.[50] Not much later, however, on February 20, Winchkler reported to the Ministry of Foreign Affairs that Soviet welcome was an accomplished fact. He claimed that, based on discussions with Jungerth, he was able to set a date to the forthcoming visit of the delegation.[51]

The trip of the delegation was arranged by Jungerth, the man chosen to be the minister in Moscow, who arrived in the Russian capital on April 24.[52] He spoke to David Shtern, the head of the Second Western Division of the Commissariat for Foreign Affairs, on April 28 about the need to discuss the practical aspects of the matter.[53] Resolution of the issue must have come about very rapidly because the delegation left Budapest three weeks later on May 23. Haste is also shown by a memorandum from Arkadii Rozengolts, the Commissar for Foreign Trade, addressed to his subordinates. In this he admonished them for not having reported to him the program of the Hungarian delegation due to arrive in Moscow in a few days or who from the commissariat would receive them and chaperone them in Moscow. He was also distressed because no arrangements had been made to secure the funds required for the reception and provisions of the delegation.[54] It became evident later that the Hungarian side had decided not to send a top-level official delegation but one consisting primarily of businessmen, industrialists, company directors and some government administrators. Its sole purpose was a preliminary evaluation of the opportunities for business activities. It is also surprising that the minister in Moscow emphasized that the members of the delegation "did not expect to receive any orders for merchandise."[55]

The list of the members of the delegation was approved by the regent who agreed that Minister of Commerce Tihamér Fabinyi take charge of arranging the trip. The detailed program of the delegation was cleared with the Soviet missions in Vienna and with the Inturist office in that city.[56] In the absence of archival material we learn from newspaper articles that the delegation was led by Félix Bornemissza a navigation expert and an official of the Royal Hungarian Office for Foreign Trade (Magyar Királyi Külkereskedelmi Hivatal). The other members of the delegation were: András Csató, József Willerstorfer, the CEO of the Hungarian Cloth Factory, Inc. (Magyar Posztógyár, Rt.), János Orphanides, vice president of the Ganz-Danubius Machine, Railway Car and Shipbuilding Inc. (Ganz-Danubius Gép-, Vagon- és Hajógyár, Rt.), Géza Rulf, the CEO of the International Lifestock Marketing Inc. (Nemzetközi Állatértékesítési Rt.), Gyula Koch, the administrator of the State Stud Farm at Mezőhegyes (Mezőhegyesi Állami Ménesbirtok), Jenő Mátyás, the director of the Rimamurány-Salgótarján Iron Works, Inc. (Rimamurány-Salgótarjáni Vasmű Rt.), and Miklós Wettstein, the director of the Fantó United Hungarian Petroleum-Industry, Inc. (Fantó Egyesült Magyar Ásványolaj-ipari Rt.).[57] One could read in the May 3 issue of the *Pesti Tőzsde* that the economist István Görgey, the parliamentary representative of the Party of National Unity, who used economic arguments during the debates on the side of the government in favor of resuming diplomatic relations, was also a member of the group. The article assumed that Miksa Fenyő, the managing director of GYOSZ would also go but his and Görgey's presence in the group cannot be substantiated.[58] The Soviet press clearly stated that the delegation consisted of eight members.[59] Selection of the members of the delegation was made in order to send a signal because experts and industrialists were selected who represented navigation, the Hungarian smelting industry, machine manufacturing, the textile industry, oil refinery, and horse breeding.

We can rely on two sources when we wish to determine the substance of the delegation's negotiations in the Soviet Union. One of these is a more than fifty-page report by Félix Bornemissza which he presumably prepared for his superiors at the end of June or early in July shortly after the return of the delegation on June 17. In spite of its length this report is interesting primarily from the perspective of cultural history. It focuses mainly on the views of a contemporary Hungarian economic expert on the Soviet Union and on Soviet reality. The official analyzed the political and economic situation in the Soviet Union, its constitutional system and its policies of enlarging its armed forces. All this can be ascertained from other sources as well. He does not cover the perspectives discussed at the meetings or the issues which had been debated. At the end of the report he briefly draws his conclusions and presents a detailed review of import and export possibilities.[60] A much broader and more detail oriented report was prepared by Miklós Wettstein who discussed one of the most important issues affecting Hungary, namely the import of crude oil and his discussions with the representatives of Nefteexport.[61] In addition to these Willerstorfer also gave an interview about his business experiences in the Soviet Union to the economic weekly, *Pesti Tőzsde.*[62]

We can reconstruct the essence of the negotiations from these building blocks. The program of the delegation can be found in Bornemissza's report. It arrived in Moscow on May 25 and was received at the station by Deputy Commissar for Foreign Trade Ivan Lorents, by the director of Inturist, and by Jungerth. On May 26 they had a discussion with Lorents and visited the AMO-Stalin automobile factory. On May 27 they were received by Rozengolts at the Commissariat for Foreign Trade. On May 29 and 31 they negotiated with the representatives of the Soviet export and import enterprises. Between June 1 and 7 they traveled in the Ukraine and in southern Russia. There they visited the large modern socialist city of Dneproges built to serve the huge Dnieper hydroelectric power station. They also saw the large agricultural combine, Gigant, built in the 1920s next to Rostov with German capital, and the tractor factory in Kharkov. On June 8 and 9 they again negotiated with the commercial and industrial leaders in Moscow. On June 11 and 12 they negotiated in Leningrad with the leaders of the maritime port about the harbor facilities, about the activities at the shipyard and about the transport possibilities. On June 14, prior to departure they said goodbye to the commissar and deputy commissar of the Commissariat for Foreign Trade at the commissariat's building.

Bornemissza summarized his impressions as follows: "It is difficult to predict much about the business deals to be made with Russia. It is a fact, however, that both the Russians and we have export materials which are mutually needed. As a matter of prestige Russia will not show much interest so that it should not become evident that it does not enjoy much credit in other countries. My conviction, based on careful structuring and continuous contacts, is that we will be able to do good business with them." He considered it essential that a "commercial presence" be established at the Hungarian Legation in Moscow which would continuously watch the Soviet market, conduct negotiations with Soviet commercial organizations and advise Soviet import agencies about available Hungarian materials. Among the potential export materials he mentioned diesel engines for vehicles and ships, metal industry products such as iron plates, roller bearings, spring steel, etc., machine parts, e.g. axles and wheels, industrial raw materials like bauxite and aluminum oxide, technical equipment and, finally, agricultural products such as frozen pork, horses, cattle and seeds. Among the potential import goods he mentioned chemicals, hemp, linen, wool, silk, and rubber products.[63]

Willerstorfer, who had returned a few days before the rest of the delegation, stated that in his opinion the Hungarian machine manufacturers had the best chance for exporting to the Soviet Union but that there was a chance for exporting bauxite and aluminum oxide as well. He confirmed that the improved Soviet textile industry has grown to the point where it used so much raw material that the export to Hungary of Soviet raw materials, like wool, would decrease.[64]

It became evident only from a circular issued by the Commissariat for Foreign Trade which Soviet export and import organizations' representatives negotiated with the Hungarian delegation. On July 8 the commissar for foreign trade instructed the leaders of the organizations who had negotiated with the Hungarians to send him the subjects of these negotiations. On the letterhead of the circular the following addressees were listed: the oil exporter Nefteexport, the cereals, grain and feeds exporter-importer Exportkhleb, the textile importer Textilimport, the iron and metal products importer Soiuzmetimport, the Mashinoimport, the electrical industry importer Tekhnopromimport, the Vneshtorgtrans transportation company and the Commissariat for Heavy Industry.[65]

It can be seen that the Hungarian delegation gathered information widely and visited every potential enterprise. Yet the negotiations caused some disappointment in Moscow and Boris Rozenblum, the director of the Economic Division of the Commissariat for Foreign Affairs later said that the trip of the delegation "had no practical results whatsoever."[66] It is true, however, that the Hungarian side repeatedly emphasized that the goal of the trade delegation was solely the exploration of the business terrain and the gathering of information. It was not to serve as a beginning for the signing of trade agreements. In the Hungarian sources we can find expressions that describe the activities of the delegation as a "study tour."[67]

Wettstein also stated in an interview to the press that the trip of the trade delegation was purely informational in nature and that its members wanted to study the situation of the Soviet industry, agriculture and commerce. They also wanted to get some information about the future potential for trade between the two countries.[68] The nature of the negotiations is also reflected by the composition of the delegation because one half of the group consisted of people who had leadership positions in a variety of business enterprises (Willerstorfer, Orphanides, Wettstein, and Mátyás) while the other half consisted of mid- or high-level government officials (Bornemissza, Csató, Rulf, and Koch). Willerstorfer was also the head of the division of the Commercial Statistical Value Assessment Committee, with the rank of commercial chief counselor and thus was also a government official.

One of the meritorious events of the Moscow negotiations can be found only in Wettstein's report and in a much later report of Jungerth, dated December 9, 1935. These reveal that during the trip of the trade delegation major emphasis was placed on the question of the revival of the Danubian transport project and, within the Soviet export issues, on the export of oil. According to Jungerth, the Commissar for Foreign Trade made it clear to the Hungarians that oil export "would be difficult" because domestic use had increased and export to Hungary would be possible only if production would be increased. The Soviet official encouraged the Hungarians by saying that an increase in production was being considered and thus it could be discussed again at a later time.[69]

Wettstein believed that claiming an increase of domestic use was only an excuse for the Soviets to reject the large-scale Hungarian import requirements. He drew this conclusion during the discussions with Nefteexport that the Soviet side seemed to be willing to undertake the export of about half of the Hungarian oil imports of seventeen thousand tank-car loads. Later, however, on intercession by the Commissar for Foreign Trade, the Soviet side retreated and made an offer only for the delivery of a low BTU artificial oil mixed with mazut fuel oil. Wettstein could therefore reasonably assume that the increase of domestic consumption was used only as an excuse:

Unfortunately the Russian crude oil export to Hungary has run into difficulties because the hopes of increasing the domestic crude oil production have not materialized. Thus, in view of the increase in domestic consumption, the large-scale growth of domestic industry, and the mechanization of agriculture, domestic consumption has greatly increased and the recent drillings have not produced the expected results. The Russian senior circles naturally tried to hide the lack of success in recent oil well drilling and blamed the increase of domestic consumption for the export difficulties.

This document proves that, in contrast to Wettstein's statement given to the press, the gathering of information was not the sole purpose and that the Hungarian delegation had very definite ideas.[70] In his report Bornemissza bitterly comments that at the moment "there was little chance" for importing Russian oil.[71] This was a setback because, as discussed earlier, the representatives of the Hungarian petroleum industry have endeavored ever since the 1920s to make the overly dependent industrial productivity of the country independent of Romanian oil imports and assure the continuity of domestic refining.

Endeavors to Attain a Monopoly in Trade Relations with the Soviet Union

During the travel of the trade delegation it became obvious that the resumption of diplomatic relations would not automatically resolve the business policy and financial problems facing the development of trade between the two countries. One of the issues which remained pending was the regulation of the system of payments. The Soviet state enterprises continued to get a variety of import articles in exchange for vouchers while they demanded instant payment for crude oil exported from Russia. In addition, they wanted to link their commodity exports with their imports from Hungary in a way disadvantageous for the Hungarian importers. This is well illustrated in Wettstein's report:

> The counter-value was paid by the Russians with a twenty-one month voucher in Western currency and these vouchers were discountable in Paris. The cost of imported crude oil would be met by the sums of money received in exchange for the Russian vouchers, i.e. only twenty-one months later. Yet the Russians insisted that delivery of petroleum products was subject to immediate payment in Western currencies. Consequently, if it should prove impossible to negotiate a more equitable exchange in payment for export and import goods, our lack of Western currency would force us to postpone purchase of petroleum for twenty-one months. There are negotiations under way to arrange that the vouchers received from the Russians should not only be discountable but also sellable. This would make it possible to make imports start in parallel with the beginning of exports.[72]

The final accreditation of the envoys and the establishment of the legations were delayed by both parties for more than a year and the appointment of a Soviet trade representative never took place. To increase Hungarian exports to the Soviet Union it was essential to resolve the problem of financing them. I have found no data suggesting that the responsible Hungarian economic organizations ever discussed the merits of state guarantees. Citing French press information some organs suggested that French or Swiss capital would be willing to support Hungarian exports with a favorable discount of the interest. Accordingly the French banks would, in exchange for the price of merchandise exported to the Soviet Union, primarily engines and railway equipment, discount the Soviet vouchers with a 10 percent interest discount.[73] Subsidization of the Hungarian-Soviet trade was eventually undertaken by an international financial group, the Emden Bank, named for Max Emden. The businessman was the owner of an international chain of department stores and he also owned the majority of shares in the Corvin Department Store in Budapest. To manage the financing he established an independent company, Stella Trading Corporation. Representatives of the Hungarian government participated in its organizing session. In this way the government gave a free hand to private capital to financially support Hungarian-Soviet trade.[74]

The contemporary economic annuals serving as trade registers suggest that Stella was directed by a combination of Hungarian and foreign capitalists with the support of the Hungarian government. According to the 1934 entries the principal shareholders of the Corvin Department Store, Inc. were Max Emden and his son Hans Erik Emden.[75] After the company had undergone some change, the Board of Directors included, other than the Emden son, two prominent members of the former trade delegation, János Orphanides, József Willerstorfer, and Ferenc Neuhaus, a Hungarian shareholder of the Corvin Department Store. Orphanides, originally trained as an engineer, was at this time one of the most influential manufacturers because he served on the Board of Directors of several highly important companies. He was a vice president of the Ganz and Hofherr-Schrantz Boards. By lobbying, the Stella Company gathered supporters from government circles and its Board of Directors included László Hoffer, a parliamentary representative of the Party of National Unity.[76] According to the Soviet Legation Hoffer was one of the confidants of the Hungarian prime minister.[77]

The key figure at Stella was Aleksandr Urievich, a man of Polish descent. Since the early 1930s he had been in close contact with Emden who considered discounting Soviet vouchers as one of his principal business activities. Urievich, claiming that he had considerable experience in Soviet markets and that he was in contact with the highest trade organizations in Moscow and with the trade mission Vienna, offered his services to Emden after the start of diplomatic relations between Hungary and the Soviet Union. He also offered his services to Stella, via Emden, offering to assure a position for it in the Soviet market. In the autumn of 1934 he went to Moscow and established contacts with Gyula Lengyel. He asked this official, of Hungarian descent, to put him in touch with the industrial exporter Promexport, with the lumber products exporter Exportles, the petroleum industry exporter Nefteexport and other representatives of state industrial enterprises in order to negotiate with them about the export of their products to Hungary and for the import of Diesel engines from Hungary. He also inquired about the position the Commissariat for Foreign Trade might take about the establishment of a Hungarian-Soviet joint company in which, from the Hungarian side, Stellla would be the principal shareholder. Lengyel conveyed the lack of interest by the Commissariat for Foreign Trade in the establishment of such a joint company.[78]

Returning from the Soviet capital Urievich went to the Soviet Legation where he claimed that the Commissariat for Foreign Trade had accepted his proposal to convert Stella into a joint company of which he would be the Hungarian director.[79] At the same time the Economic Division of the Commissariat for Foreign Affairs advised the legation in Budapest that the responsible parties in Moscow did not approve the ideas about establishing a joint company and that Stella would enjoy no advantages whatsoever in any commercial transaction with the Soviet Union.[80] The Soviets made it clear to the Hungarian government as well that it did not wish to grant the company any monopolistic privileges.[81]

Contrary to the intentions of the Soviet side a significant portion of the Hungarian interests later on tried to enter the Soviet markets with Stella undertaking the financing of the individual exports. It was with Stella's assistance that Hofherr-Schrantz sold its tractors in 1935.[82] One of the sensitive areas of Hungarian exports to the Soviet Union, the horse exports, also came about with the mediation of Stella. In the matter of selling the horses the name of Gyula Csobaji, a landowner in Békés County and the owner of several stud farms, was mentioned repeatedly in both Hungarian and Russian sources. On August 26, 1935, he succeeded in signing a contract with Exportkhleb, the Soviet import enterprise, about the sale of five hundred breeding stallions. A report of the Hungarian Legation in Moscow reveals that Csobaji and Ferenc Neuhaus, the director of Stella, negotiated together in Moscow.[83] Contrary to expectations the company and the landowner could not reach an agreement on the matter of financing. According to Csobaji Stella confronted him with unacceptable conditions and considered the 3 percent commission too low.[84]

In connection with the sale of the horses Stella became embroiled in other conflicts. In engaging in the business promising great financial returns Stella cut across the interests of another influential Hungarian consortium. It was the Hungarian-Egyptian Trade Corporation, owned jointly by the Anglo-Hungarian Bank and the Pest Hungarian Bank of Commerce. The managing director of the Hungarian-Egyptian Trade Corporation, ever since its establishment in 1931, was Miklós Horthy, Jr. the younger son of the regent.[85]

After the resumption of diplomatic relations the leadership of the AMB again believed that the conditions were favorable for renewing the negotiations about the establishment of a joint enterprise. The Hungarian-Egyptian Trade Corporation charged Miklós Horthy, Jr. to find out from the Royal Hungarian Office for Foreign Trade, the organization charged with coordinating export and import activities with the Soviet Union, how individual companies could participate in the exchange of merchandise with the Soviet Union. The second charge to Horthy was to ascertain the conditions required for the establishment of a joint Hungarian-Soviet enterprise.[86] The Russian archival sources for 1935–1936 reveal a number of comments about the younger Horthy and his company. In a report from the Soviet minister it is stated bluntly that young Horthy and the AMB want to gain exclusive export rights for the Soviet livestock market.[87] Hoping to achieve this, the AMB commissioned Max Schlesinger, the German businessman who successfully negotiated during the second half of the 1920s between Hungarian interests and the Soviet state import agencies. It was at this time that Schlesinger engaged in a conflict with Csobaji and Stella. Allegedly the German businessman threatened to artificially increase the sales price of horses on the domestic Hungarian markets if Csobaji were to exclude the company represented by him from business with Russia. The Hungarian landowner, in response, declared that he had no intention of doing business with blackmailers and was willing to take his complaint to the regent if necessary.[88]

The 1935 annual report of the Soviet Legation in Budapest devoted a separate paragraph to the sustained efforts made by the AMB and the Hungarian-Egyptian Trade Corporation. It is worthwhile to quote this verbatim because it clearly reflects the attitude of Soviet diplomacy vis-à-vis the establishment of a joint Hungarian-Soviet trade enterprise. It also indicates the reasons for rejecting it. The unalterable position stated:

> Taking notice that, under the conditions prevailing in Hungary, such a company would become a commission agency and an interceder between the Soviet economic organizations and the Hungarian exporters and importers and noting that it had a very small initial capital (100,000 pengős), it would be unable to finance individual transactions. The legation had explained to the interested people that it was not reasonable to establish such a company and recommended that they should turn with concrete proposals to our export organizations in Moscow or to our trade mission in Vienna.[89]

The same fate befell Stella's proposal. Had this proposal been met it would have meant that under the aegis of a joint commercial enterprise the entire Hungarian-Soviet trade would have been held by a single company. It did not help the reputation of the company that after a while light was thrown on Urievich's previous activities and fraudulent deals. The Soviet Legation in Budapest found out that earlier he had been active in Vienna on behalf of some Austrian businessmen but that the Soviet Trade Mission and Inturist severed all their relations with him.[90] In addition the Polish agent got Max Emden into trouble. Emden believed that there was profit to be made from financing Hungarian exports to the Soviet Union and therefore he invested some capital into the activities of Stella.

The scandal exploded during the winter of 1935. Urievich sold seven Soviet vouchers, valued at one million French francs, which the banker resold to a French bank. On becoming mature the Parisian bank presented them to the Soviet Trade Mission in Milan where it was determined that the vouchers were forgeries. The Parisian bank and the Soviet Trade Mission in Milan then filed a complaint against Urievich. He was arrested and during the interrogation claimed in his defense that he had received the vouchers from a third person, since deceased. It is also true that Hans Erik Emden, testifying in the case and releasing the information, stated that the scandal had nothing to do with Hungary.[91] In spite of this the publicity of the affair was a good excuse to bring up the harmful activities of Urievich affecting Hungarian business. In the Hungarian press the agent who caused great harm to Russian-Hungarian trade was accused of using his contacts in Hungary to thwart serious transactions and with some exaggeration the press stated that if, "The Russian-Hungarian trade did not develop to the extent that the government wanted this was primarily due to Urievich."[92]

The lack of legal regulations and the absence of a bilateral commercial agreement or, at least, of an agreement of compensation and the lack of an adequate organization of the Soviet Trade Mission in Budapest, favored those endeavors and financial manipulations in Hungary which were directed toward securing a monopolistic position in the Soviet markets. The first secretary of the Soviet Legation in Budapest, Semen Mirnii, drew the attention of his superiors to this situation. He warned the Commissariat for Foreign Affairs that as long that there was not an official Soviet coordinator for the purchases and sales of the Soviet Union in Hungary or, in the worst case, through the Berlin or Vienna trade mission, the Hungarian companies and banks, hoping for fabulous profits, would hold commerce with the Soviet Union firmly in their hands.[93]

Negotiations about Terms of Payment

Bornemissza, gathering information in Soviet Russia, considered it important not only to create conditions that would coordinate Hungarian commercial activities in Moscow, but also prepared a document on the internal regulations that governed the economic relations of the Soviet Union with other countries. He did this to facilitate the drafting of a future economic agreement. Tihamér Fabiny, the minister of commerce, forwarded this material to the other concerned ministers with the comment that this could be the starting point, at a forthcoming inter-ministry meeting, for the discussion of a future Hungarian-Soviet agreement.[94]

Because of the difficulties in getting the various ministries interested in reaching an agreement to coordinate their activities the drafting of the proposed agreement proceeded very slowly. In a telegram to Jungerth, on April 15, 1935, Kánya stated that the text of the proposed agreement was still being prepared by the Economic Policy Department of the Ministry of Foreign Affairs. The minister of foreign affairs told his envoy in Moscow that, according to the wishes of Hungarian diplomacy, the text of the future agreement would be based on a system of compensatory trading. This meant that Hungary wanted to continue the 1:2 ratio in Hungary's favor. He added that the draft was legal and administrative and therefore it would deal with economic policy matters only to the point where they became indispensable components of a trade agreement.[95]

The position of Soviet diplomacy on this issue was quite different. The Soviet government wanted to sign an agreement with Hungary modeled on the agreement the Soviets signed with Czechoslovakia on March 25, 1935. It regulated in detail the legal consequences ensuing from trade agreements such as the personal and economic protection of the Soviet citizens (merchants) in Hungary.[96] In addition, perpetuating the 1:2 trade ratios in the agreement was totally unacceptable to the Soviet government. In July 1935 the leader of the Soviet Trade Mission in Berlin went to Budapest and recommended that henceforth the compensation ratio should be 1:1. This meant that, at whatever dollar value the Soviet Union would make purchases in Hungary, raw materials of the same dollar value would have to be purchased by Hungary in the Soviet Union.[97]

Hungarian documents reveal that during the negotiations the Ministry of Commerce was willing to reach a compromise, namely the establishment of a compensation ratio of 100:75. According to the Hungarians this would have meant that Hungarian exports to the Soviet Union would have been 75 percent compensated by Hungarian purchases in the Soviet Union and that the remaining 25 percent would be paid for by the Soviets in hard foreign currency. The justification for maintaining compensation ratio favorable for Hungary was made evident by a memorandum from the Ministry of Commerce. The memorandum stated that,

> We must insist on a 100:75 ratio because the cost of transit of our exports to Russia and the cost of transporting the raw materials from Russia require hard currency that we would be unable to produce....In Russia the pressure of world competition is great and therefore the Hungarian exports in that direction would require such a large surcharge that the Hungarian imports could not bear it.

Hungarian exports to Russia would become profitable only if a certain portion of the export merchandise would, in exchange for hard currency,...be qualified for a higher surcharge.[98]

The signing of a trade agreement was made urgent not only by the need to regulate the order of financing Hungarian exports to the Soviet Union but also for reviving Hungary's commercial connections with the East. In the 1930s Hungary's principal commercial partner in the Middle East was Iran and Hungarian exports had to travel to that country by a wide detour via the Red Sea and the Persian Gulf. The fastest and least expensive route would have been across Soviet territory through the cities of Batumi and Baku. The principal Hungarian exports to Iran were horses and electrical products, mainly light bulbs and switches.

The situation was stated precisely in a letter from the United Light Bulb and Electricity, Inc. (Egyesült Izzó- és Lámpaárugyár Rt.). In this letter the leaders of the company turned for help directly to the Ministry of Foreign Affairs and asked that the ministry, through the legation in Moscow, seek a transit permit for the latest shipment to Iran consisting of 5,000 kilograms of light bulbs. In the letter they explained that Hungarian materials having to go via the Persian Gulf took three months to arrive in Iran and thus the Hungarian exporters were at a considerable disadvantage vis-à-vis the exporters of those countries that were allowed to ship their products to Iran through the Soviet Union. The commercial transit permit was issued by the Commissariat for Foreign Trade and thus this document could be obtained only through official diplomatic intercession and through a formal diplomatic note.[99]

Jungerth interceded with the Commissariat for Foreign Trade but did not succeed. Stating that because there was no commercial agreement between Hungary and the Soviet Union, the responsible organization denied the transit request of United Light Bulb, Inc. The Hungarian minister tried to find out from the Iranian ambassador what the real reasons for this denial might have been and what the Iranian practices were in such situations. The Persian ambassador told him that the decision of the Soviets was not unique and was not discriminatory against Hungary. Soviet commercial agencies always followed this path vis-à-vis other countries as well. For example, there were active commercial relations between Iran and Poland and Iran and Finland. The Soviet Union had a commercial agreement with Iran but did not have one with Poland or Finland and therefore the Soviet authorities denied transit of materials from these countries across territory under their control. The Hungarian envoy mentioned the instance when Hungary, on one occasion, transported horses to Iran across the Soviet Union but that on that occasion the Soviet government made an exception and granted the permit in response to a request by the Iranian government. In his report about his conversation with the Iranian ambassador Jungerth argued that this situation was another reason for finally getting the commercial negotiations between the two countries started.[100]

Seeing the Hungarian party's inflexibility in changing the compensation ratios, the Soviet government, after the autumn of 1935, was unwilling to sign any compensation-based agreement and insisted that an agreement with another country, for example Czechoslovakia, be taken as the model. Hungarian diplomacy would have been willing to agree to this only if the agreement could be bastioned with those security arrangements recommended by the minister of the interior and by the minister of defense. Miklós Kozma, the minister of the interior, considered the first paragraph of the Soviet-Czechoslovak agreement to be unacceptable because it guaranteed the citizens of the contracting parties freedom of travel, freedom of settlement, and the unfettered practice of their profession. According to the minister of the interior the existing Hungarian legal regulations did not permit such privileges to be granted to Soviet citizens.[101] The Ministry of Defense also expressed its concerns about granting a freedom of movement to Soviet merchants traveling in Hungary.[102] Considering these concerns the Economic Policy Department of the Ministry of Foreign Affairs recommended that Hungary and the Soviet Union not undertake a commercial agreement but follow the model of the February 15, 1936, Soviet-Romanian merchandise transport and payments agreement. Thus they should engage in a payments agreement which would make it possible to eliminate the necessity of clarifying the legal issues ensuing from commercial transactions and limit itself to an agreement of the payment method subsequent to the shipment of merchandise.[103]

In order to discuss this matter a meeting of all the concerned ministers was called for February 25, 1936, in the Ministry of Foreign

Affairs with all ministers attending. It was decided at the meeting that the Ministry of Foreign affairs should officially contact Bekzadian and tell him that Hungary was prepared to negotiate with the Soviet government about a commercial agreement, modeled on the Soviet-Romanian compensation pattern. The Hungarians stipulated that if the Soviet diplomacy did not accept the Hungarian proposal and if thus the vitally important issue of transit could not be resolved, in the final analysis Hungary would be willing to negotiate along the lines of the Soviet-Czechoslovak commercial agreement.[104] On April 11, 1936, Semen Mirnii, the first secretary of the Soviet Legation in Budapest, informed the Ministry of Foreign Affairs that the Soviet government was prepared to initiate negotiations with representatives of the Hungarian government to reach an agreement on payments based on the Soviet-Romanian system of compensation.[105] The Ministry of Foreign Affairs appointed Jungerth to represent the Hungarian government at the negotiations which took place in Moscow during the spring and summer of 1936. At these negotiations the Soviet Union was represented by Andrei Sabanin, the head of the Legal Department of the Commissariat for Foreign Affairs and by David Shtern, the head of Second Western Division of the Commissariat of Foreign Affairs.

The first meeting took place on April 25. During the negotiations the only issue about which there was no agreement and which ultimately led to the failure of the negotiations was the question of the banks participating in the transfer of funds upon the completion of the export-import transactions. The Soviet-Romanian compensation agreement that was to serve as the model required that the Romanian importers deposit the cost of the imported Soviet merchandise in the Romanian National Bank in an account opened for the State Bank of the USSR (Gosudarstvennyi bank SSSR, or Gosbank). Romania could export merchandise to the Soviet Union that was equivalent in price to the amount deposited in the above account.

By comparison the Hungarian plan differed in that the payments would not have been made through the Hungarian National Bank (MNB) and the State Bank of the USSR but through a British commercial bank in London. The Soviets believed that the Hungarian proposal was based on a lack of confidence in the Gosbank. While they agreed that this form of arrangement for the payments would not be detrimental to the conduct of the business, Jungerth believed that they made a prestige issue of it stating that it was unacceptable to have the two national banks turn to a private bank for security because they did not trust each other.[106] Even though Jungerth endeavored to convince the Soviets that the Hungarian proposal was not discriminating against the State Bank of the USSR and that there was absolutely no lack of confidence in it, the Soviet counter proposal, submitted forthwith, mandated that the payments derived from the mutual exchange of merchandise would have to be made in pounds sterling by the MNB to the State Bank of the USSR and to the account of the Soviet bank at the MNB. The MNB viewed the Soviet to be leading to a "clearing agreement," meaning that the settlement of the accounts receivable and the debts would have been done by an inter-bank remittal and would not involve cash payments.[107]

Jungerth, observing the comportment of the Soviet negotiators, did not believe that there would be any accommodation on their part and tried to convince his superiors in Budapest that, because Hungary was a regular purchaser in the Soviet Union, accepting an arrangement of settlements between the two national banks did not represent a danger for the Hungarian commercial interests if Hungary continued to purchase more raw materials in the Soviet Union than what the Soviet import agencies purchased in Hungary.[108] The MNB, however, was unwilling to accept the Hungarian diplomat's compromise suggestion and the positions became rigid and the negotiations were suspended in August 1936 with the proviso that during the autumn the MNB would send a financial expert to continue the negotiations and clarify the financial questions.[109] The available documents confirm that the trip of the MNB official to Moscow did not take place at that time or at any time thereafter and that, while Jungerth repeatedly urged resumption of the discussions, the negotiations were never reopened.

Plans for the Development of a Danubian Transport Route

Increase in trading between Hungary and the Soviet Union required a rapprochement of the ideas on business policy principles and, most importantly, an agreement at the governmental level on a payments system. It also required an increase in the intensity of trading, an enlargement of the commercial infrastructure which had a major influence on the total cost of exports and imports, and a more rapid and less expensive transport system.

During the 1920s trading with the Soviet Union was largely limited to two routes. One was by rail and this was burdened by duties and a variety of transit fees. In this case Hungarian merchandise had to cross Czechoslovak and Polish or Romanian territory and the railways of all three countries charged transit fees which varied depending on the nature of the merchandise. Because of the difference in the width of the track in the Soviet Union all the merchandise had to be transferred at the Polish-Soviet and Romanian-Soviet border to Soviet freight cars which meant a delay and an increase in cost.

The other route, longer and even more expensive and, therefore, less used was the maritime one through Trieste. Along this route the Hungarian merchandise could reach its destination only by a long detour. Furthermore, the available company documents show that in the 1920s and 1930s Soviet orders were transmitted to the Hungarian companies by foreign agencies, naturally in exchange for a commission fee. This is what happened to the Manfred Weiss Company in 1925 and 1926 when Soviet import agencies ordered agricultural machines from it. The sale was arranged by Austrian middle men, agents of the Austrian partner in the joint Soviet-Austrian enterprise, the RATAO.[110]

All these factors significantly increased the costs of Hungarian exports. For this reason, after the start of diplomatic relations, the Hungarian economic leadership considered the revival of the Danubian transport route to be of the greatest importance. This waterway was a major component of the European economic traffic prior to World War I. The Hungarian experts wanted this waterway, which by multilateral international agreements had been declared to be an international river, to be opened up for commercial intercourse between the two countries. The Danube enjoyed a number of natural and infrastructural properties which made it possible to increase riverine transportation and usage and increase the volume of Hungarian-Soviet merchandise between the two countries. The river, abounding in water, had a number of navigable tributaries, such as the Tisza, the Dráva and the Száva. Also, the Danube in its lower reaches was frozen for only a relatively short time, on the average for 40–50 days. Along the Danube there were also a number of cities, Vienna, Bratislava (Pozsony, Pressburg), Budapest, Belgrade, Brăila, Galați and others, which were well equipped with warehouses and had efficient loading and unloading capabilities. Danubian navigation could have established direct contacts between the large capacity Hungarian ports like Csepel and Mohács and the very large Soviet port cities in the northern and eastern basins of the Black Sea, namely Odessa, Nikolaev, Novorossiisk, Batumi, and others. Regent Horthy was strongly in favor of this project.

We find economic statistical data in both Soviet and Hungarian sources which show that utilization of the Danubian transportation route would have been a substantially more economical and profitable solution than the rail or maritime transfers. Thus, for instance, according to Soviet calculations, one ton of Soviet grain transported to Bratislava via Trieste would have cost, in round numbers, forty-three Austrian schillings while using the Danube the cost would have been, again in round numbers, twenty-four schillings. The situation was similar for other Soviet products such as iron ore, tobacco products and lumber. The cost of shipping one ton of these products to Vienna via Trieste would have been fifty-seven schillings and shipping it along the Danube would have cost only twenty-four schillings.[111]

Similarly, a technical expert at the Ministry of Commerce calculated the share of the Hungarian railways if the merchandise to be exported were shipped not through Poland but, with a transfer, through Csepel. During the summer of 1935 the Soviet Union ordered 30,000 tons of railway equipment from the Diósgyőr factory of MÁVAG. It seemed logical that the MÁV would send the merchandise, filling three thousand railway cars, to the nearby Czechoslovak border from where it would have traveled through Poland to the Soviet Union. In this case the MÁV would have profited 117,000 pengős for the ninety-five kilometer stretch, while on the remaining distance the Polish National Railways would have collected the transport fee. If the merchandise had been shipped from Diósgyőr to Csepel the196 kilometer trip would have benefited the MÁV to the tune of 195,000 pengős but part of this fee would have accrued to the Port of Csepel and to the Magyar Folyam- és Tengerhajózási Rt. (Hungarian River and Ocean Shipping, Inc.). Because the Danube was declared to be an international waterway the exporters would not have had to pay the otherwise huge customs duties.[112]

The only problem was that at the Romanian riverine ports, Brăila and Galaţi, levies were imposed under various titles for transfer and storage. These fees accrued partly to the Romanian authorities and partly to the International Commission of the Danube. This could be avoided only if the merchandise were loaded on ships which could leave the river and enter the Black Sea. Even though the Soviet authorities doubted if Hungary had such river- and seaworthy vessels, initially they believed that it would be appropriate to establish a direct contact between Budapest and Odessa over water.[113] Not long after the return of the commercial delegation the Ganz shipyard completed the first "Apollinaire" type ship that could carry merchandise both on the river and also on the sea. The ship, named *Budapest*, was launched on August 14, 1934, and had its first trial run from Óbuda to Alexandria via Istanbul, Beirut, and Haifa in October and November. The event was welcomed in the press indicating that it was the realization of the Hungarian merchants' dream of a direct water route, without transshipping, from Hungary to countries in the East.[114]

After the first Hungarian ship of this type was launched and had completed its maiden voyage, Bornemissza gave a talk about his negotiations in Moscow on the use of shipping in transporting the merchandise. He indicated that in the Soviet Union there were favorable opportunities for Hungarian water transports because an improvement in the canal system allowed exit from the Black Sea to the Baltic and to the Caspian Sea. He added that, "The Russians were very interested in this form of transport and had constructed these canals without building ships or even in engaging in the development of such vessels. Their eyes were opened at the time of the visit of the Hungarian delegation and they became enthusiastic seeing that their activities might have a useful purpose." He claimed that during the Moscow and Leningrad negotiations the Soviet authorities made commitments which, if realized, would grant Hungary advantages over other countries in transporting merchandise from the Soviet Union and also on its internal waterways. Accordingly they would reduce the port duties for the Hungarian ships to one sixth, would be willing to rent Hungarian seagoing vessels and were prepared to negotiate a separate shipping agreement. This would have been very helpful to Hungarian commercial shipping because then the *Budapest*-type vessels could have gone from Csepel via the Danube and Odessa to the Dnieper and Dniester and so create contacts with the industrial developments along the course of the two Soviet rivers.[115]

According to another press item the Soviet government wanted to make the Csepel port a logistics base where Soviet exports and imports could meet. Developing Csepel into a Hungarian-Soviet transfer center and making it suitable for the reception of seagoing vessels might have been initiated by the launching of the first river and seagoing freighters. From the Soviet perspective Csepel could have been a distribution center for Soviet raw material exports toward the Western markets. It could have also become the major center for the Danubian Soviet flotilla.[116]

The condition for the achievement of these plans was the signing of a navigation agreement by the two countries. Reaching such an agreement would have been facilitated by the fact, already referred to repeatedly, that Horthy considered a direct Hungarian-Soviet shipboard commerce and the development of the Csepel port into a maritime transfer point a priority and had taken steps in that direction. At the time when Bekzadian presented his credentials Horthy raised the issue of commercial ties and of the development of Danubian shipping.[117] At the 1936 New Year's reception for the diplomatic corps Horthy again urged a discussion of this matter and recommended that the Soviet Union order the newly constructed riverine vessels in Hungary. Bekzadian reported that one week prior to this reception he participated in a hunt with the regent and the prime minister. There were only twelve guests and he and the departing Austrian minister were the only diplomats. He mentioned particularly that at the breakfast he was seated next to Horthy which could not have been a coincidence.[118]

It is also evident, however, that during the negotiations of the Hungarian trade delegation in Moscow the Soviets made no promises that would have given preferential considerations to the Hungarian commercial flotilla in transporting Soviet merchandise. Boris Rozenblum, the director of the Economic Department of the Commissariat for Foreign Affairs wrote to Bekzadian at the end of 1934 that other than for the transport of anthracite the Soviet Union had no desire to rent the barges of the Hungarian shipping company and would prefer the Czechoslovak companies.[119] In spite of the fact that the Danubian route of transport had substantial natural and infrastructural advantages, Moscow made it clear that a joint regulation of the Danubian and Black Sea shipping route would be considered only if the Soviet Union did not have to make economic sacrifices.[120] On behalf of the Soviet diplomatic leadership Krestinskii declared that signing a shipping agreement was of no significance to the Soviet Union.[121] He, Litvinov, and Rozenblum indicated that even if such an agreement were signed it would have primarily a political significance because it would enable Soviet diplomacy to make a gesture toward Horthy, who wanted this, and to his circle.[122] Evidently this was the reason why the Soviet economic experts initially made restrained and polite comments in which they did not *ab ovo* set aside the Hungarian endeavors for a joint arrangement of the transportation relations.

The Hungarian government delivered the first draft of the agreement on February 20, 1936,[123] to which Semen Mirnii, the first secretary of the Soviet Legation, responded only on March 27. It was on this basis that the negotiations about a shipping agreement could get started in Moscow. At the negotiations Hungary was represented by Jungerth, by the first secretary of the Hungarian Legation, Egon Cindric, and in April and May by Bornemissza, making a return visit to Moscow. The Soviet Union was represented by Rozenblum and Shtern. The negotiations were conducted within the framework of the payments agreement discussions and the outcome of the shipping discussions was always dependent on the outcome of the compensation issues. The most significant difference between the negotiating parties was caused by paragraph one of the proposal which was supposed to determine the status of the freighters in the domestic waters of the other country. The nature of the problem was that because the Danube was considered an international waterway the Hungarians could not prevent the Soviet ships to travel under a Soviet flag on the Hungarian segment of the Danube. The Soviet authorities were unwilling to agree that the Hungarian ships could travel under a Hungarian flag on Soviet rivers. This was considered to be incompatible with the rights of sovereignty and was viewed as a potentially dangerous precedent for Soviet relations with other countries.[124]

At the first meeting, on April 27, the Hungarian delegates seeing the inflexibility of the Soviets used the argument that this preference was strictly limited to ships carrying Hungarian merchandise and to the Hungarian ships rented by the Soviets.[125] Even though throughout the negotiations the Soviets insisted that the movement of ships on inland waterways was the exclusive monopoly of the Soviet Union, they admitted that on occasion they granted permission to Finnish ships to sail on the Neva or that flotillas of neighboring Asian countries use the Asiatic border rivers. The Hungarian delegation recommended that instead of defining the use of inland waterways they should focus on discussing the "most favored" principle according to which the Soviet Union would not exclude Hungary in the future from the advantages of inland waterway use when they had granted this privilege on occasion to other countries. According to the arguments used by the Hungarians, Hungarian seagoing ships would sail only in the northern and eastern basins of the Black Sea, on the rivers flowing into the Black sea, such as the Bug and the Dnieper, and on the Azov Sea which had been declared to be a Soviet inland sea.[126]

The Hungarian documents suggest that eventually a compromise was reached and that the Hungarians were inclined to accept the Soviet views. The minutes of a ministers' meeting in the Ministry of Foreign Affairs stated that the "navigation agreement was fully negotiated."[127] It is certain, however, that there were no additional negotiations subsequent to the meeting of July 16, 1936, because the Soviets made the enactment of the shipping convention subject to the signing of the payments agreement.[128] Soviet documents reveal that the Soviet government acted on the tactical recommendation contained in the May 17 report of its minister in Budapest. Bekzadian repeated the earlier Soviet point of view according to which the signing of a navigation agreement was of no interest to the Soviet Union and that it was purely a gesture when they seemed to agree with the Hungarian demands. The minister also recommended that there should be no haste in answering and that, for the time being, they should not express their disinterest in signing a convention. They should only delay the course of the negotiations. Because the Soviet Union would certainly sign a payment agreement with Hungary, which was far more important than the navigation agreement, the Soviet Union could, after signing the international treaty, cite the achieved results and without any political odium reject the Hungarian endeavors to have the navigation agreement signed.[129]

It seems likely that at the time the negotiations were terminated, the Hungarians could not have been satisfied with the results achieved. In later Hungarian documents we can encounter expert opinions on foreign affairs according to which Hungary's retreat before the Soviet demands, namely yielding on the matter of navigation on Soviet inland waters, had practically no impact on the transport of merchandise. Yet it would create an awkward situation for Hungary because it would deprive it from the use of the principle of reciprocity, which was a feature in international law.

The Balance of Hungarian-Soviet Trade Relations in the 1930s

It is of interest to study the effects of the resumption of diplomatic relations on the freight traffic between Hungary and the Soviet Union. To show this I selected the year of the start of diplomatic relations and the four years thereafter. In this period the principal Hungarian imports were asbestos and pig iron with some coal being shipped in 1938. The most frequent Hungarian export articles were iron and metal products, such as steel tubes, wires, springs, etc., portable steam engines, seeds and forage plants. In 1935 a small number of horses were also sold. If we study the composition of the merchandise exported to Hungary by the Soviet Union and exported from Hungary to the Soviet Union we can get a good picture about the structure of the products imported and exported. Taking the pengő value of the traded merchandise as the base we can calculate the balance even though the volume of trade was quite modest. The nature of the Soviet exports was simple and consisted entirely of industrial raw materials. The Hungarian exports to the Soviet Union between 1934 and 1939 consisted largely of finished and semi-finished industrial products in 1934. In 1936 1 to 2 percent consisted of agricultural products. In 1935 the ratio of exported agricultural products rose to 10 percent by virtue of the number of horses exported. In 1937 Hungary exported only alfalfa to the Soviet Union and thus the presence of agricultural products became nominal within the total export. It is worthwhile to mention that according to the identical information in the Hungarian and

Soviet statistics Hungary exported no merchandise at all to the Soviet Union in 1938.

Table 7 Hungarian-Soviet Merchandise Exchange between 1934 and 1938[130]

Year	Hungarian exports		Hungarian imports	
	Tons	in 1,000 pengős	Tons	in 1,000 pengős
1934	6,941.2	1,365	179.4	96
1935	10,856+71 1,999	1,999	19,379.2	1,967
1936	412.7	125	31,953.6	1,486
1937	1,570.3	2,073	2,236.1	296
1938	–	–	355.1	71

Table 7 shows that the closing balance of the annual trade between the two countries varied considerably. 1934 finished with a strongly positive balance in Hungary's favor with 1935 being much less positive. The Hungarian advance during these two years can probably be explained by the mechanism of the compensation system which in the case of several transaction was permitted by the Soviets to be at the 1:2 ratio. Trading was still modest when compared to the period between 1929 and 1933 and did not increase by a substantial factor. This could have been comforting for the Soviet partners because it made Hungarian growth completely relative from their perspective and did not affect the evolution of Soviet foreign trading. This might have been the reason why when the text of the payments agreement was being negotiated, during 1936–1937, the Soviets were unwilling to agree to these ratios and were willing to accept only a 1:1 parity arrangement. From the Soviet perspective such an agreement was no longer of major significance because the year 1936 closed with a balance in favor of the

Soviet Union. While in 1937 Hungarian exports were considerably greater than the imports from the Soviet Union, the bilateral commerce between the two countries practically disappeared by 1938–1939 and was essentially limited to an insignificant amount of Soviet imports.

In summary we can state that while the resumption of diplomatic relations created a favorable political atmosphere for the bilateral increase of economic activities, it did not cause an appreciable improvement in the trade relations between the two countries. Thus the optimistic expectations which linked the spectacular increases of Hungarian export opportunities to the appearance of Hungarian businesses in the Soviet markets were not realized. It would have required additional steps but no commercial agreement, payments agreement or navigation convention was ever implemented. Even the commercial framework necessary for these developments never came about. The matter of the Soviet Trade Mission in Budapest was never resolved and therefore Hungarian businessmen had to turn to the Berlin or Vienna Soviet Trade Missions with their offers just like during the period prior to the establishment of diplomatic relations. Referring to Hungary's intention to join the Anti-Comintern Pact, the Soviet Union suspended direct diplomatic relations with it on March 2, 1939, and the accredited diplomatic representations in both countries were closed.[131]

Chapter Four

THE ACCOMPLISHMENT OF ECONOMIC TIES 1939–1941

The Nature of the Conditions of Hungarian-Soviet Economic Relations in the Shadow of the World War

Examining the almost two decades of Hungarian-Soviet relations after World War I, the question emerges why the economic relations between the two countries "came to fruition" only during the summer and autumn of 1940, in the shadow of World War II. The question is a very complex one. The factors contributing to the opening of the Soviet markets for Hungary included the constraints produced by the war, the changing geopolitical relations and the adaptation of the regional economic-strategic goals to them. It is of interest to examine the economic benefits, and the potential political ones, that could accrue from these agreements for Hungary and for the Soviet Union during the brief interval prior to the armed confrontation.

The most recent historical investigations have reliably demonstrated that the Soviet Union was preparing for the predictable armed clash not only with diplomatic maneuvering but also economically with an increasing concentration of its energy resources and with the development of the organizations essential for waging war. The relevant economic indicators showed that by the turn of 1937–1938, the end of the Second Five Year Plan, economic productivity in the Soviet Union was still substantially behind that of the United States, Great Britain, or Germany. Even though the Soviet leadership wanted to introduce the Third Five Year Plan in 1938 it was cast into its final form only at the Party Congress on March 10–21, 1939. The plan projected an increase of 92 percent in industrial productivity by the end 1942 when compared to the productivity of 1937.[1] This would have been a significant step because the industrial productivity in 1937 exceeded 53 percent of the total national income. An important part of the preparations for war was the improvement of the technical equipment of the Red Army and the enlargement of the economic infrastructure such as transportation equipment, railways and harbors. To create this background and to increase the rate of expansion it was essential to import the technology used in the more developed countries and to increase purchasing of finished and semi-finished industrial products. This in turn demanded the broadening of foreign trade relations without which a more intensive procurement of such products would not have been possible.[2]

Such substantial progress in the Soviet Union was based primarily on economic cooperation with Germany. The Non-Aggression Pact, indicating the political-strategic cooperation between the two countries, signed on August 23, 1939, was preceded by the commercial and credit agreement signed in Berlin on August 19. Under this agreement the Soviet Union received from its German partner a 200 million mark, seven-year credit at a very favorable annual 4.5 percent interest to be used primarily for the purchase of German merchandise, primarily industrial products. Within the negotiated framework Germany was to deliver to the Soviet Union military supplies to the value of 58 million marks.[3] This agreement was complemented by another commercial agreement signed by the two countries on February 11, 1940, which placed the transport of merchandise on a reciprocal basis thus promising a variety of agricultural and industrial products for Germany already engaged in war. During the sixteen months prior to the attack on the Soviet Union, Moscow adhered to every word of the agreement and buttressed Berlin's activities in the war with merchandise of the value of 1 billion marks consisting of grains, crude oil, anthracite and other mineral "treasures" frequently purchased from a third country.[4] As shown by recent historical studies this agreement actually was more favorable for Germany because the military supplies sent to the Soviet Union in exchange for the above were old and of poor quality and the German government did not comply fully with the terms of the agreement. Consequently the Soviet side repeatedly withheld shipments and demanded, almost as an ultimatum, that the agreement be corrected and renewed.[5]

This would explain the fact that during 1940, in one year, the Soviet Union regularized its commercial relations with its central and southeast European neighbors, with which it previously had no economic agreements. It signed a commercial and navigation agreement with Bulgaria on January 5,[6] with Yugoslavia on May 11,[7] with Hungary on September 3 and with Slovakia, independent since the spring of 1939, on December 6.[8] It is of interest that the trade agreement between the Soviet Union and Yugoslavia preceded the start of diplomatic relations between the two countries on June 24. By doing this the Soviet Union relinquished its strong position, held firmly since 1924, which tied the opening of its markets to diplomatic recognition. For the sake of completeness it should be mentioned that since early autumn, 1940, a Romanian commercial delegation was in Moscow, but because of the political tensions between the two countries an agreement could be signed only on February 26, 1941.[9]

In commercial agreements with other countries the Soviet Union always assured itself the right to establish a trade mission in the capital of the other country. Its officials were granted diplomatic immunity and the building or office of the mission was granted extraterritorial rights. In every commercial agreement with eastern European countries there was an appendix which dealt with the opening and legal status of the trade missions. It was thus for the missions opened in Sofia, Belgrade, Budapest, and Bratislava. The budget proposal of the Commissariat for Foreign Trade for 1941 reports on almost two dozen Soviet trade missions in other countries world-wide, including the one in Budapest.[10]

Looking at these trade agreements from a legal perspective we find that they were all of the "most favored" type in which the contracting parties guaranteed for each other that exports and imports, duties, shipping and harbor dues and transportation facilities would be receiving all the benefits that would have been granted to a third party. The articles contained the provisions usually found in commercial agreements, such as the regulations concerning telegraph, telephone, and postal service and the proceedings of a court of arbitration. The merchandise transport and payments agreements, linked tightly to the commercial and navigation contracts, were of a type known as "contingency agreements." The essence of these agreements was that the parties determined the value of the exports and imports in advance meaning that one country could export merchandise of a given value to the other in exchange for imports of the same value from that country. This made it possible to maintain a balance while both countries obtained raw materials or the industrial and agricultural products they needed. The emphasis was on the total value of exports and imports and they mutually determined the quantity of the merchandise within that value. The Soviet-Bulgarian agreement set this value at 4.1 million dollars, the Soviet-Yugoslav one at 3.2 million, the Soviet-Hungarian one at 3.7 million and the Soviet-Slovak one at 2.4 million.[11]

The most burning issue of the Hungarian economy during 1939–1940 was the shortage of raw materials caused by the blockage of many of the purchasing routes by the war. This was the chief motive for the economic rapprochement with the Soviet Union. After the outbreak of the war Great Britain and Germany both declared a maritime blockade for shipments destined from across the ocean towards each other's harbors, in order to make the enemy country economically destitute. In 1939 Great Britain introduced the "navicert system" which meant that all shipments to Europe originating from its colonies, or using the shipping lines under its control, required a special permit. This affected all imports to Hungary coming from the American continent or from the eastern end of the Mediterranean.

The extent of the problems in the area of raw material procurement can be estimated from data and statistics in the Hungarian documents. Rolf Krausz, an official in the Economic Policy Department of the Ministry of Foreign Affairs and a former commercial attaché accredited to the Baltic States, wrote a detailed report, on November 13, 1939, on the perspectives of the Hungarian-Soviet commercial ties. He estimated that the annual loss of imports, due to the escalating war that had started on September 1, was approximately 44 million pengős.[12] In 1939 the value of Hungarian imports was set at 400 million pengős[13] of which 84 million pengős were for industrial raw materials.[14] The situation was not improved by Hungary's major successes in the territorial revision process during 1939–1940 when its area was enlarged by poorly industrialized regions low in mineral resources. Krausz stated that the return of the southern portion of Slovakia and of the Subcarpathia did not reduce the country's raw material supplies but actually raised the demands by 15 percent.[15]

During 1939–1940 this seriously impacted the economy because the 1938 Győr Program produced a military industry upswing lasting until 1941. As a result of this program the industrial production index rose by 21–22 percent in 1939 compared to 1938 and grew another 11 percent in 1940.[16] This economic achievement was attained, in spite of the British-German blockade, the introduction of the "navicert system," Italy's entry into the war, and by a drastic reduction of the raw material supplies. Under these conditions the completion of the Győr Program was possible only by the government introducing two strategies and applying them, at times concurrently.

One of these was the holding of the existing raw material supplies in reserve which inevitably necessitated the reduction of the export of raw materials from Hungary. One of the results of this was that the balance of Hungary's foreign trade ended on the negative side in 1940. This was without precedent since 1930 because ever since that year the annual foreign trade balance always ended with Hungary on the positive side.[17] Another step was the regulation of domestic distribution and use with the goal of restricting or, at least, moderating domestic consumption. In order to support the war material production, consuming increasing quantities of raw materials, the government introduced a number of exceptional administrative ordinances which made it possible to regulate and control the supply of raw materials and its distribution. The ordinances empowered the minister of industry to regulate the production, use and consumption of the raw materials and semi-finished products required by industry. It also made it mandatory that the raw materials be augmented by the admixture of artificial substances.[18]

Ordinance number 10.670/1939. M. E. prescribed that in order to keep certain raw materials under lock and key, to eventually release them and to implement all the necessary procedures and regulations required for the production, distribution and use of raw materials the minister of industry could set up commissions, the so-called expert commissions for industrial raw material management.[19] One year later, in view of the further deterioration of the situation, ordinance number 4.570/1940. M. E. went considerably further and sequestered all raw materials owned by and in the hands of private industry. The release of these sequestered materials, their purchase, distribution, storage, delivery and use was tied to a permit obtained from the minister of industry.[20]

The ordinances designed to assure the continuity of raw material deliveries caused innumerable complaints from economic associations and sectoral alliances. The complaints focused on the hasty and insensitive implementation of the ordinances and the lack of any attempt to attune them to the interests of the business world. There were also complaints about the expert committees, charged with implementing the ordinances, frequently overstepping their authority and that, "frequently we are faced with measures which represent restrictions in the import, distribution and domestic use of raw materials, far beyond the prescription of the law and seriously affecting certain groups of merchants and manufacturers."[21] The representatives of the business arena felt that these rules, imposed from above, offended the principles of a free market, were excessive, and unfairly favored the interests of the army vis-à-vis the interests of industrial, agricultural and commercial private enterprises.[22] The legal basis for the implementation of the above ordinances was Act II of 1939 (National Security Act) which in Paragraph 212 stated that the government, meaning the Prime Minister's Office, could directly, or by organizations under its control, regulate and supervise all raw materials, products, production, distribution and use of items and materials for sale and may determine the methods of production and use of said materials. It also declared that concerning raw materials and other items the government could act contrary to existing laws.[23]

Secondly the new situation required the urgent exploration of new raw material markets. The essential raw materials for Hungary's economic infrastructure were acquired before the war from forty-six different countries.[24] Subsequent to this Hungary had to find a new base for raw materials or at least for a substantial part of them, namely a large country from which a large part of the critically important raw materials, essential for the maintenance of industrial productivity, could be secured.

After territorial increases the area of the Soviet Union in 1939 was 21 million square kilometers and the population increased to 170.5 million.[25] Between the two World Wars the Soviet Union's oil reserves were estimated to represent 37.4 percent of the world's crude oil reserves. The European part of the Soviet Union was considered the greatest source of iron ore with the Soviet Union providing 18 to 21 percent of the world's iron ore production prior to World War II. It provided 41 percent of the world's manganese and 15.5 percent of chromium. Equally rich and inexhaustible were the supplies of asbestos, essential for the building trade, and of anthracite from the mines in the south-Ural area.[26] In 1939 the iron ore, manganese and chromium provided the majority of the raw materials for the productivity of the machine industry which exceeded the overall Hungarian industrial productivity by 53 percent and of the productivity of the metal industry which exceeded said productivity by 54 percent.[27] Prior to the Second Vienna Award serious attention had to be paid to the Soviet lumber capacity because 44.7 percent of the Soviet Union's area was covered by forests and the lumber produced during the first half of the 1930s was about 210 million cubic meters.[28]

Negotiations in Moscow. The Establishment of Trade Relations

According to contemporary sources the commercial negotiations were initiated by Hungarian diplomacy. The immediate impetus was the fact that the Red Army pouring into Poland on September 17, 1939, reached the former Polish-Hungarian border on September 25–26, 1939. Over the next two days they made contact with the Hungarian border forces in several places, including the Tatár and Verecke Passes. Consequently the two countries now had a common border approximately 150 kilometers long.

It is known from the Hungarian historical literature that in May 1939, shortly after the break of direct diplomatic relations, Hungarian diplomacy proposed that Budapest and Moscow normalize their relations. Negotiations on this matter began in Paris on August 7, between Jungerth and Iakov Surits, the Soviet ambassador in Paris. Even though Moscow had reached its decision about regularizing diplomatic relations as early as the beginning of September, József Kristóffy, the new Hungarian minister in Moscow, presented his credentials only on October 25. Nikolai Sharonov, the Soviet minister in Budapest, presented his credentials even later, on December 7. The "strained coexistence" led in 1939 to several border incidents[29] and therefore the Hungarian minister when presenting his credentials to Mikhail Kalinin, requested that the two countries sign a frontier defense convention to prevent further bloodshed. Both Hungarian and Soviet documents indicate the Soviet head of state gave a noncommittal response to this request.[30]

The economic problems and particularly the shortfalls in the availability of raw materials had become so severe in Hungary that on November 15 an inter-ministry meeting was called at the Ministry of Foreign Affairs to discuss the normalization of Hungarian-Soviet economic relations. The principal question was how it would be possible to fully exploit the economic-political advantages originating from stable relations. It was stated at this meeting that in order to normalize Hungarian-Soviet economic relations it would be preferable to sign a single, general economic agreement. Individual articles or appendices of such an agreement would then also deal with the problems of cooperation and traffic at the new common border. It was also stated that because Hungary's raw material supplies were adversely affected by the blockades established by the belligerent nations, arrangements should be made that at least a part of the Hungarian raw material needs be met from the less risky and still intact Soviet market. In this instance the British and German blockade would not affect the Hungarian-Soviet exchange of merchandise and the transport problems could be eliminated easily at the common border.[31] We can conclude on the basis of contemporary Hungarian sources that, at the turn of 1939–1940, Hungarian economic leaders considered the Soviet Union to be a raw materials market free of the dangers of war.

On November 24 Kristóffy, in a memorandum, made a proposal to Deputy Commissar for Foreign Affairs Vladimir Potemkin for a trade pact, regulation of cross-border traffic and establishment of direct rail connections. Kristóffy also suggested that a three-member commercial delegation be sent to the Soviet capital to discuss the above matters and to map out the export and import possibilities. The Hungarian delegation would consist of a representative of the MNB and of the Office for Foreign Trade and a joint representative of the Pest Hungarian Bank of Commerce (PMKB) and MÁH.

Soviet diplomacy delayed and appeared initially to be in no hurry to agree with the Hungarian proposals about the signing of a trade pact. In spite of the repeated urging of the Hungarian minister no answer was received for several months. On December 30 Potemkin submitted a summary of his conversations with Kristóffy and a plan for a decision to the Politburo. It is impossible to tell what the effects of this basic document had on the Soviet decision-making mechanism. The deputy commissar suggested in his memorandum that the question of the Hungarian-Soviet economic relations had to be approached from a political angle but for this very reason he did not consider it advisable to refuse the proposal of the Hungarian government to send a three-member delegation. Potemkin also told the Party leadership that he assumed that Hungary also wished to initiate discussions from a political perspective. He thought that Hungary had plans connected to the Kremlin's Balkan policies and perhaps hoped that, jointly with Sofia and with Moscow's backing, it could slice off certain areas from Romania's territory.[32]

As a result of the pressure by the purchasing demands of Hungarian businessmen, supported by Hungarian diplomacy, Moscow later relented but agreed only to the two countries signing a compensation agreement to the value of the amount of dollars equivalent to 400,000 pengős. According to the exchange rate of the day this was equivalent to approximately 80–100,000 U.S. dollars. In this fashion Hungary would have purchased lumber and semi-finished wood products from Galicia, now under Soviet control, in exchange for railway equipment, such as wheels and axles, and oil pipes made of steel manufactured in Hungary.[33] On June 4, 1940, András Csató, the representative of the PMKB and MÁH and Mór Orován, lumber merchant and director of the Forest Owner and Timber Exploitation, Inc. (Erdőbirtokos és Fakitermelő, Rt.), arrived in Moscow in order to negotiate a business agreement. Csató was thoroughly familiar with the economic policies of the Soviet Union having served during the first half of the 1930s in Berlin as a representative of the Office for Foreign Trade. His job at that time included the representation of Hungarian interests vis-à-vis the trade organizations of the Soviet Union in the German capital. As described earlier, he was also a member of the first official Hungarian trade delegation which visited Moscow in May and June 1934.[34] These negotiations had little if any effect on the progress of the events and in some respects they can be considered to be symptomatic. Yet two episodes deserve to be highlighted.

First, that the Hungarian businessmen stated at the beginning of the negotiations that Hungary was prepared to import considerably more merchandise from the Soviet Union than for the 400,000 pengős originally suggested. The businessmen told their Soviet partners that if the Soviet organization would satisfy the raw material needs of at least the Manfréd Weiss and MÁVAG companies, a purchase agreement could be reached at a much higher level. The Hungarian minister informed the Commissariat for Foreign Affairs about this in an official communication.[35] It is made evident in Csató's report that this maneuver was to establish a close link between the shipping of Hungarian industrial products and additional raw material imports from the Soviet Union. He claimed that, if the Soviet shipments of pig iron, metals and petroleum would satisfy at least 50 percent of the needs of Manfréd Weiss and MÁVAG for the manufacture of products to be shipped to the Soviet Union, MÁVAG could export materials monthly for about 120,000 dollars and Manfréd Weiss for 70,000. Csató also requested the shipment of chemical industry raw materials and wool in addition to the earlier mentioned lumber products and materials required to keep the two giant companies in business.[36]

Secondly, it became obvious that a long-term resolution of the infrastructural problems was a prerequisite for an agreement on trade. So far as lumber products were concerned the Soviet lumber mills in Galicia were quite close to the Hungarian border and thus the only sensible method of transportation would be by rail. The Hungarians claimed that no other methods could be even imagined.[37] Similarly to the discussions in the 1930s the shipping route of Budapest-Danube-Black Sea-Novorossiisk was mentioned for all non-lumber products. For Hungary, however, at this time this route could no longer be profitable particularly because in the meantime the two countries acquired a common land frontier. The Hungarian companies did not wish to purchase goods from a base in Novorossiisk because the three Hungarian river and seagoing freighters were scheduled to travel to Istanbul and the extension of the route to Novorossiisk would have meant substantial financial losses.[38] Although it appears as a daring idea, knowing the above problem it does not seem incidental that during the negotiations Mór Orován suggested the possibility of establishing a Soviet transport warehouse in Budapest.[39]

The earlier delaying Soviet tactics, refusing to engage in official negotiations, changed during the summer of 1940. A major contribution is made to the retrospective assessment of the events by the fact that on July 4, 1940, Viacheslav Molotov, the Foreign Affairs Commissar, personally informed Kristóffy that the Soviet government was prepared to sign a commercial agreement with Hungary.[40] This sudden change in the Soviet position was due to the changes in the geopolitical situation.

On June 26 the Soviet Union gave Romania an ultimatum about its territorial demands and occupied Bessarabia and Northern Bukovina. The Soviet action triggered a protest from Germany because according to a secret codicil to the August 23, 1939, Soviet-German Non-Aggression Pact, the Molotov-Ribbentrop Pact, only that part of Romania was considered to be in the Soviet sphere of interest which formerly belonged to tsarist Russia, namely Bessarabia. Bukovina, which until the end of World War I was part of the Austro-Hungarian Monarchy, was not assigned to the Soviet Union in the pact.[41] The political power plays of the Soviet Union in southeast Europe and in the Balkans suggest that it wanted to take a strong stand in the European political arena so far as the future fate of Romania and Bulgaria was concerned.[42] The pact did not name Romania or Hungary but Article 3, which required notification concerning any matter affecting both countries, was always interpreted by Soviet Russia to affect the small countries adjacent to it or located in the geographic area between the two countries. Thus the territorial problems between Romania and Hungary and their resolution could not be a matter of indifference to the Soviet Union. This is supported by the fact that at the July 4 meeting Molotov clearly stated the Soviet point of view about Hungarian-Romanian relations. According to Molotov the Soviet Union considered the Hungarian territorial demands vis-à-vis Romania to be fully justified and that the Soviet Union would so state at a potential international meeting which had the future of Transylvania on its agenda.

We can say that the role of Budapest and the quality of Hungarian-Soviet relations began to improve in the Soviet perspective after June 26, 1940, in the context of the Soviet ultimatum and of its consequence, namely the Soviet-German confrontation. Another important component in this change was the evolution of the Soviet political game vis-à-vis Bucharest. Moscow did not have any particularly significant economic basis for its relations with Budapest and therefore its willingness to have a commercial treaty signed was based primarily on political motivations. It can also be stated that the German expansion gradually enveloping all of central and southeastern Europe, required an increased Soviet presence in that area. In preparing this it seemed appropriate to establish a more serious economic presence in Hungary which adapted itself to the changing conditions. This would not only increase the economic relations and move away from a stalemate, but would also hold the promise of serious political benefits.

Subsequent to the Soviet agreement, the Hungarian government, the very next day, on July 6, decided that in preparing the text of the Hungarian agreement proposal, would take the Soviet-Bulgarian and Soviet-Yugoslav commercial agreements as a model.[43] On July 16, at the Ministry of Commerce, the leaders of the Office for Foreign Trade and of the five greatest Hungarian industrial concerns, Rimamurány-Salgótarján Iron Works, Manfréd Weiss, Láng Machine Industry, Ganz Machine-Railway Carriage, and Ship Building Company, and the representatives of MÁVAG held a meeting where they outlined the Hungarian demands. Initially the leaders of these organizations set the cost of the raw materials to be imported from the Soviet Union and required for the continuing operation of the Hungarian companies at fifteen million pengős. In this the largest item were the 400 wagons of pig iron, 200 wagons of ferro-manganese, 20 wagons of ferro-chrome and non-ferrous metals. In exchange for the raw materials MÁVAG offered railway axles, hoops, and pairs of railway wheels, Manfréd Weiss offered steel pipes, Ganz offered electric engines and ships, Láng offered Diesel engines and the Rimaurány-Salgótarján Iron Works offered metal sheets and steel wire.[44]

The instructions for the delegation starting for Moscow, the negotiating tactics and the composition of the delegation were determined at an inter-ministry meeting at the Ministry of Foreign Affairs on July 23. Unfortunately the minutes of this meeting could not be found and therefore we have to deduce from Minister of Foreign Affairs István Csáky's July 25 submission to the Council of Ministers that the most pressing issue, namely the financial arrangements for payment of the merchandise, was not determined in advance. Consequently the Hungarian tactics can be defined by the "let's get as much raw material as possible from the Russians" slogan. In his submission to the Council of Ministers, the Minister of Foreign Affairs stated it explicitly that, "the principal purpose of the negotiations in Moscow was to squeeze as much raw material out of the Russians as possible."[45] A substantial delegation consisting of fifteen persons, (thirteen officials, an interpreter and a secretary) started for Moscow. Alfréd Nickl, envoy extraordinary and minister plenipotentiary, head of the Economic Policy Division of the Ministry of Foreign Affairs, was designated as the leader of the delegation. A high official of the affected expert organizations, the Ministry of Commerce, the Ministry of Finance, the Ministry of Agriculture, the Ministry of Industry, the Ministry of Justice, the Hungarian National Bank and the Office for Foreign Trade constituted the membership of the delegation.[46]

The large delegation left Budapest on August 3. They first went to Berlin from where they flew to Moscow on August 7. We know little about the reason for the three day Berlin detour. We learn from a later report of Lajos Krivátsy-Szűcs, a counselor of the Department of Justice, that the members of the delegation exchanged information with the German commercial organizations and ministries but that the Germans were reluctant to reveal to their Hungarian colleagues the details of the German-Soviet commercial agreements.[47]

The head of the delegation was received the day after his arrival in Moscow by Anastas Mikoyan, the commissar for foreign trade. They agreed that the negotiations would be conducted by two subcommittees. Subcommittee no. 1 was to discuss the composition and value of the shipments while Subcommittee no. 2 was to draft the commercial and shipping agreements and the agreements on trading and payments. The Soviet contingent on Subcommittee no. 1 was headed by Dmitrii D. Mishustin, the head of the Contract Section of the Commissariat for Foreign Trade and Subcommittee no. 2. was headed by Aleksei. D. Krutikov, the deputy commissar for foreign trade.[48] Nickl later wrote about the atmosphere of the discussions:

> The negotiating techniques of our discussion partners differed from the methods generally used in such negotiations. The high ranking officials charged with heading the committees strictly limited the discussions to their own areas of expertise but even here they had to wait for new instructions on every important issue. The language of discussion on our part was mostly French with some German,

while the Soviets used Russian conveyed through interpreters. They rigidly insisted on texts of agreements that they had used previously in other contexts. I was impressed throughout the discussions with their intelligence, expertise and courtesy.[49]

In the negotiations lasting from August 8 to September 3 opinions diverged on two fundamental issues. One of the debates evolved over the matter of the accreditation and legal status of the Soviet Trade Mission in Budapest. We have seen that at the 1924 and 1934 negotiations about the establishment of diplomatic relations between Hungary and the Soviet Union this issue was also a problem area. The Hungarian government wanted to avoid at all costs the setting up of a Soviet trade mission in Budapest consisting of many members and engaged in a wide range of activities. The government particularly opposed the opening of missions in various parts of the country.[50] This matter actually was dealt with in the official report produced at the start of diplomatic relations on February 6, 1934. This document limited the membership of the Soviet Trade Mission to three people having diplomatic immunity, limited the legal rights of the Soviet representative organizations in Budapest and forbade the employment of former Hungarian citizens.[51] With these conditions the freedom of movement and legal standing of the Soviet Trade Mission was successfully curtailed. The current Hungarian delegation was concerned that if this matter was again revised the advantages gained in 1934 might be jeopardized. Therefore, initially the delegation held on to the view that there was no need to include any decisions on this issue in the agreement because the major principles had been established in 1934.

The Soviets stubbornly insisted on revising the regulations claiming that in 1934, or since, no trade mission had been established in Hungary and that the Soviet-Bulgarian and Soviet-Romanian agreements authorized the activities of the trade missions. They claimed that this had to set a precedent for the Hungarian agreement. They also demanded that the trade mission be allowed to open branch offices in provincial cities. The Hungarian delegation was forced to yield but insisted that the article authorizing the establishment of provincial offices be removed. It also endeavored to achieve that the leading officials of the future trade missions not be endowed with consular privileges. The final solution was a compromise where the Commissariat for Foreign Trade was not to open provincial offices but the head of the trade mission in Budapest and his two associates were granted diplomatic immunity.

In order to minimize the loss of prestige the Hungarians endeavored to make this compromise reciprocal. Even though on August 14 Nickl still argued that the Hungarian government was not planning to establish a commercial mission in Moscow because foreign trade was not a state monopoly in Hungary, one day later he sketched the structure of the Hungarian trade representation. Accordingly a commercial attaché would be appointed to the Hungarian Legation in Moscow and the Hungarian industrial organizations, and the financial institutions supporting them, would be represented by a foreign trade representative. The primary commercial and the related political matters would be handled by the attaché but the concrete deals would be made by the commercial and financial representative under his supervision. The Soviets considered reliance on the principle of reciprocity in the agreement unacceptable claiming that the Soviet foreign trade organizations had a peculiar nature. They finally agreed that the principle of reciprocity would not be included in the agreement but that there would be a gentleman's agreement under which Moscow would recognize the activities of a trade delegate in the Soviet Union.

The Hungarian concessions were based to some extent on the advice of Gustav Hilger, the head of the Commercial Section of the German Embassy in Moscow, who was consulted confidentially by the members of the Hungarian delegation. He considered it impossible for the Hungarian delegation to achieve the establishment of the legal position of the trade mission on the basis of reciprocity. We know from a report of Krivátsy that it was on the recommendation of the German diplomat that the delegation accepted the Soviet demand that the office of the Soviet Trade Mission in Budapest be entitled to extraterritorial status.[52]

The assumption that when the trade agreement was made Soviet diplomacy was guided primarily by long-term political considerations is supported by the nature of the second major controversial issue. At the time of the Hungarian-Soviet commercial negotiations the Soviets wanted to limit the framework of the merchandise exchange at 1.7–1.8 million dollars which was less than the ultimately much more modest

Soviet-Slovak one. In contrast, by comparison to the approximately 15 million dollars that the Hungarian industrial establishments had set as the value of their raw material requirements, István Schlick, a member of the Hungarian commercial delegation and the head of the Commercial Policy Division of the Ministry of Commerce, recommended the horrendous export potential of 25–30 million dollars to the Soviets.[53] Acceptance of this figure would have meant that that the Soviet trade organizations would have to export merchandise of the same value to Hungary. At the initial conversation between Mikoyan and Nickl the latter stated that, "Hungary had no limits on the amount of Soviet raw materials it could use." This incredibly exaggerated offer evidently gave the Hungarian group greater opportunities to maneuver and made it possible to reach an agreement after numerous compromises that kept the final figure from being below Hungarian requirements.

The unexpectedly low value of the Soviet offer surprised the Hungarian delegates who had endeavored during their discussions with the Soviets to create a tight correlation between the Soviet imports and Hungarian industrial production. They argued to the end that Hungary could guarantee the delivery of the finished and semi-finished industrial machinery, asked for by the Soviets, only if the Soviet would satisfy the raw material requirements for the production of this equipment. It hit the Hungarians like an icy shower that the Soviets made no offer to furnish the most essential raw material of the machine industry, namely iron ore. Mikoyan emphasized that he did not wish to link the raw material issue to the equipment ordered from Hungary and "consoled" the Hungarians that iron ore could be procured from other areas such as the Benelux countries, northern France or Yugoslavia. Mikoyan stated categorically that they could furnish no iron of any kind to Hungary because the developing Soviet industry needed all they had.

In addition, the 1.7–1.8 million dollar Soviet offer did not contain the raw materials needed by Hungary, such as pig iron, steel, manganese, ferro-manganese and lubricating oils. It was limited to lumber, cellulose, super-phosphate and naphthalene. On demand from the Hungarians, however, the Soviet offer was first raised to 2.3 million dollars and later to 3.2 million and the list of offers was enlarged to include cotton, asbestos, manganese ore, lubricating oil and chromium. This then began to come near to the lowered Hungarian demand of 4.5 million dollars. The gradual meeting of Hungarian demands was probably due to the Hungarians' yielding on other issues, such as the ominous trade mission, and the delay of the arrangements for railway transportation. In addition, the Soviets wanted to use this approach to eliminate the Hungarian demands for iron ore.

The Hungarian delegation still insisted on receiving a certain amount of iron ore. The situation is well illustrated by the following conversation between Nickl and Krutikov. The Hungarian diplomat stated that if he returned home without iron ore it would mean that he "had suffered a defeat" and he begged his Soviet partner to "Exercise an act of mercy and satisfy at least the Hungarian delegation's request for wolframite." The Soviet diplomat responded, "If every defeated enemy could go home with a list of material like the Hungarian delegation, every one of our negotiating partners would be pleased to consider himself defeated. I regret that I am unable to exercise the requested act of mercy because, as I have stated repeatedly, we cannot give wolframite to Hungary."[54] The final result was again a compromise. The level of the Hungarian-Soviet merchandise exchange was set at 3.7 million dollars but the list of the Soviet contingent did not include the iron ore, so vigorously requested by the Hungarian delegation. It also did not include other items such as the wolframite, required as a component of steel alloys, essential for the electrical industry or copper and bronze which were key components of machine manufacturing.

Signing of the documents took place in the evening of September 3. The agreements were prepared in four copies, two each in Hungarian and Russian. Nickl and Mikoyan signed the following documents: 1. The commercial and shipping agreement; 2. the memorandum attached to Article 3 of the agreement regulating the bans and limitations on exports, imports and transports; 3. addendum no. 1 to the text of the agreement about the legal status of the Soviet Trade Mission in Budapest; 4. addendum no. 2 to the text of the agreement about the use of arbitration panels; 5. the merchandise and payments agreement; 6. the two lists of merchandise attached to the text of the agreement; and 7. an exchange of letters indicating that the above agreements would take effect, at least temporarily, on September 15.[55]

In addition to the general clauses of the trade pact, Article 11 presented the proposed opening of direct railway contacts after the two governments reached a particular agreement on it. Article 12 provided that until an agreement was reached between the two countries on telegraph, telephone and postal connections the pertinent international regulations would apply.[56] The thought-provoking essential regulations which held the promise of meeting Hungary's needs were contained in the merchandise and payments agreement. The first article of this agreement stated that the quotas set up could be changed at some future time by mutual agreement between the two governments. Article 3 stated that also by mutual agreement, and the consent of the affected government, trades could be transacted in exchange for hard currency within the 3.7 million dollar limits.

The two largest items on the import lists were 820,000 dollars worth of fir lumber and 4,000 tons of wool and various textile components valued at 460,000 dollars. Other large items, worth 120,000 dollars, included phosphates and super-phosphates required for the production of fertilizers, 5,000 tons of manganese and 1,000 tons each of chromium, lubricating oil and machine oil. Smaller contingents consisted of coal, asbestos, and the naphthalene and turpentine needed for the manufacture of chemicals. The two major items on the export list were 800,000 dollars worth of transport items and 700,000 dollars worth of electrical motors and generators. The agreement specified exports to the Soviet Union of 3,600 pairs of railway coach wheels, 6,000 railway axels, 4,000 tons of steel tubing, 250,000 dollars worth of Diesel engines and steam engines.[57]

After his return Nickl prepared a detailed report for the Ministry of Foreign Affairs and summarized the results of the negotiations as follows: "The outcome of the negotiations is favorable….During the negotiations we were able to secure for Hungary significantly larger amounts of valuable raw materials than the Yugoslav, Bulgarian, or Finnish delegations. It is noteworthy that the Swedish and Danish delegations, having been in Moscow for two months, have been unable to reach any agreements, while we were able to reach a viable agreement in one month that also showed promise for future developments."[58] We can conclude from the press and from primary sources that the feeling of success was buttressed by the complete failure of the Romanian trade delegation that had been in Moscow all through the autumn of 1940. The Romanian fiasco was reflected in the gloating and somewhat cynical comments of the leading managers of the Hungarian economy. The domestic economic publications stated that the Soviet negotiators were much more understanding toward the Hungarians than toward the Romanians.[59] It is also typical what György Perényi-Lukács, a secretary of the legation wrote to the Minister of Foreign Affairs László Bárdossy: "Among the members of the Romanian delegation I saw familiar and unfriendly faces. The Romanians are delighted that their negotiations are making no progress and thus they do not have to go home."[60]

Difficulties in the Fulfillment of the Agreement on the Transport of Merchandise and Terms of Payment

The agreement on the transport of merchandise and on terms of payment and the two attached lists of contingencies set the limits of expenditure for the exchange of merchandise for only one year. The agreement did prove to be only a framework for discussion and therefore the transfer of individual goods required a new agreement between the Soviet trade organizations and the Hungarian industrial corporations in which the conditions of the sale, such as advances, standards, rate of manufacturing, delivery dates, and penalties had to be defined. As stated above, Articles 1 and 3 allowed Hungary a certain range of maneuvers. According to Article 3 Hungary could order merchandise in excess of the sum set for payments, namely the 3.7 million dollars, provided the additional payments were made in hard currency.

On October 30 the representatives of MÁVAG, Manfréd Weiss, the Rimamurány-Salgótarján Metal Works, and Ganz were asked to come to the Office for Foreign Trade to compile the additional Hungarian offers. The dissonance between Hungarian demands and Soviet intentions became clear immediately. The businessmen made offers for sales of 10–11 million dollars in excess of the 3.7 million dollars agreed upon and in exchange expected to receive an equal value of raw materials essential for Hungarian manufacturing.[61] The list of the business delegation going to Moscow included representatives of the above industrial organizations and of the MNB and PMKB. Nándor Rosslav, the head of the Office for Foreign Trade was appointed the leader of the delegation.[62]

The Hungarian businessmen arrived in Moscow on December 5 and started negotiations with the involved Soviet enterprises and with the officials of the Commissariat for Foreign Trade.[63] At the commissariat not much hope was given to the Hungarians. Mishustin roundly declared that during the first year the Soviet Union intended to export to Hungary only the merchandise included in the framework of the agreement, that no additional shipments would be made and thus there was no need to increase the merchandise to be exported.[64] When first heard this acted like a cold shower but did not yet mean the "defeat" of Hungarian diplomacy.

In order to determine the results of the Hungarian-Soviet trade agreements and to draw the appropriate conclusions we must examine the fate of the two largest items on the list of merchandise, the 820,000 dollars worth of lumber and the 800,000 dollars worth of ship delivery. The members of the Hungarian trade delegation were still in Moscow when the decision of the German and Italian arbitrators in Vienna was announced which returned to Hungary a 43,000 square kilometer area of Northern Transylvania. The regional and economic conditions of this large area were well known. The Székely Counties, and Máramaros and Beszterce-Naszód Counties had been considered to be the center of the lumber industry. The Vienna Award changed Hungary from being a lumber importer into a lumber exporter. It is characteristic that when Minister of Foreign Affairs Csáky talked to Sharonov, the Soviet minister in Budapest, he assessed the economic consequences of the Second Vienna Award saying that, "Hungary got nothing but woods and mountains. All the essential minerals necessary to build an independent country, remained outside of the new borders."[65]

The Hungarian delegates learned about the Vienna Award in the Soviet capital just at the time when they had finalized the value of the principal items, including lumber with the Soviets. Thus there was no possibility for modifying this item. As a consequence of the geographic and economic changes resulting from the Vienna Award it was inevitable that the importation of lumber and lumber products should be modified. This was made possible by Article 1 of the merchandise transportation and payments agreement.

Rosslav told Mishustin that because of the return of Northern Transylvania Hungary did not wish to make a deal on lumber imports and recommended that the lumber be replaced by other goods. Principal consideration should be given to such items which Hungary in the past obtained from the Baltic States, from western Belorussia and from Bessarabia. These included linseed, cattle-turnip seeds, and pomace.[66] The need to replace the lumber imports was emphasized by the Hungarian Legation in Moscow in a diplomatic note which precisely delineated the type and quantity of merchandise to take the place of the lumber imports, namely 5,000 tons of pomace, 750 tons of cattle-turnip seeds and 300 tons of flax seeds. The recommendation contained in Kristóffy's note was initially rejected by the Soviets because, in Rosslav's view, the Soviet Union has been unable to fully integrate economically the new territories that had come under its authority.[67] Within the Soviet economic leadership there clearly was some uncertainty about whether they should accede to the Hungarian request urging the replacement of the lumber contingent. Yet there might have been other reasons than the ones suggested by Rosslav. The experts at the raw lumber exporting agency, Exportles, in a document analyzing Hungary's 1940 lumber imports and 1941 import forecast, believed that Hungary's 1940 lumber imports were greater than the 1939 ones and that, in spite of the return of heavily wooded Northern Transylvania, lumber export to Hungary from Finland, Norway, Sweden, and Slovakia would continue at the same level in 1941.[68] In the end, however, Moscow accepted Budapest's request and agreed in January 1941 that the 820,000 dollar lumber import be replaced by a 400,000 dollar raw phosphate import and a 420,000 dollar import of wool.[69]

The compensation and trade agreement specified the date of delivery of the agreed upon merchandise within one year and thus the transactions should have been completed by September 15, 1941. The raw materials to be sent by the Soviets were immediately available in the Soviet Union but the manufacture of the heavy industry products to be shipped from Hungary, such as ships, transformers, generators, and railway equipment, required more time. Therefore the Soviets, immediately after the arrival of the Hungarian business delegation in Moscow, insisted that export of the raw materials to Hungary would take place only after the Soviets were satisfied that the contract on the major import item, the ships, had been satisfied. For this reason the Soviet export agencies delayed meeting their obligations to ship the oil derivatives, wool, phosphates and manganese ore until Mashinoimport could complete the purchase of the ships.

In Hungary it was the Ganz shipyard that had the necessary engineering and financial resources to build the ships. The Hungarian company signed the contract with the Soviet importing agency on December 29, 1940, for two 4,000 ton capacity ships, each being worth 950 thousand dollars.[70] It is evident that the conditions set down in the contract went considerably beyond the 800,000 dollars defined in the payments agreement and were, in fact, more than twice as much. To be sure, this was not made impossible by the original agreement. Most of our information about the way this agreement was reached comes from the Ganz archives. They relate the behind-the-scenes discussions between the company and the Hungarian government. This reveals that that the Hungarian government was willing to assure the supply of raw materials from the Soviet Union by any means and practically forced Ganz to enter into the contract.

The leaders of Ganz had emphasized to the representatives of the government, during the summer of 1940, that in the best of conditions the completion of the ships might be accomplished during 1942 but was most likely in 1943.[71] The Soviet side, however, insisted after the signing of the agreement that the delivery of the ships had to take place by the September 15, 1941, deadline. There remained only one possible solution. On March 23, 1939, the Ganz shipyard signed a contract with two newly established Hungarian maritime freighter companies, the Hungarian Orient Line Sea Navigation Company, Ltd. (Magyar Orientvonal Tengerhajózási Rt.) and the Commercial Sea Navigation Company, Ltd. (Kereskedelmi Tengerhajózási, Rt.) for the construction of two 4,000 ton seafaring vessels. The two companies provided the advance payment and construction of the ships began. At the same time the government exerted considerable pressure on Ganz to cancel the contract and let Mashinoimport have the two ships. A later *Aide Memoire* of the Ganz Company described the events as follows: "The expressed demand of the Hungarian government that the company make the two ships available under the terms of the Hungarian-Soviet agreement was firmly rejected by the interested parties. After lengthy discussions, during which the government assumed a threatening attitude, the two companies were forced to agree to cancel their contract with Ganz."[72] It is a fact that it was due only to the Ganz-Mashinoimport contract that the representatives of the Soviet export organizations even talked to the Hungarian business delegation under the leadership of Nándor Rosslav. At the beginning of 1941, in accordance with its obligation under the contract, the Soviet company paid an advance representing 25 percent of the purchase price, approximately 475,000 dollars.[73]

During the negotiations between Ganz and Mashinoimport the government exerted considerable pressure on Ganz making a variety of promises. The Soviet enterprise insisted on a number of changes in the technical plans submitted by Ganz which ultimately led to an increase of eighty-six thousand dollars in the cost of production. In a note prepared about the construction of the ships it was stated that, "The Soviets made excessive socially significant demands so far as internal designs were concerned. They wanted a casino room, bathrooms, etc." This note reveals that at the stage of construction the requested changes could still be made but that the alterations requested by the Soviets, such as the cabins, would have made the ships impossible to sell in any other country.[74] With the additional costs of production the lowest price Ganz could put on the ships was 1,950,000 dollars but the Soviets were unwilling to purchase them for more than 1.9 million. At this point Rosslav stepped in and "told" the Ganz representative in Moscow to sign the agreement based on 1.9 million dollars. According to a Ganz document, Rosslav made a promise that he would see to it that the missing 50,000 dollars were paid to the company "by putting a charge on the Hungarian raw material imports or by some other way."[75]

The government's other promise related to the manufacturing process. It was a concern that the Soviet exports lacked precisely those items, iron sheets, bronze and copper, which were essential for building ships and thus these items had to be supplied from sequestered Hungarian supplies. The government promised that it would provide all the necessary items for the construction, namely 900 tons of sheet metal, 61 tons of copper and 38 tons of bronze. The last two items were to be obtained, by confiscation, from obsolete and no longer usable equipment of the Hungarian textile industry.[76] Ganz, however, was forced to file a complaint on January 21, 1941, with Minister of Industry and Trade József Varga, because, in spite of the government promises, the two 450 ton units of sheet metal, promised for the end of November or the beginning of December, had not arrived at the factory. The company asked the minister to make immediate arrangements for the delivery of the 900 tons of iron from existing supplies.[77] The promised iron items were delivered only during the second half of March, 1941, which caused the fear that the completion of ship construction would be delayed by 2.5 months. (In the December 29, 1940, contract Ganz agreed to deliver the ships in Galați for their maiden voyage with a deadline of December 15, 1941, for the first one and January 15, 1942, for the second one.) The delay would have been very harmful because meeting the promised delivery date was subject to a penalty clause according to which 1 percent of the payments would have been deducted each week after the eight week of the delay.[78]

Dealing with Infrastructural Issues

During the commercial negotiations in Moscow the Hungarians repeatedly emphasized that unless the infrastructural barriers were eliminated no effective exchange of goods could take place between the two countries. The Hungarian delegates in the Russian capital would have liked to achieve that direct rail communication be made an item of the trade agreement and submitted a detailed proposal for their regulation. The Soviets, however, wanted to separate the infrastructural issues from the trade agreement and recommended that a separate railway agreement be signed. They argued that this was appropriate only after the trade agreement had been signed.[79] The Hungarian delegation agreed and the future regulation of the problem was guaranteed by Article 11 of the trade agreement which stated that the parties were required to sign a separate railway traffic agreement.

Shortly after his return on September 16, Nickl met Sharonov, the Soviet minister in Budapest, and expressed his satisfaction with the trade agreement. Nickl also indicated the need to address and resolve the infrastructure problems. He stated that for Hungary the establishment of a direct railway link with the Soviet Union was a matter of great importance and would become even more important after the onset of autumn because the Danube would be frozen for forty to fifty days and all water transport would come to a halt. According to the Soviet minister the Hungarian diplomat was worried that no discussion of the railway issue had been started.[80] Kristóffy, the Hungarian minister in Moscow, repeatedly urged the Commissariat for Foreign Affairs, during the autumn of 1940, to prepare a Soviet counter-proposal for the railway traffic agreement.[81] On November 23 Nickl met with the newly accredited representative of the Soviet Trade Mission, Nikolai Vozhzhov, and again stated that the conditions specified in the trade agreement could be met only if the infrastructural barriers were removed and rail, mail, telephone and telegraph connections were established between the two countries.[82] In response to the repeated Hungarian requests the Commissariat for Transportation drafted the Soviet counterproposal by the end of November and the Soviet government indicated on December 19 that it was prepared to receive Hungarian plenipotentiaries to negotiate a rail and postal traffic agreement.[83]

On January 20, 1941, a seven member delegation started out for the Soviet capital under the leadership of György Perényi-Lukács, secretary of legation and head of the Transportation Section of the Economic and Political Division of the Ministry of Foreign Affairs. The members of the delegation included Károly Forster, the executive director of the Hungarian Royal Mail Service, Miklós Tarkőy, deputy director of the Hungarian Royal Railways (MÁV) and other MÁV officials.[84]

The first issue that could be resolved rapidly was an agreement on the start of mail, telephone and telegraph services. Foster tried the direct telephone connection between Moscow and Budapest on January 27 and was able to talk with Budapest.[85] The agreement on establishing direct mail, telephone and telegraph connections was signed on February 4. The agreement opened direct telephone communication between Moscow and Budapest, via Lvov[86] and assured a telephone connection with other far away countries as well. It made every form of international telephone communication possible. Included were regular and emergency calls, official and private calls, weekly or monthly subscriptions, etc. In Hungary conversations with Soviet citizens were possible only from special telephone booths located at the post offices. Due to the agreement the fee for a three minute call from Budapest to Moscow or Leningrad was reduced by one third. The agreement also established a direct telegraphic connection between the two countries which made it possible for Hungarian citizens to exchange telegrams also with Japan and with the United States. The cost of sending telegrams from Budapest to Moscow was also substantially reduced.[87]

In accordance with the agreement mail traffic could also begin between the two countries after the end of February but initially only indirectly through Germany. Opening a direct mail contact between the two countries would become possible only after a rail link had been established. Perényi-Lukács assessed the outcome of the negotiations as follows: "The negotiations took place in a surprisingly favorable, almost friendly atmosphere and we experienced the greatest courtesy and helpfulness from the Soviets. This was true at both the conference and dinner tables."[88]

Reaching an agreement on rail connection was a much slower process. In principle the rail connection between the two countries could be established along three different routes. In the end they all converged on Csap, the railway center in Hungary, which was connected with Lvov (Lemberg), the capital of the former Austrian province of Galicia. The shortest route between the two cities would have been along the Munkács-Szolyva-Lavochne line. Until 1939 Lavochne was a busy international railway center between Czechoslovakia and Poland and its railway station was designed for the reception and transshipment of large amounts of merchandise.[89] The biggest problem was the adjustment from the Hungarian rail gauge to the much wider Soviet one. An agreement in principle was reached to resolve this difficulty by building parallel narrow and wide gauge tracks between the Hungarian border station Volóc, and the Soviet border station Lavochne. Of the distance between the two stations 14.5 kilometers were in Hungary and this distance was broken up by a total of six viaducts. In addition, on the Hungarian side, close to the border, there was a 1.7 kilometer-long tunnel through the Beskids and three shorter tunnels.

Establishing a wide gauge tract on the Hungarian side would have required much larger investments in both time and money. Parallel with the old viaducts new ones would have to be built and the tunnels would have to be widened to twice their previous width. On February 3, 1941, a mixed committee consisting of MÁV and Soviet State Railway representatives went to the border. Its task was to assess the status of the viaducts and tunnels on this tract and determine the time required for the necessary repairs and expansions. In its report the committee stated that because of the expected substantial amount of traffic it would be pointless to begin on the Hungarian side because the double track construction would take at least several months and might take one year to complete.[90] This is why the Hungarian delegation made the recommendation in Moscow that each side place only one additional rail. The Soviets should place one rail between the wide gauge ones at a standard distance from one of them while the Hungarians would add an extra line outside of the standard ones to fit the Soviet carriages. This would obviate the need for new viaducts and for the complete rebuilding of the Beskids Tunnel. According to preliminary calculations these activities would have taken approximately fifty days to complete while the changes on the Soviet side would have taken only twenty-five days. The reason for this was that on the Hungarian side substantial investments would have to be made to enlarge and improve the Volóc station and because the Beskids Tunnel required considerable maintenance.[91]

The agreement relative to the direct passanger and freight rail traffic between Hungary and the Soviet Union was signed on March 3, but was dated March 1. About a dozen attachments were appended to the agreement which regulated accounting, fares, the method of managing travelers and acceptance of merchandise at the border, and other technical problems. The document was endorsed on the Hungarian side by Tarkőy and on the Soviet side by S. I. Bagaev, the deputy commissar for transportation.[92] According to the agreement the trains arriving from Hungary would have gone as far as Lavochne and it was there that merchandise and passengers would have been transferred to the Soviet train. Trains coming from the Soviet Union on the wide gauge would have proceeded to the station at Volóc and it was there that the merchandise and the passengers would have been transferred to the Hungarian trains.[93] The parties agreed that during the period of repairs and reconstruction of the tracks the trains arriving from the Soviet side would all go to Lavochne and that the passengers and merchandise would be moved there to the Hungarian trains.

The train ride between Budapest and Moscow took, on the average, 50–52 hours, depending on traffic.[94] The first direct express train left Moscow for Budapest late in the evening on March 20 and arrived in Lavochne on the evening of March 22. This train brought back the flags captured during the 1848–1849 Revolution and War of Independence[95] but the only people on the train were the railway personnel. There were no paying travelers. In addition to the Honvéd flags there was a huge amount of mail which had to be transferred and thus the train arrived at the Hungarian border station, Volóc, one hour late.[96] The early passenger data suggest that the trains were not used much for passenger traffic and the wagons remained essentially unoccupied. The Miskolc office of MÁV, familiar with traffic to the Soviet Union, reported that until March 28 only five people bought a ticket for Lavochne.[97]

It is the irony of fate that Prime Minister Bárdossy, on June 16, 1941, precisely ten days before he announced to Parliament the state of war with the Soviet Union, notified Kristóffy by telegram that on the Hungarian side the combined gauge railroad track had been completed to Volóc and that there was no problem with starting the bi-directional traffic on June 20. MÁV asked the Soviet Railway Administration to send an engine with the Soviet gauge to Volóc on June 20, to test the tracks built on Hungarian territory.[98]

In addition to the postal and train traffic there was another infrastructure problem the resolution of which was much in Hungary's interest. The "navicert system," introduced by the British authorities in 1939, which controlled the commercial maritime transport of goods across the Atlantic from the overseas colonies and from North and South America made the delivery of goods to Europe very difficult and made imports of raw materials from the American continent to Hungary impossible. Consequently, after the second half of 1940 there were only two possible routes for the shipment of imported goods. The first one went by way of the Persian Gulf, via Basra, from where the goods could be forwarded by train, trucks and, again by ships. This was a very complex and cumbersome route because it required a number of transfers of the merchandise and because this route went through areas under British control, such as the Baghdad railway.[99] The situation was made even worse when Great Britain broke off its diplomatic relations with Hungary on April 6, 1941.

A route unaffected by the war and quite safe was through the Pacific Ocean port of Vladivostok connected to the European parts of the Soviet Union by the Trans-Siberian railroad. This made it possible to carry the merchandise to its destination. Resolution of the matter became critically urgent because by the end of 1940 a huge amount of merchandise destined for Hungary was accumulated in American and Japanese ports. It was estimated to amount to 300–400 wagon loads[100] and had been paid for by the Hungarian buyers. It only waited for transportation.[101] Transport across the Soviet Union was an uncertain affair until it was regulated by formal agreements. The reason for this was that the Soviet Union did not join the October 3, 1924, international tariff agreement which made the railway transport tariffs in Europe uniform from one country to the other. Thus the Soviet government could set the freight rate at whatever level it chose and which it considered most advantageous for itself. Also, the start of regular transport was contingent on the opening of a direct rail connection which again caused problems, increased costs and delays. The merchandise had to be transferred twice, once from ships in Vladivostok to railway cars and then from the wide gauge Soviet tracts to the Hungarian railway cars.[102]

At the August-September 1940 negotiations in Moscow the Hungarian delegation would have liked to have the transit options mentioned in Articles 3 and 11 of the agreement. It was only a modest victory that the Hungarian request was accepted by the Soviet side only so far as Article 3 was concerned.[103] In the case of Article 11 the request was rigidly refused even though this article was the more important one from the Hungarian commercial interests' perspective. It was not clear from Article 3 what the issues related to transport were and what the responsibility of the Soviet Union was in this matter. No direct reference was made in this article about these two issues. In Article 3 the two contracting parties agreed that in some instances, such as public safety, public health, animal health, plant protection, artistic and antiquarian values, etc, prohibitions and limitations could be set up in import, export and transit, provided that these were in effect against all other countries as well. Thus the transit issue was mentioned only once and in the context of an individual and specific governmental action. Article 11 which stated in a factual manner that there was an agreement about the necessity of establishing a direct rail connection also stated that traffic on the railways of the two contracting parties would not be treated with less consideration or at a different rate than those granted to the "most favored nations." Nickl suggested during the negotiations that without a mention of traffic Article 11 would be suffering from "certain cosmetic blemishes" and expressed his hope that the standalone railway traffic agreement would contain regulations about transit traffic as well.[104] It could not have been incidental that, so far as traffic was concerned, both parties interpreted the commercial agreement from the perspective of their own interests and in their own way. The Hungarian business delegation negotiating in Moscow at the turn of 1940–1941 wanted to clarify the traffic issues even before the trade agreement was signed. Consequently Rosslav, the leader of the delegation, raised this matter at the very first discussion he had with Mishustin. According to Hungarian sources twelve trains left Vladivostok for Europe every day. Rosslav asked for 1 percent of this transport capacity, approximately 6 railway cars, every day. The original request asked for 2,240 tons of copper, 50 tons of nickel and 40 tons of other metals, 129 tons of iron alloys and raw rubber. The importance of the issue is shown dramatically by the fact that from Hungary, by telegram, additional traffic requests were introduced to the business delegation in Moscow, such as for instance for 88 tons of wool, and 50 tank cars of oil.[105] Rosslav argued that under Article 3 there could be no doubt about Hungary's transit rights[106] while the Soviets stated that the agreement made no special reference to this matter.[107]

The Hungarian delegation also tried to use as an argument the belief that getting the copper and the nickel was essential for the Manfréd Weiss Company to be able to comply with its obligations toward the Soviet Union and deliver the steel tubes for the oil pipeline. Initially the Soviets claimed that the Trans-Siberian line was so heavily burdened that until March 1 they were not willing to assume the responsibility for the relatively small shipment of 50 tons of nickel.[108] In order to exert some pressure Kristóffy submitted several diplomatic notes in support of the transit requests but the Commissariat for Foreign Affairs denied the requests claiming the absence of a separate agreement.[109]

It became possible to move away from dead center only during the negotiations of the Hungarian delegation which went to Moscow to reach an agreement on the infrastructure. The experts of the Commissariat for Transportation agreed to discuss the possibility of transit across the Soviet Union in parallel with the discussions of the railway transport.[110] Yet no article on transit was included in, or even mentioned in, the railway traffic agreement but there was an oral agreement that the appropriate Soviet agency would review each application for transit individually. After the earlier rigid rejections this appeared to be a significant triumph. The Commissariat for Transportation, however, tied the issuance of individual permits to strict bureaucratic and financial conditions. The companies wanting to import merchandise had to apply for a transit permit in writing to the head of the Soviet Trade Mission in Budapest indicating the nature of the merchandise, its quantity and provenance. The applications had to be endorsed by the Hungarian Office for Foreign Trade. In addition, the Hungarian shipping agents handling the transport had to reach a separate agreement on the counterpart shipments with the Soviet state enterprise, Iransovtrans, which was under the supervision of the Commissariat for Transportation.

It became evident later that for the transport rights Iransovtrans wanted part of the transit merchandise for payment instead of hard currency. The amount and quality of the goods to be kept would have been established at each occurrence. In exchange it made a commitment that within 60 days of its arrival in Vladivostok the rest of the merchandise in the shipment destined for Hungary would be delivered at the Soviet-Hungarian border to the Hungarian companies.[110] The Hungarian government believed that the transit costs would amount approximately to the value of half of the merchandise but that the economic loss created by the transfer of half of the merchandise was acceptable in view of the difference between the cost of the merchandise overseas and the cost of the same merchandise in Hungary.[111] In the Hungarian professional trade journals articles appeared which suggested that the Soviet trade organizations could demand up to 70 percent of the transit merchandise. It caused little confidence that because of the heavy use of the Trans-Siberian railway Moscow retained the right to select the goods it would permit to transit.[112]

It became obvious that the Soviet Union would select the raw materials, destined for Hungary from the American hemispheres, according to its own economic interest and with attention to its own raw material requirements. It is clear from the history of the discussions about the permits for transit that the possibilities hidden in the Hungarian-Soviet commercial ties had to be viewed by Budapest with consideration of the economic rationale and the stringent demands of the situation while Moscow always approached them from a perspective of purely political advantage. This may be the reason why later it did permit the transit of goods to

Hungary because their rejection, in the face of the vigorous Hungarian pressure for their approval, would have caused a minor breach in the positive evolution of Hungarian-Soviet relations after the summer of 1940. At the same time the Soviet Union buttressed the transit permits with conditions which made their fulfillment extremely difficult. Even if fulfilled they could not have caused any particular damage or loss to the capacity of railway transportation and to international obligations.

Soviet Participation at the Budapest
International Fair

The social sensation of the spring of 1941 was the Soviet Union's participation at the International Fair in Budapest (BNV). For broad segments of Hungarian society this was the first opportunity to see the commercial products of Soviet industry and agriculture, the consumer goods produced in that country, the cultural life in the Soviet Union and the scientific and technical accomplishments achieved since the 1917 October Revolution. The exposition in the Soviet pavilion was arranged and displayed by experts from the Commissariat for Foreign Trade. "Soviet reality" was thus documented by a Soviet presentation and from a Soviet point of view. Such a thing had not occurred since 1919. It is perhaps due to this that in the remembrances about the fair it is frequently said that the participation of the Soviet Union in the BNV was initiated by Soviet diplomacy partly because during 1940–1941 it endeavored to establish good relations with Hungary and wanted to demonstrate this in a variety of ways. According to this interpretation the return of the Honvéd flags of the 1848–1849 Revolution and War of Independence was part of the same Soviet diplomatic offensive that backed the construction of a Soviet pavilion at the 1941 BNV.[113]

According to both Hungarian and Soviet archival sources the truth of the matter was that it was the Hungarian government that asked the Soviet government to present its country at the 1941 BNV. Because most of the pre-1945 documents of the BMV were destroyed during the war, it is difficult to ascertain what precise reasons moved the leadership of the BNV to make this decision. Material in the Soviet archives reveals that the invitation of the Soviet Union to the BNV was not without some preliminary activity. There is evidence that the directors of the BNV had invited the Communist state to participate in at least one earlier BNV, namely the 1925 one.[114]

It is a fact that József Varga, the minister of industry and trade, submitted to the Council of Ministers on January 24, 1941, a request from the leadership of the BNV, addressed to him, in which it asked his approval for inviting the Soviet Union to the upcoming fair. The BNV leadership informed the minister that it had already asked the Ministry of Foreign Affairs which had indicated that it would not object to the invitation. The directors of the fair justified the request by saying that the matter was not only one of commercial policy but that it "affected in some ways general political, foreign affairs and domestic policy matters." The initiative of the BNV leadership can be best understood when seen in the context of the events that took place during the preceding months. It was evidently related to the positive developments in Hungarian-Soviet trade relations and, therefore, it is not surprising that the Council of Ministers approved the request without a dissenting vote.[115]

On February 1 the Hungarian Legation in Moscow presented the diplomatic note with the official invitation of the directors of BNV to the Commissariat for Foreign Affairs. The invitation stated that the goal was the increase and improvement of the commercial and touristic ties between the two countries. The BNV directors also asked the Commissariat for Foreign Affairs that, in addition to tourism information, the material displayed at the fair would also include those Soviet products which were sought after not only in Hungary but also in other neighboring countries.[116]

The Soviet decision to accept the invitation was made at the highest state decision-making level, that is, the Communist Party's Politburo. The laconic minutes of the Politburo reveal that 32,500 dollars were appropriated from the nation's hard currency reserves for the construction of the Soviet pavilion and for the expenses associated with the Soviet presence at the BNV.[117] The importance for Hungary of the Soviet participation at the BNV is shown by the fact that Bárdossy wanted to invite Mikoyan to the fair which would have raised the Soviet participation to a higher level.[118]

The domestic press presented the preparations for the exhibit as a major sensation. To the left of the Stefánia Road entry an area was designated as the "Nations' Plaza" where six foreign countries erected national pavilions. There was one each for the Soviet Union, Germany, Switzerland, Slovakia, and Japan, with two additional ones for Italy. The Soviet pavilion, erected on the basis of plans made in Moscow, was the largest of all of the foreign country exhibits at the fair. It covered an area of 1,000 square meters, while the two Italian pavilions covered areas of 800 and 600 square meters and the German one stood on an area of only 260 square meters. The material for the exhibit left Moscow in three sixty ton trucks on April 15. The remainder of the exhibit, almost six wagon loads, shown previously in Leipzig, was brought from a Soviet warehouse in Germany. A three-member committee that left Moscow on April 17 was sent to Budapest by the Commissariat for Foreign Trade to set up the exhibit in an artistic way.[119] Initially there were some articles in the Hungarian press suggesting that there would be an official information agency in the Soviet pavilion to inform the interested visitors about the economic relations between the two countries.[120]

The Soviet state export enterprises that were most important from the perspective of Hungarian imports and which had a display in the Soviet pavilion included Promexport (industrial products), Exportlen (textile industry raw materials), and Neftesindikat (oil industry products). Other organizations that had a display were Exportkhleb (grains), Soiuzpushnina (furs and pelts), and Raznoexport (tobacco, volatile oils, medicinal plants, etc.). The cultural area was represented by a book distribution organization, Mezhdunarodnaia Kniga, a motion picture distributor, Soiustorgkino, and the state tourism organization, Inturist.

The thirty-sixth BNV, lasting from May 2 to May 12, was opened by Regent Horthy who then visited all the foreign national pavilions including the Soviet one. He was accompanied by his wife, his daughter-in-law, Mrs. István Horthy, Prime Minister Bárdossy, Lord Mayor Károly Szendy, and István Hollósy the director of the BNV.[121] The Soviet pavilion was later visited by a number of prominent politicians including, on May 3, the German Minister of Finance Lutz Graf Schwerin von Krosigk and the Hungarian Minister of Finance Lajos Reményi-Schneller. On May 5 it was visited by Archduke József Ferenc, accompanied by the Minister of Industry and Trade József Varga. On May 6 it was visited by the Slovakian Minister of Commerce Gejza Medrick.[122]

In connection with these visits by important people a number of anecdotal stories are preserved. The first of these relates to Horthy who apparently was not in the least distressed by the large symbols of the Communist movement displayed on the façade of the pavilion. These were the hammer and sickle and the red star which now were the state symbols of the Soviet Union. In an interview in 1981, Béla Geiger the press secretary and interpreter of the Soviet Legation in Budapest who was of Hungarian descent, recalled this event as follows:

> When the throng of people decreased it was announced by the Hungarian authorities that the regent wanted to view the exhibit. He did not, however, want to make the visit known to the public. For this reason he came only accompanied by his wife and by László Bárdossy. Mrs. Horthy was very pleased and our minister asked the regent to write something in the visitors' book. Horthy looked at Bárdossy with considerable distress and did not know what to do. There were some awkward moments. Our minister then suggested to Horthy that he should only enter his name and the date of the visit. This is what happened.[123]

Sharonov recorded the visit of Archduke József Ferenc in his diplomatic diary:

> On the day the exhibit opened and after I had received the regent and showed him the exhibit, Archduke József Ferenc asked me to convey his sincere thanks to my government for having returned to Hungary the flags kept in the Soviet Union. I told him that I would be pleased to do so. Then the archduke asked me to write to Moscow and convey his request: "I collect the autographs of famous people. Please do everything you can to have Mr. Stalin send me his autograph." I promised that I would write. The archduke then said that it was certainly not easy to obtain Stalin's autograph but that he hoped that his request would be honored.

The minister also noted that Minister of Commerce Varga and Lord Mayor Szendy expressed their profound thanks for the Soviet Union having participated at the fair "in such difficult times."[124]

Even though these two stories contain some questionable recollections and some inaccuracies[125] they do indicate the manifestation of a wide interest in the material displayed in the Soviet pavilion. The domestic press unanimously reported that the most popular of all of the national exhibits was the one of the Soviet Union and that in front of the Soviet pavilion there were long lines of people waiting to get in all the time and there were also some tumultuous disturbances.[126] Allegedly on May 4 the German and Hungarian politicians visiting the fair could progress through the Soviet pavilion only after the Soviet personnel provided protection for the group by keeping the throngs besieging the pavilion away from them.[127] Order could generally be maintained only by special security arrangements. By the entrance to the pavilion a gangway was constructed of timbers and ropes to admit the public in a more orderly fashion. Yet the number of visitors increased to the point where at one time the personal safety of Béla Geiger was in jeopardy.[128]

The Problem of the Dangers of Soviet Propaganda

Contemporary photographs of the BNV's Soviet pavilion show that in front of the entrance mounted police were maintaining order.[129] This was not only to control the crwds but also to prevent any activity on the part of the Hungarian Communists. There were rumors all over town that the presence of large crowds massed before the Soviet pavilion might be used by the workers to stage a demonstration. To date I have found no direct data or documents substantiating these rumors and even the paper of the Social Democratic Party stated that at the Soviet pavilion every stratum of society was curious to see the exhibits.[130] Even though Béla Geiger stated that not only Communists and communist sympathizers came to the exhibit but everybody who wanted to learn something about the Soviet Union. He attributed the enormous interest and the obvious success of the exhibition to, "An expression by the working masses of their sympathy toward the Soviet Union." According to him, at one time the Hungarian authorities wanted to close the exhibit.[131] There is no evidence at all for the veracity of this statement.

In contrast, Kristóffy, the Hungarian minister in Moscow, assessed the events believing that at the BNV many fell under the influence of the totally deceptive and completely misleading Soviet propaganda, and he felt that behind the success of the Soviet exhibit there was consciously organized political propaganda.[132] Even though in the sources currently available to us there is no evidence for any direct Comintern propaganda there were a number of visual tools at the exhibit, such as documentary films lauding the Soviet Union, prospectuses, albums, etc., which, according to some, could have had an indirect impact on the visitors.[133]

The fears of the Hungarian leadership, based on ideological grounds, about a potential surge of Communist agitation linked to the developing commercial relations focused largely on the arguments involving the legal status of the Soviet Trade Mission in Budapest. During the negotiations in Moscow the Hungarian delegation was unable to achieve that the agreement include specific regulations about the total number of people in the trade mission or its precise legal status. In personnel matters the protocol was limited to the decision that the head of the mission and his two associates would be eligible for the rights and privileges granted to the members of the diplomatic missions. Just a few days after signing the trade agreement the Politburo, on September 6, appointed the head of the trade mission in Budapest, Nikolai Vozhzhov, who arrived in Budapest during the first few days of November.[134] His first discussion with Pál Práger, the chief executive of Ganz, took place on November 15.[135]

During the subsequent weeks the staff of the mission rose to five. There were also a large number of Soviet engineers who came to Hungary to inspect the industrial plants of the Hungarian companies and to check on the specifications and manufacturing processes of the goods to be shipped to the Soviet Union. Most of these engineers came during the first half of 1941, usually remained in Hungary for up to two months and during this time they were considered to be members of the trade mission. After a while the Hungarian leadership became acutely aware of this because the confidential exchange of letters of February 6, 1934, about the establishment of a trade mission, which actually took place only in 1940, limited the personnel to three people. The Soviets were correct, however, when they claimed that the September 3, 1940, protocol did not tie their hands so far as the personnel situation of the mission was concerned. It appears that Hungarian diplomacy endeavored to stop any further increase in the personnel of the trade mission and therefore returned to the content of the confidential exchange of letters of February, 1934. Interpreting the time line of the agreement differently, the Hungarian side argued that although the September 3, 1940, protocol specified the status and responsibilities of the mission in considerable detail, this did not supersede the limitation of personnel agreed upon in the protocol six years earlier. It was the result of this diplomatic swordplay that Kristóffy, citing the confidential exchange of letters of February 6, 1934, ordered on April 19, 1941, that the Hungarian Legation withhold the issuance of visa to two additional members of the trade mission in Budapest until the Commissariat for Foreign Affairs issued specific information about the purpose of the trip of these two to Hungary.[136]

In Hungary a sense of dislike or, at least a lack of confidence, was manifested in military circles about the trade agreement and the evolving Hungarian-Soviet business connections. The main reason for this was that, as a logical consequence of the agreement, there was a marked increase in Soviet commercial experts and engineers entering Hungary. In one instance the Army Chief of Staff Henrik Werth advised Minister of Foreign Affairs Csáky that according to his [Werth's] information the Soviets wanted to install a four-member engineering supervision group at the Ganz shipyard. Werth believed that the establishment of such a group in "the munitions factories," permanently and without reservations, was undesirable and dangerous. He therefore advised the ministry that if the Soviets would really ask for it, the number of the group should be limited absolutely to the smallest possible number, that a permanent liaison officer was to be assigned to supervise the activities and that the freedom of movement of the group was to be restricted to the shipyard.[137]

In the absence of other source material I have learned of the number of personnel associated with the commercial representation from a Bulgarian archival source that I discovered recently during my work in Sofia. After the German invasion all diplomatic relations between Germany and its east European allies, Hungary, Slovakia, and Romania, and the Soviet Union came to a stop. The exchange of the diplomatic representatives of the Soviet Union in Hungary and in Slovakia (who were also interned in Hungary) for the Hungarian and Slovakian diplomats interned in the Soviet Union took place with the assistance of the Bulgarian and Turkish governments. The Soviet citizens interned in

Hungary were exchanged on July 10 at the Bulgarian-Turkish border at the Svilengrad railway station. For the management of the exchange the Bulgarian government appointed a special representative of the Ministry of Foreign Affairs, Ivan Stanchev, secretary of legation, who after his arrival on the scene prepared a list of the Soviet officials who had been taken to that site.[138] According to this list the total number of the staff of the Budapest and Bratislava Soviet missions, including the trade representatives, was sixty-one persons of which eight people, including the Soviet engineers in Budapest, belonged to the personnel of the trade mission.[139]

My studies to date have not revealed any documents or data that would indicate any direct propaganda activity by the diplomats employed at the foreign mission or by Soviet officials who did not enjoy diplomatic immunity. The mistrust in the Soviet engineers coming to Hungary was perhaps not entirely without foundation, not because they might have incited the workers in the companies they visited but because of the industrial spying they might have engaged in. Thus, for instance, Viktor Korolev who was sent by the Commissariat for Transportation to Budapest to study the Manfréd Weiss and MÁVAG plants and to place an order for railway axles and arrange for their deliveries also visited a number of other industrial plants including the Hungarian Steel Products, Inc. (Magyar Acélárugyár, Rt.), where military equipment was being manufactured.[140] In his report of the visit, written in long hand, he gave a relatively thorough report about the factory and about the activities taking place there. During the days when Germany attacked the Soviet Union he had an opportunity to chat with the workers with whom he talked about the works and living conditions in the Soviet Union.[141]

The Balance Sheet of Hungarian-Soviet Commercial Relations and the Lessons Learned from It

Statements by high-ranking government officials clearly reflect the attitude of the Hungarian government toward the entire system of bilateral Hungarian-Soviet agreements. Minister of Finance Lajos Reményi-Schneller emphasized the importance of Hungarian-Soviet economic cooperation from the perspective of raw material supplies.[142]

Minister of Foreign Affairs Csáky, speaking in the House of Representatives in Parliament on November 13, correctly assessing the global political importance of the Soviet state, declared, "Our relations with Soviet Russia are above board and normal. No doubt they noted in Moscow at the time of the economic negotiations that the Hungarian government is seriously endeavoring to deepen its economic ties with the Russian empire....The Hungarian government is fully aware of the economic and political weight of the Soviet Russian empire."[143] At the November 15 budget debate the Minister of Industry and Trade József Varga, emphasized the beneficial effects of the agreements.[144]

After a careful review of the domestic press and the archival sources it is fair to say that in addition to the government the Hungarian political elite unanimously assessed the trade agreement and its economic effects on Hungary positively. I have not found any assessment or statement that raised the fear of Communist propaganda relative to the agreement.[145] At the Ministry of Foreign Affairs budget debate in the House of Representatives, on November 13, not only the Government Party Representative József Hoss and the Subcarpathian Representative Mihály Demkó, the economic advisor of the governor of Subcarpathia, but even the extreme right-wing representatives, Ferenc Rajniss[146] and Kálmán Rátz,[147] argued in favor of the agreement. The way Rajniss spoke of Hungarian-Soviet relations illustrates the typical attitude of the political elite: "The proper Russian-Hungarian relations, which has led to the resumption of trade agreements, excludes any and all propaganda in this country and all it expects from us is to view the internal life in Russia as being a purely Russian affair."[148] Kálmán Rátz felt that the rate of Hungarian-Soviet economic rapprochement was too slow and recommended a much more forceful economic penetration to include the development of water transport routes and the establishment of consulates having commercial rights in the Soviet port cities, industrial centers, and in Central Asia.[149]

On the basis of an oral agreement reached at the August 1940 Moscow negotiations the Hungarian government began to construct a structure for the Hungarian trade-representative system in the Soviet Union. In the autumn of 1940 a commercial attaché was appointed to the Hungarian Legation in Moscow. This attaché was Rolf Krausz who had worked earlier in the independent Baltic States as an accredited trade representative and who, from this vantage point studied and followed the economic situation in the Soviet Union. In addition to Krausz, a banking expert, Oszkár Haris, spent several months in Moscow during the spring of 1941 as a non-diplomatically accredited permanent representative of the two large Hungarian Banks, PMKB and MÁH, which were deeply interested in financing Soviet exports. Starting about this time Arzén Rankó functioned as a "Russian rapporteur" in the Royal Hungarian Office for Foreign Trade, responsible for coordinating the commercial matters relative to the Soviet Union.[150]

Examining the trends of the merchandise exchange, in tables 8 and 9, we can see that the 1940 trade agreement resulted in some successes in economic relations, particularly during the first half of 1941. There was a definite increase in Soviet exports toward Hungary.

Table 8 Trends in Hungarian-Soviet Trade[151]

Year	Hungarian exports		Hungarian imports	
	Tons	in 1,000 pengős	Tons	in 1,000 pengős
1939	–	–	918.5	253
1940	5.98	36	1,071.9	531
1941 (1st half)	2,416 + 14,365[152]	1,536	21,104.0	10,819

Table 9 The Soviet Union's Share in the Total Hungarian Export and Import[153]

Year	Soviet share in Hungarian exports	Soviet share in Hungarian imports
1939	–	0.05%
1940	0.01%	0.09%
1941 (1st half)	0.19%	1.48%

In spite of this the increase was not large enough to fill the Hungarian leadership with satisfaction. In the Hungarian documents we can repeatedly find government opinions which stated that changes in Hungarian industrial production were required in order for the Hungarian-Soviet commercial agreement to be implemented as soon as possible. This was considered critical for Hungary in order to get the raw materials absolutely essential for the Hungarian economic infrastructure. The intent to make the Hungarian-Soviet trade agreements more effective and centrally controlled can be seen clearly in the government's April 17, 1941, press release which stated: "The unusual economic conditions and particularly the raw material problems make it necessary for the state, through its appropriate agencies, to increase the supervision over the merchandise certain companies want to import or export. There is a particularly urgent need to oversee Hungarian-Soviet trade relations because in this highly important and recently inaugurated commercial relationship it happened repeatedly that proper deals on the goods were not possible." The government advised the companies involved in Hungarian-Soviet business relations that in the future only those companies would be granted an export and import license who had previously reported every such activity to the Interstate Department of the Office for Foreign Trade.[154] One of the victims of the government's centralizing effort was the Ganz Company.

After Hungary entered the war against the Soviet Union on June 27, 1941, the Hungarian-Soviet trade agreement and the transactions produced under its terms became impossible. On the future fate of the ships which were almost completed at the Ganz shipyards there was a fundamental difference of opinion between the company and Minister Varga. The leaders of the company believed that the unconditional sale of ships, to be completed in the near future, would represent a hazard to the company because after the war a peace treaty would decide the fate of the ships. The company advised Varga that because the company had made sacrifices for the benefit of the country they should be absolved of any obligations to meet the demands of the Soviets for compensation. In the company's opinion in case of wartime compensations the sum of the Soviet demands for compensation would be the same as the total value of the Soviet shipments. This would equal the basic capital of the company and inevitably would lead to its bankruptcy. The leader of the company had been informed that the value of the Soviet exports to date equaled 2.5 million dollars, or 12.5 million pengős, which was the precise amount of the company's capital stock.[155]

Table 8 shows that the total value of the Soviet shipments was approximately 10.8 million pengős but the concerns of the Ganz Company were not entirely without reason. It seems likely, from the archival sources, that these concerns had their roots in the past. The Ganz Company experienced serious difficulties after the end of World War I. During that war the government of the Austro-Hungarian Monarchy requisitioned the Ganz ships but under the terms of the peace treaty the ships had to be delivered to the original purchaser, Greece, and therefore the company had to build identical ships at its own expense.[156] This had no effect on the minister of commerce and ignoring the Ganz Company's losses he "forbade" the company from continuing to build the ships according to the Soviet specifications when that country was at war with Hungary. The minister also directed the company to choose a building construction type that would eventually make the ships marketable to and suitable for use by the Hungarian armed forces.[157]

The balance sheet of the trade under the commercial agreement was worked out by the Ministry of Foreign Affairs after the diplomatic relations between Hungary and the Soviet Union were severed by the war. According to these data Hungary had imported 345 tons of wool, 915 tons of wool waste, 15,600 tons of phosphates and 250 tons of cylinder oil from the Soviet Union. The Hungarian exports consisted of one generator, 3,800 railway axles, 1,300 tons of steel oil pipes, and 14,365 vacuum tubes. The Soviet Union had made a down payment of 800,000 dollars and a cash payment of 450,000 dollars while Hungary opened an account at the State Bank of the USSR for 1,250,000 dollars of which approximately 500,000 dollars worth of raw materials had not been delivered. In the total Hungary ended up with a deficit in its trade with the Soviet Union. When the war broke out Hungary owed 400,000 dollars to the Soviet Union.[158]

The Hungarian government wished to resolve the matter of credits and debits derived from the trade with the Soviet Union by a unilateral liquidation. The matter was governed by ordinance No. 5.910/1942 M.E. It ordered that within thirty days of this ordinance taking effect the Hungarian companies had to report to the Office for Foreign Trade all the credits and debits which were derived from the legal trades under the trade agreement or originated from the fact that all trading had become impossible. The report had to include the origins of the credits and debits, the current status and total sums. The accuracy of the statements could have been checked by accountants sent out by the office. The existing debts had to be paid into an account, established for this purpose, at the Office for Foreign Trade. The sums so deposited were to satisfy the outstanding demands from the State Bank of the USSR, if the Office for Foreign Trade determined that these demands were valid. Which demands to satisfy, and to what extent, were decisions to be made by the Office for Foreign Trade. According to the ordinance the Office for Foreign Trade, prior to making a decision had to apply to the committee established by the Minister of Finance for a recommendation. This committee consisted of a chairman and four members. The chairman was appointed by the minister of finance and the members were appointed by the minister of trade and transportation, the minister of industry, the minister of justice and the Hungarian National Bank.[159] The Hungarian state wanted to compensate the loss of the companies which were owed money by the Soviet Union from the funds owed by other companies to the Soviet Union, ignoring the fact that the approximately 400,000 dollars owed by the Hungarian companies properly should have gone to the treasury of the other country.

Ganz put its debt to Mashinoimport at approximately 3 million pengős which included an advance payment of 475,000 dollars. Ganz, at the same time, estimated its demands to be 1.5 million pengős, meaning that it admitted a debt of 1.5 million pengős.[160] The president of the Foreign Trade Office refused to recognize the 1.5 million pengős owed to Ganz and ordered the company to deposit the entire 3 million pengő debt in an account established for this purpose by the Foreign Trade Office.[161] This represented slightly less than one quarter of Ganz's entire base capital of 12.5 million pengős.

The Hungarian-Soviet trade relations of 1940–1941 make further studies and discussions seem appropriate. A subject, just as timely today, is the question of how far the state can go in assuming a role in economic questions and activities and what the limitations and controls should be. It is evident that in the midst of wartime conditions the government brutally interfered with free market processes and employed force in the distribution of economic assets particularly in the acquisition and distribution of the raw materials essential for the functioning of the economic infrastructure. It can be said that by the summer of 1940 many aspects of a "state capitalism" had come into effect in Hungary not entirely dissimilar from the Soviet "state socialist" economic system which was completely rejected by the Western capitalist world. The government pressure exerted on the Ganz Company and the losses endured by the company due to the government's political actions and, finally, the unilateral solution in the name of the interest of the state should make us very thoughtful about the wisdom of state intervention.

SUMMARY

From the end of World War I to the beginning of World War II the political leadership of both Hungary and of the Soviet Union continued to hold the justifying concepts according to which the Hungarian counterrevolutionary system came into power as a result of its fight against the proletarian dictatorship while the genesis and victory of the Soviet Communist regime was attributed to the Civil War and to the fending off of intervention by the capitalist countries. Similarly much of society in both countries, to some extent, continued to hold the negative reflexes which originated from the memory of the short-lived Soviet regime in Hungary and from the memory of the international intervention and the Civil War in the Soviet Union. All of this, however, did not keep the realistically thinking diplomats in both countries from coming into contact with each other, overcoming the ideological perspectives, and recognizing the common political and economic goals of the two countries. Actually, political and economic relations between the two countries began to emerge while the two diametrically opposite internal political systems were still in the stage of consolidation. The documents I have found overwhelmingly show that the Hungarian government, and particularly, the foreign affairs apparatus, approached the Soviet Union, and all the international movements which favored the foreign policy endeavors of the Soviet state, not on the basis of ideological premises but on the basis of pragmatic definitions. The members of the Hungarian government and the diplomats were just as much concerned about the public opinion of their constituencies as they were about the more or less real dangers of Communist propaganda.

Many of the Hungarian contemporaries felt, after the 1920 Peace Treaty of Trianon, that one of the possible escape routes from the economic isolation of the country would be the opening of Soviet markets to Hungarian exporters and importers. The question came to the fore during the 1920s and again at the time of the Great Depression because an increase in the exchange of merchandise between the two countries would have improved the condition of Hungarian economy struggling to find an arena for the placement of its goods. It is puzzling that during the 1920s and early 1930s the Hungarian government could not take advantage of the opportunities offered by the relative proximity of the Soviet markets, and trade between the two countries continued to be small in volume and low in intensity. Until 1924 there had been several opportunities to meet the conditions set up by the Soviet side because at that time Soviet diplomacy would have been satisfied with a temporary commercial contract equivalent to a de facto recognition of the Soviet Union. This would have been entirely in agreement with the interests of the entrepreneurial and financial circles putting pressure on the government.

After the spring of 1924, however, the Soviet foreign policy shapers demanded considerably more, namely the de jure recognition of the Soviet Union. This could not be avoided by Germany, Great Britain, Italy, and Austria. Later it was done by France and Japan with Hungary following behind them. To be sure, the start of diplomatic relations in 1934 did not automatically lead to a completion of commercial relations. The trade between the two countries, other than the minor upswing in 1934 and 1935, remained vestigial and by the end of the 1930s essentially disappeared. In 1938 and 1939 the Hungarian exports were reduced to zero. Because of some business policy and differences of opinion on financial matters between the two countries it was not possible to achieve a framework for a trade agreement or even a payments and shipping agreement during this period.

Meaningful economic relations could be established first under the shadow of World War II and it was only during the brief half-year period, from the early autumn of 1940 to the late spring of 1941, that a number of bilateral trade agreements were signed between Hungary and the Soviet Union. The economic changes generated by the war made it critical for Hungary to cooperate with the Soviet Union in the commercial arena. At the same time such a move appeared favorable to the Soviet Union's political-strategic perspectives as well because of the changes in the geopolitical constellation of the world.

The first two items in the system of interstate agreements were the trade and shipping agreement signed on September 3, 1940, and the merchandise exchange and payments agreement attached to it. These agreements, creating the basic infrastructural conditions for the start of bilateral trade, were followed on February 4, 1941, by a postal service agreement and, on March 1, 1941, by a rail traffic agreement. These agreements offered an important growth opportunity for the severely constrained Hungarian industry suffering from a critical shortage of raw materials. It is safe to say that in the period under discussion these months were the most productive ones in Hungarian-Soviet trade relations, differing markedly from the earlier period.

The first conclusion that we can draw from my study is that the evolution of trade relations between the two countries was not determined primarily by ideological convictions. The intensity and volume of trade were influenced much more strongly by the political and diplomatic considerations and conditions ensuing from the international position of the two countries and by the problems of the business structures, business policies, and financial and infrastructural (transport) matters.

The second conclusion is that even though political consideration could limit the evolution of trade perspectives during the interwar period in Hungarian-Soviet relations, Hungary's perspectives were controlled by precisely the inverse situation. The economic exigencies and the rational interests of the economy were the factors which exerted a significant force on the willingness of the government to act in the political sphere. The perspective of economic cooperation contributed to the creation of the conditions for a political rapprochement. It can also be seen that the profit-oriented business enterprise sphere, ignoring the ideological perspectives, always stood in the background of the change in Hungarian-Soviet trade relations. Its activities regularly forced the Hungarian administration to take the necessary steps.

During the 1920s 70–75 percent of Hungary's trade was with the same five countries, namely with the successor states of the Austro-Hungarian Empire, Austria, Czechoslovakia, Romania, Yugoslavia, and with Germany. The dominant forces governing Hungarian exports and imports were Austria and Czechoslovakia. Their share in the total Hungarian export and import activities gradually decreased at the turn of the 1920s and 1930s and Hungarian business turned increasingly toward the German and Italian markets. The documents I have found suggest that within this trend the enormous market capacity of the Soviet Union became progressively more apparent to the contemporaries. It is my opinion that in addition to the Hungarian foreign trade orientation toward the restoration of the economic unity of the Danube Basin and toward Italy and Germany there was another starting point, namely the development and exploitation of Hungarian-Soviet economic relations. The composition of the merchandise making up the commercial traffic between the two countries shows clearly that the structure of the Hungarian and Soviet economic production would have been complementary. The Soviet Union produced and exported the strategic essentials and raw materials for which Hungary had a desperate need while the Hungarian leadership developed precisely those branches of industry which produced the goods which the Soviet Union would have purchased in great numbers due to its relatively backward machine industry.

NOTES

Notes to Introduction

1. For a detailed discussion, see Zsuzsa Bekker and Mária Hild, "Köz-gazdaságtan a két világháború között" [Economics between the two World Wars], in *Magyar közgazdasági gondolkodás (a közgazdasági irodalom kezdeteitől a II. világháborúig). Gazdaság-elméleti olvasmányok 2* [Hungarian Economic Thought (from the Beginning of the Economic Literature to World War II). Readings in Economic Theory 2], ed. Zsuzsa Bekker (Budapest, 2002), 535– 541.

Notes to Chapter One

1. For details on the conditions of the Russian archives, see Éva Mária Varga, "Hungarica-kutatás az oroszországi levéltárakban" [Hungary-related research in the Russian archives], *Levéltári Szemle* 53, no. 4 (2003): 3–18.
2. For the changes of the organization of the Commissariat for Foreign Affairs between 1917 and 1945, see Anatolii V. Torkunov, ed., *Ocherki istorii Ministerstva Inostrannikh Del Rossii*, vol. 2, *1917–2002 gg.* (Moscow, 2002), 7–330.
3. For the function of the Politburo, see Oleg V. Khlevniuk, *Politbiuro: Mekhanizmy politicheskoi vlasti v 1930-e gody* (Moscow, 1996).
4. Vilmos Bélay and Mária H. Kohut, *A Kereskedelemügyi Miniszté-riumi Levéltár (1889–1899), a Kereskedelem és Közlekedésügyi Minisztériumi Levéltár (1935–1945). Repertórium.* (Levéltári leltárak 12.) [The Ministry of Commerce Archives (1889–1899), the Ministry of Commerce and Communication Archives (1935– 1945). Repertorium. Archival Inventories 12] (Budapest, 1961), 18.

5. Peter Pastor, ed., *A moszkvai magyar követség jelentései 1935–1941* [The Reports of the Moscow Legation, 1935–1941] (Budapest, 1992), 7. Attention was drawn to these reports of the Moscow legation in Andor Gellért, "Magyar diplomaták Moszkvában. A magyar-szovjet viszony a magyar királyi követség titkos jelentései tükrében" [Hungarian diplomats in Moscow. Hungarian-Soviet Relations as Reflected in the Secret Reports of the Royal Hungarian Legation in Moscow], *Új Látóhatár* 26, no. 1 (1975): 17–37. During the 1960s these reports were microfilmed and returned to Hungary by Elek Karsai and are presently in the Microfilm Collection of the National Archives of Hungary on four rolls under Number X–9581.

6. Known as Mihály Jungerth until 1933. At that time he Hungarized his name to Arnóthy-Jungerth. His personal and diplomatic career rapidly became of interest to historians. See István Dolmányos, "A magyar-szovjet diplomáciai kapcsolatok egy napló tükrében (1920–1939) [The Hungarian-Soviet diplomatic relations as reflected in a diary, 1920–1939). *Valóság 9,* no. 1 (1966): 73–85. Certain parts of his diary were published in Mihály Jungerth-Arnóthy, *Moszkvai napló* [Moscow Diary], ed. Péter Sipos and Mihály Szűcs (Budapest, 1989), 5–49. His ministerial duties in Sofia between 1939 and 1944 have been presented by Penka Peikovska, "Bâlgarskijat dnevnik na Mihály Jungerth-Arnóthy, ungarski p'lnomoshchen ministr v Sofija prez 1939–1944" [Bul-garian log of Mihály Jungerth-Arnóthy, Hungarian plenipotentiary minister in 1939–1944], *Izvestija na dârzhavnite arkhivi* 63 (1992): 87–139. During the spring and summer of 1944 he became the Permanent Deputy Minister of Foreign Affairs in the Sztójay government. For details, see Pál Pritz, "A magyar külügyi szolgálat 1944-ben a német megszállástól október 15-ig [The Hungarian foreign service in 1944 from the German occupation to October 15], *Múltunk* 44, no. 4 (1999): 120–137.

7. In his autobiographical notes typed at the end of 1944 and the beginning of 1945 he stated that his appointment to Ankara was due to his familiarity with the Soviet Union. Mihály Jungerth-Radnóthy, "Curriculum vitae," 972. f., 9. ő.e. 102–111. fol., Poli-

tikatörténeti és Szakszervezeti Levéltár (hereafter cited as PSZL).
8. Jungerth, *Moszkvai napló*, 104.
9. Andrei Gromyko, ed., *Dokumenty vneshnei politiki SSSR* (hereafter cited as *DVP SSSR*), vol. 17, *1 ianvaria–31 dekabria 1934 g.* (Moscow, 1971), 106–107. After 1992 this series was renewed with the title of *Dokumenty vneshnei politiki*, under a new editorial board. This board had a different approach, included the archival designation of the documents and referred to their textologic peculiarities.
10. *Iratok az ellenforradalom történetéhez, 1919–1945*, vol. 3, *Az ellenforradalmi rendszer gazdasági helyzete és politikája Magyarországon, 1924–1926* [Documents for the History of the Counterrevolution, vol. 3, The Economic Situation and Policies of the Counterrevolutionary Regime in Hungary, 1924–1926], ed. Dezső Nemes and Elek Karsai (Budapest, 1959), 686–689 and 736–740.
11. József Búzás, "A szovjet-magyar kereskedelmi kapcsolatok történetéhez, 1919–1938" [On the History of Soviet-Hungarian Trade Relations, 1919–1938), *Századok* 89, nos. 4–5 (1955): 588–633.
12. Ibid., 587–598.
13. Attila Seres, "A szovjet piac 'meghódítása' és a magyar tőke Trianon után. Iratok a szovjet-magyar vegyes kereskedelmi társaság történetéhez (1923)" [The conquest of the Soviet market and Hungarian capital after Trianon. Documents for the history of the Soviet-Hungarian Joint Trade Enterprise (1923)], *Századok* 140, no. 1 (2006): 79–125. See also the appropriate chapter of this volume.
14. József Búzás and András Nagy, *Magyarország külkereskedelme 1919–1945* [Hungary's Foreign Trade, 1919–1941] (Budapest, 1961), 126–147 and 290–304.
15. János Lukács, *Magyar-orosz kapcsolatok 1914 óta* [Hungarian-Russian Relations since 1914] (Budapest, 1945); Gyula Juhász, "A két világháború közötti szovjet-magyar diplomáciai kapcsolatok történetéhez" [To the history of Soviet-Hungarian diplomatic relations between the two World Wars], in *A Marx Károly Közgazdaságtudományi Egyetem tudományos ülésszaka* [The Scholarly Sessions of the Karl Marx Economic Science University], no ed.

(Budapest, 1968), 360–377; and János Péter, *A magyar-szovjet diplomáciai kapcsolatok történetéből 1939–1941* [From the History of Hungarian-Soviet Diplomatic Relations, 1939–1941] (Budapest, 1979). János Péter, a former minister of foreign affairs used Soviet archival sources for his book which he could access by diplomatic pathways. István Máté's essay is along the same lines. István Máté, "Adalékok a magyar-szovjet diplomáciai kapcsolatok két világháború közötti történetéhez, különös tekintettel az 1934–1939 közötti időszakra" [Addenda to the history of Hungarian-Soviet diplomatic relations between the two World Wars, with particular reference to the period between 1934 and 1939], *Clio (Fiatal Kutatók Közleményei)* 3, no. 2 (1986): 229–295.

16. Pál Pritz, *Magyarország külpolitikája Gömbös Gyula miniszterelnöksége idején. 1932–1936* [Hungary's Foreign Policy at the Time of Gyula Gömbös' Prime Ministry, 1932–1936] (Budapest, 1982), 141–149. Gyula Juhász's political views had changed over time and he revised his synthesis of diplomatic history twice. In the third edition "hostility toward the Soviet" received substantially less emphasis. Gyula Juhász, *Magyarország külpolitikája, 1919–1945* (Hungary's Foreign Policy, 1919–1944], 3rd ed. (Budapest, 1988).

17. György Ránki, *Gazdaság és külpolitika. A nagyhatalmak harca a délkelet-európai gazdasági hegemóniáért. 1919–1939* [Economics and Foreign Policy. The Battle of the Great Powers for the Economic Hegemony of Southeastern Europe, 1919–1939] (Budapest, 1981).

18. György Kövér, "A Szovjetunió és Közép-Kelet Európa. Gazdasági érintkezés a két vilagháború között" [The Soviet Union and east central Europe. Economic contacts between the two World Wars], *Történelmi Szemle* 29, nos. 3–4 (1986): 481–489.

19. János Honvári, ed., *Magyarország gazdaságtörténete a honfoglalástól a 20. század közepéig* [Hungary's Economic History from the Conquest to the Middle of the Twentieth Century] (Budapest 1995), 337–455; and Péter Gunst, *Magyarország gazdaságtörténete (1914–1989)* [Hungary's Economic History 1914–1989] (Budapest, 1996), 29–85; Béla Csikós-Nagy, *A XX. század magyar gazdaságpolitikája. Tanulságok az ezredforduló küszöbén*

[Twentieth Century Hungarian Economic Policy. Lessons at the Threshold of a New Millennium] (Budapest, 1996); Zoltán Kaposi, *Magyarország gazdaságtörténete* [The Economic History of Hungary] (Budapest, 2002), 271–320; Miklós Zeidler, "Társadalom és gazdaság Trianon után" [Society and economy after Trianon], *Limes* 15, no. 2 (2002): 11–18.

20. Honvári, *Magyarország gazdaságtörténete a honfoglalástól*, 441; Csikós-Nagy, *A XX. század magyar gazdaságpolitikája*, 102.

21. Soviet statistical reports covering the period of July 1, 1927, to June 30, 1928, used the traditional Soviet fiscal year. The second half of 1928 was reported as a separate, independent period. Sergei N. Bakulin and Dmitrii D. Mishustin, eds., *Vneshniaia torgovlia SSSR za 20 let. Statisticheskii spravochnik* (Moscow, 1939), 23; and A. D. Chistov, ed., *Vneshniaia torgovlia SSSR za 1918–1940 gg.: Statisticheskii obzor* (Moscow, 1960), 22 and 515–517.

22. László L. Pap, "A Szovjetunió külkereskedelmi forgalma" [Foreign Trade of the Soviet Union], *Magyar Statisztikai Szemle* 12, nos. 1–6 (1945): 80–95.

Notes to Chapter Two

1. Data of the wartime losses can be found in most professional works. Some of the manuals on economic history, published after the regime change, include: Csikós-Nagy, *A XX. század magyar gazdaságpolitikája*, 39–43. Gunst, *Magyarország gazdaságtörténete (1914–1989)*, 29–44; and Kaposi, *Magyarország gazdaságtörténete*, 262–278.

2. Csikós-Nagy, *A XX. század magyar gazdaságpolitikája*, 64–65.

3. Gunst, *Magyarország gazdaságtörténete (1914–1989)*, 36–38.

4. Zeidler, "Társadalom és gazdaság Trianon után," 13.

5. The statistical data from 1913, the last year of peace, show that 75 percent of the Hungarian exports went to Austria and to the other components of the Monarchy, mainly Czechoslovakia, Poland, and Bosnia. Approximately the same percentage of imports came from these areas. See "A Magyar Szentkorona országainak 1913. évi külkereskedelmi forgalma" [The foreign trade activities of the

Lands of the Hungarian Holy Crown in 1913], *Magyar Statisztikai Közlemények,* Új sorozat 53, part 1 (Budapest, 1915), 41.

6. Lajos Reményi, *Külkereskedelempolitika Magyarországon 1919–1924.* Gazdaságtörténeti értekezések 5 [Foreign Trade Policy in Hungary 1919–1924. Economic History Dissertations 5] (Budapest, 1969), 82, 203, and 230–231.

7. Gunst, *Magyarország gazdaságtörténete (1914–1989),* 38–40.

8. Reményi, *Külkereskedelempolitika Magyarországon 1919–1924,* 90.

9. Gunst, *Magyarország gazdaságtörténete (1914–1989),* 37.

10. For the data, see V. B. Zhiromskaia, ed., *Naselenie Rossii v XX veke: istoricheskie ocherki* (Moscow, 2000), 1:143.

11. For details of the damages caused by the World War, the Civil War and the international intervention, see Rem A. Belousov, *Ekonomicheskaia istoriia Rossii—XX vek,* bk. 2, *Cherez revoliutsiiu k NEPu* (Moscow, 2000), 124–147.

12. Efim G. Gimpel'son, *NEP i sovetskaia politicheskaia sistema: 20-e gody* (Moscow, 2000), 18–38.

13. Nicolas Werth, *Istoriia sovetskogo gosudarstva, 1900–1991* (Moscow, 2003), 158.

14. For the complete text of the decree, see G. D. Obichkin, ed., *Dekrety sovetskoi vlasti,* vol 2, *17 marta–10 iiulia 1918. g.* (Moscow, 1959), 158–160.

15. Y. P. Bokarev, "Rossiiskaia ekonomika v mirovoi ekonomicheskoi sisteme (konets XIX–30–e gg. XX v.)," in *Ekonomicheskaia istoriia Rossii XIX–XX vv.: sovremennyi vzgliad,* ed. Vladimir A. Vino-gradov (Moscow, 2001), 442–445.

16. Carole Fink, "NEP vo vneshnei politike. Genuezskaia konferentsia I rapallskii dogovor," in *Sovetskaia vneshniaia politika v retrospective, 1917–1991,* ed. Aleksandr O. Chubar'ian (Moscow, 1993), 60–69.

17. The first segment of the Soviet commercial network abroad was the ARCOS (All Russian Cooperative Society) established on June 9, 1920. It was recognized in London as a legal entity but its three officials did not receive diplomatic immunity. Valerii A. Shishkin, *Stanovlenie vneshnei politiki poslerevoliutsionnoi Rossii (1917–1930 gody) i kapitalisticheskii mir: ot revoliut-*

sionnogo "zapadnichestva" k "natsional-bol'shevizmu." Ocherk istorii (St. Petersburg, 2002), 98–99.

18. We learn much later, from a Hungarian source in 1940, about the number of the Soviet state trade enterprises which were in charge of and supervised imports and exports. These minutes state that there were twenty such organizations. According to Soviet economic experts this number had not changed since the establishment of the Soviet state. Notes about the third session of the subcommittee no. 2 of the Hungarian-Soviet trade negotiations, Moscow, August 14, 1940, K 69, 1940–I–5. t., 760. cs., 24–27. fol., Magyar Országos Levéltár [National Archives of Hungary] (hereafter cited as MOL).

19. The concept of "one hand" in the professional economic literature was used as accepted terminology between the two World Wars applicable not only to the Soviet economic management system but also for the definition of the western-European export and import associations and syndicates that enjoyed monopolistic privileges. Such organizations, consisting of banks, industrial, transportation and commercial enterprises, as well as of associations of economic interest groups, operating with government support, came into being in western Europe during the 1930s and particularly during the first years of World War II. In Hungary similar, government-supported monopolistic organizations appeared, partly because of the difficulties in marketing but also in order to call for increased government subventions and advantages. István Hegedűs, *Az egykéz* [The One Hand] (Budapest, 1938), 5–21.

20. Bokarev, "Rossiiskaia ekonomika," p. 456. The foreign debts of the tsarist government reached 12.5 billion gold rubles. See Iurii. A. Petrov, "Rossiiskaia ekonomika v nachale XX v.," in *Rossiia v nachale XX veka*, ed. Andrei N. Sakharov et al. (Moscow, 2002), 189.

21. Maksim M. Zagorul'ko, ed., *Inostrannye kontsessii v SSSR: 1920–1930 gg.: dokumenty i materialy* (Moscow, 2005), 8.

22. The GYOSZ submission to the government, Budapest, s.d. (August, 1924), K 64, 10. cs., 1924/24. t., 405/1924. res. pol., 89–92. fol, MOL.

23. Notice from Minister of Finance Frigyes Korányi to Kálmán

Kánya, the permanent deputy minister of foreign affairs, September 19, 1924., K 64, 10. cs., 1924/24. t., 405/1924. res. pol. 192–193. fol., MOL.

24. *Magyar Törvénytár, 1921. évi törvénycikkek* [Hungarian Law Code. 1921 Acts], annotated by Gyula Térfy (Budapest, 1922), 220–221. Essentially the same matter was raised in Paragraph 227 which stated that Hungary considered all international agreements made as a member of the Austro-Hungarian Monarchy, prior to the Trianon Peace Treaty, null and void. Ibid., 271.

25. Ibid., 260. Hungary also agreed to hand over to the Allied powers all assets (cash, shares and products), which it received from the Brest-Litovsk Peace Treaty.

26. For Soviet foreign policy at the time of the Geneva and Hague Conferences, see Shishkin, *Stanovlenie vneshnei politiki,* 135– 139.

27. This amount was later reduced to 50 billion. See Semen S. Khromov, ed., *Inostrannye kontsessii v SSSR: istoricheskii ocherk, dokumenty* (Moscow, 2006), part 1, 5–6.

28. Summary of Minister of Foreign Affairs Bánffy to Kánya, Genoa, April 19, 1922, K 69, 789. cs. (Conference material), 3. dossier, 136–145. f., MOL.

29. Bánffy to Kánya, Genoa, April 27, 1922, ibid., 146–152. fol., MOL.

30. It is now known that the Soviet delegation went to Genoa via Berlin. Fink, "NEP vo vneshnei politike," in *Sovetskaia vneshniaia politika v retrospective*, ed. Chubar'ian, 60–69.

31. Magda Ádám, "The Genoa Conference and the Little Entente," in *Genoa, Rapallo and European Reconstruction in 1922*, ed. Carole Frohn-Fink and Jürgen Axel-Heideking (Cambridge, 1991), 187–199.

32. Attila Seres, "Magyar-szovjet titkos tárgyalások Genovában, 1922-ben. Bánffy Miklós magyar külügyminiszter feljegyzései" [Secret Hungarian-Soviet negotiations in Genoa in 1922. The Hungarian Minister of Foreign Affairs Miklós Bánffy's notes], *Fons 8,* no. 3 (2001): 397–411.

33. Recommendation for the reestablishment of economic relationship with Russia, Budapest, s.d. (1922), K 69, 88. cs., 109/1922. t., 57.947/1922. sz., 513–514. fol., MOL

34. "A miniszterelnök a génuai konferenciáról" [The Prime Minister on the Genoa Conference], *Budapesti Hírlap,* April 27, 1922, 1–3.

35. Andrei Gromyko, ed., *Dokumenty vneshnei politiki SSSR,* vol. 5, *1 ianvaria–19 noiabria 1922 g.* (Moscow, 1961), 727,

36. Minutes of the Politburo meeting, Moscow, March 8, 1922, f. 17, op. 3, d. 257, l. 15, Rossiiskii gosudarstvennii arkhiv sotsialno-politicheskoi istorii (hereafter cites as RGASPI).

37. Gromyko, ed., *DVP SSSR,* 5:156–157.

38. Jungerth's report to Bánffy, Reval, July 20, 1922, K 69, 85. cs., 1922/108. t., 76.065/1922. alapsz., 82.684.1922. sz., MOL.

39. László Buday, *Magyarország küzdelmes évei* [Hungary's Years of Struggle] (Budapest, 1923), 93–94.

40 Agreement between the Association of Hungarian Crude Oil Refining Companies and the Neftesindikat, Berlin, September 18, 1922, K 69, 2/1922. sz., 760. cs., 11–16. fol., MOL.

41. Károly Koffler, "Magyarország és Oroszország" [Hungary and Russia] *Magyar Gyáripar* 14, (October 1, 1924): 1–3.

42. Notes of Simon Krausz about the discussions with the Soviets. Berlin, March 2, 1923, Z 96, 83. t., 3616. sz., 21–36. fol., 64. cs., MOL.

43. Letter from Office VI/2 of the Ministry of Defense to Permanent Deputy Minister of Foreign Affairs Kálmán Kánya, Budapest, August 30, 1923, I/89. f., 19.029/1923. sz., (B/172. tek.), Hadtör-ténelmi Levéltár [Military History Archive] (hereafter cited as HL).

44. "A Magyar Szentkorona országainak," 57 and 541.

45. Buday, *Magyarország küzdelmes évei,* 135.

46. "Oroszország" [Russia], *Külkereskedelmi Hírek,* May 11, 1924, 1.

47. "Oroszország lótenyésztése" [Russia's horse breeding], *Állator-vosi Lapok,* July 15, 1925, 152.

48. Buday, *Magyarország küzdelmes évei,*132.

49. Report of Minister Szilárd Masirevich from Vienna to Minister of Foreign Affairs Daruváry, Vienna, July 3, 1923, K 69, 147. cs., 1923/10. t., 76.439/1923. alapsz., 78.559/1923.sz., MOL.

50. Chistov, ed., *Vneshniaia torgovlia SSSR,* 423–427.

51. See the report from Vulfson, the Soviet commercial representative in Vienna to M. I. Frumkin, the deputy commissar for foreign

trade, Vienna, August 26, 1925, f. 413, op. 2, d. 1991, l. 23–25, Rossiskii Gosudarstvennii Arkhiv Ekonomiki (hereafter cited as RGAE).

52. V. B. Ginzburg, "O konsignatsionnikh dogovorakh," *Vneshniaia targovlia*, June 6, 11–12.

53. Sándor Kóródi, "A szovjet-oroszországi export megindítása és egyéb kiviteli célkitűzések" [Start of exports to Soviet Russia and other export goals], *Pesti Tőzsde*, August 12, 1931, 4.

54. Unfortunately our data on international discount rates of the Soviet letters of exchange are derived during the first half of the 1930s only from the newspapers citing Hungarian government sources. See for example "Winchkler István Berlinben tárgyalt a szovjet külkereskedelmi képviselettel" [István Winchkler negotiated with the Soviet foreign trade representatives in Berlin], *Pesti Napló,* November 12, 1933, 9.

55. Submission of the Hungarian Foreign Trade Institute Inc. to Minister of Commerce Béla Kenéz, Budapest, September 10, 1931, K 69, 380. cs., 54.180/1931. sz., MOL.

56. "Magyarország és az orosz üzlet. Beszélgetés Kóródi Sándorral, a Magyar Külkereskedelmi Intézet Rt. vezérigazgatójával" [Hungary and the Russian business. Conversation with Sándor Kóródi, the CEO of the Hungarian Foreign Trade Institute Inc.], *Pesti Tőzsde*, March 3, 1932, 1.

57. Gunst, *Magyarország gazdaságtörténete (1914–1989)*, 47–49.

58. Búzás and Nagy, *Magyarország külkereskedelme 1919–1945*, 39–45.

59. Contract between Hofherr-Schrantz and the Soviet representative in Berlin, May 7, 1924, f. 413, op. 10, d. 194, l. 6–13, RGAE.

60. Report on the annual activities of the Soviet Trade Mission in Berlin, in 1923–1924, to Moscow, March 17, 1925, f. 413, op. 2, d. 2008, l. 133, RGAE. Some of the details of the MÁVAG contract are not available and the date of signing the contract is not known.

61. Shishkin, *Stanovlenie vneshnei politiki*, 295–297.

62. Telegram from N. K. Klishko, the head of the Administrative Division of the Commissariat for Foreign Trade to B. S. Stomoniakov, the leader of the Soviet Trade Mission in Berlin, Moscow, May 16, 1924, f. 413, op. 10, d. 194, l. 4, RGAE.

63. O. B. Mozokhin and V. P. Iampolskii, "O privechenni inostranno-go kapitala v ekonomiku SSSR. 1920–e gg.," *Istoricheskii arkhiv*, 2002, no. 1:101.

64. Zagorul'ko, ed., *Inostrannye kontsessii v SSSR*, 8–9.

65. Belousov, *Ekonomicheskaia istoriia*, bk. 2, *Cherez revoliutsiiu*, 375–376.

66. Zagorul'ko, ed., *Inostrannye kontsessii v SSSR*, 590–591.

67. Report from Stomoniakov to G. L. Piatakov, the president of the GKK, Berlin, February 2, 1923, f. 8350, op. 1, d. 1440, l. 1, Gos-udarstvennii Arkhiv Rossiskoi Federatsii (hereafter cited as GA RF).

68. For Klein, see Ágnes Pogány, "Bankárok és üzletfelek. A Magyar Általános Hitelbank és vállalati ügyfelei a két világháború között" [Bankers and clients. The Hungarian General Bank of Credit and its corporate clients between the two World Wars], *Replika* 8, no. 25 (1997): 65.

69. Telegrams sent by Sándor László in July–August, 1918, Z 40, 9. cs., 257. sz., MOL.

70. Extract from the GKK minutes, Moscow, April 5, 1923, f. 8350, op. 1, d. 1440, l. 30, GA RF.

71. Litvinov's note to Piatakov. Moscow, March 14, 1923, f. 8350, op. 1, d. 1440, l. 15, GA RF.

72. Note from the Commissariat for Naval Affairs to the GKK, Moscow, March 26, 1923, f. 8350, op. 1, d. 1440, l. 26, GA RF.

73. Notes of the Supreme Economic Council on the Nikolaev Shipyards. Moscow, s.d. f. 8350, op. 1, d. 1440, l. 6–10, GA RF.

74. Zagorul'ko, ed., *Inostrannye kontsessii v SSSR*, 14.

75. Ibid., 17–19.

76. Note from the Commissariat for Transportation to the Main Directorate of the Navy. Moscow, November 21, 1922, f. 1884, op. 1. d. 451, l. 4, RGAE.

77. Zagorul'ko, ed., *Inostrannye kontsessii v SSSR*, 20–21.

78. "Smeshannie aktsionernie obshchestva," *Vneshniaia torgovlia*, February 23, 1923, 38.

79. Report of Ghika to Bethlen, Hamburg, December 8, 1922, K 69, 141, cs., 1923/10. t., 53.882/1923. alapsz., 125.755/1922. Sz, MOL.

80. "'Rabota Russko-Avstriiskogo Torgovogo AO 'RATAO,'" *Vneshniaia torgovlia,* October 18, 1924, 29.

81. "O smeshannikh obshchestvakh," *Vneshniaia torgovlia,* July 15, 1924, 29. The data consist of rounded off figures. It should be noted that because of the enormous inflation, the ruble was not used for a while as a method of payment in the domestic markets after the 1922–1924 Soviet fiscal reforms. The term "ruble" used in Soviet statistics usually meant the gold ruble which remained the basic unit for calculation in commercial transactions.

82. György Kövér, "Egy magánbankár a XX. században—Krausz Simon" [A Private banker in the twentieth century—Simon Krausz], *Valóság* 30, no. 9 (1987): 56–62.

83. Krausz's notes on the discussions with the Soviets. Berlin, March 2, 1923, Z 96, 64. cs., 83. t., 3616. sz., 21–36. fol., MOL; and Stomoniakov's report to I. S. Ganetskii, a member of the GKK and of the Board of the Commissariat for Foreign Trade, Berlin, March 2, 1923, f. 8350, op. 1, d. 1440, l. 11–13, GA RF.

84. Piatakov's memorandum to the Supreme Economic Council and to the Commissariat for Agriculture, Moscow, March 20, 1923, f. 8350, op. 1, d. 1440, l. 20, GA RF.

85. Memorandum from the Supreme Economic Council to the GKK, Moscow, March 26, 1923. f. 8350, op. 1, d. 1440, l. 24, GA RF.

86. Memorandum from the Agricultural Commissariat to the LKB. Moscow, March 28, 1923, f. 8350, op. 1, d. 1440, l. 25, GA RF.

87. Letter from the Soviet Trade Mission to the AMB. Moscow, May 5, 1923, Z 96, 64. cs., 83. t., 3616a/XX/6. sz., 160. f., MOL.

88. This sum was stated in paper crowns and, according to the June 1923 rates, one gold crown was worth 1,820 paper crowns. The foreign exchange rate for British pounds on the same date showed that one pound was worth somewhere between 38,000 and 39,500 crowns. The U.S. dollar was worth 8,300–8,700 crowns.

89. Structure and bylaws of the Russian-Hungarian Trade Corporation, Budapest, June 25, 1923, Z 96, 64. cs., 83. t., 3616/I. sz., 165–179. f., MOL.

90. Minutes of the initial meeting of the Russian-Hungarian Trade Corporation, Budapest, June 28, 1923, Z 96, 64.cs., 83. t., 3616/I sz., 237–240. f., MOL.

91. Pro domo notes of the "first review" of the registration application of the Russian-Hungarian Trade Corporation, Budapest, August 24,

1923, VII/2. e., 3398. d., Cg. 20788/1924. sz., Budapest Főváros Levéltára [Budapest City Archives] (hereafter cited as BFL).

92. Minutes of the ad hoc meeting of the Russian-Hungarian Trade Corporation, Budapest, September 19, 1923, Z 96, 64. cs., 83. t., 3616/II/1. sz., 283–286. F., MOL.

93. The AMB letter to Daruváry. September 21, 1923. Ibid. 3616/I/8. sz., 270–271. f.

94. Minutes of the meeting of the Russian-Hungarian Trade Corporation, Inc. Budapest, October 17, 1923. Ibid. 3616/I/1. sz., 313–316. f., MOL.

95. Stomoniakov's report to Litvinov and to Ganetskii, Berlin, November 1, 1923, f. 413, op. 5, d. 1169, l. 20–21, RGAE.

96. Krestinski's report to Litvinov. Berlin, November 13, 1923, f. 04, op.11, op. 67, d. 938, l. 128–130, Arkhiv vneshnei politiky Rossiiskoi Federatsii (hereafter cited as AVP RF).

97. Litvinov's telegram to Krestinskii, Moscow, November 14, 1923, f. 413. op. 5, d. 1169, l. 16, RGAE.

98. Ganetskii's telegram to Stomoniakov. Moscow, November 15, 1923, f 413, op. 5, d. 1169, l. 14, RGAE.

99. Monthly report of the Russian Trade Mission, Berlin, s. d. (before December 29, 1923), f. 8350, op.1, d. 1440, l. 44, GA RF.

100. "Second Review" by the Court of Registration of the application of the Russian-Hungarian Trade Corporation, Budapest, November 15, 1923, VII/2. e., 3398. d., Cg. 20788/1924. sz., BFL.

101. Ruling of the Royal Court in Budapest, April 24, 1924, ibid.

102. Minutes of the special meeting of the Russian-Hungarian Trade Corporation, Budapest, May 9, 1924, Z 96, 64. cs., 83. t., 3616/III/2. sz., 305–306. F, MOL.

103. Ruling of the Court of Registration. Budapest, August 5, 1924, VII/2. e., 3398. d., Cg. 20788/1924. sz., BFL,

104. *Magyar törvénytár. 1875–1876. évi törvények* [Hungarian Law Code. Acts of 1875–1876] (Budapest, 1896), 120–123.

105. Viktória N. Czaga, "A cégbíróságról és a cégbírósági irattárról" [On the Court of Registration and on the Court of Registration Archives], *Üzemtörténeti Értesítő* 10, no. 10 (1991): 78–79.

106. *Magyar törvénytár. 1875–1876,* 143.

107. Ganetskii's telegram to Stomoniakov, Moscow, November 15, 1923, f. 413, op.5, d. 1169, l. 14, RGAE.

108. "Rabota Russko-Avstriiskogo Torgovogo," 21. The data are given in rounded off figures.

109. Stomoniakov's report to Litvinov and Ganetskii, Berlin, November 1, 1923, f. 413, op. 5, d. 1196, l. 20–21. RGAE. Taken as group the commercial concessions did not generate substantial losses for the Soviet economy. The ten largest commercial concessions produced an injection of 2.5 million rubles into the Soviet economy in 1923–1924. By way of the commercial concessions the Soviet Union exported merchandise of a value of 49.1 million rubles between 1923 and 1926, while importing merchandise valued at 47.6 million rubles. See, Mozokhin and Iampolskii, "O privechenni inostrannogo kapitala," 102.

110. Magyar gépek—orosz nafta [Hungarian machines—Russian naphta], *Jövő*, March 4. 1923, 6.

111. Gusztáv Gratz, *Magyarország a két háború között* (Hungary between the Two Wars), ed. Vince Paál (Budapest, 2001), 355–389.

112. The activities of this company included the provision of equipment for railways and for transportation companies, the construction and repair of transportation equipment and the planning and construction of railroads. See Sándor Nagy Galánthai ed., *Nagy Magyar Compass (azelőtt Mihók-féle) 1922–1924,* vol. 49, part 2, *Az 1925-ik évre* (Budapest, 1925), 714–715.

113. Masirevich's report to Daruváry, Vienna, May 6, 1924, K 64, 10. cs., 1924/24. t., 405/1924. alapsz., 186/1924. res. sz., MOL; Levitskii's report to Litvinov. Vienna, May 6, 1924, f. 04, op. 11, p. 67. d. 938, l. 125–126, AVP RF.

114. Aussem's notes about his discussion with Gratz, Vienna, June 4, 1924, f. 04, op. 11, p. 67, d. 938, l. 121–124, AVP RF.

115. Gustav Gratz, "Aus meinem Leben von Brest-Litowsk bis Ende des Zweiten Weltkrieges," Sammlungen und Nachlässe, B/19, no. 1, 179, Österreichisches Staatsarchiv.

116. Aussem's notes about his discussions with Gratz, Vienna, June 4, 1924, f. 04, op. 11, p. 67, d. 938, l. 121–124, AVP RF.

117. Report from I. Davidovich, the deputy head of the Soviet Trade

Mission in Vienna, to the Commissariat for Foreign Trade, Vienna, June 26, 1924, f. 413, op. 5, d. 1169, l. 8, RGAE

118. Deputy Commissar for Foreign Trade Avanesov in a telegram to the Soviet Trade Mission in Vienna, Moscow, July 26, 1924, f. 413, op. 5, d. 1169, l. 7, RGAE.

119. Aussem's report to Avanesov. Vienna, August 4, 1924, f. 413, op. 5, d. 1169, l. 6, RGAE.

120. Report from the Soviet Trade Mission in Vienna to the Commissar for Foreign Trade L. B. Krasin, Vienna, August 6, 1924, f. 413, op. 2, d. 1803, l. 4, RGAE.

121. Gratz's letter to Walko, Budapest, August 10, 1924, K 64, 10. cs., 1924/24. t., 405/1924. alapsz., 93. f., MOL.

122. Report from the Soviet Trade Mission in Vienna, to L. B. Krasin, Vienna, August 6, 1924, , f. 413, op. 2, d. 1803, l. 4, RGAE.

123. GYOSZ memorandum to the Hungarian government. Budapest, s.d. (August, 1924), K 64, 10. cs., 1924/24. t., 405/1924. alapsz., 89–92. f., MOL.

124. Telegram from Litvinov to Krestinskii, Moscow, November 14, 1923, f. 413, op. 5, d. 1169, l. 16. RGAE.

125. Litvinov's circular to the members of the Politburo, Moscow, June 5, 1923, f. 359, op. 1, d. 9, l. 9–11, RGASPI.

126. Shishkin, *Stanovlenie vneshnei politiki*, 175–239.

127. Belousov, *Ekonomicheskaia istoriia*, bk. 2, *Cherez revoliutsiiu*, 369–390.

128. The GYOSZ memorandum to Lajos Walko, Budapest, February 18, 1924, K 69, 1924/107. t.,70.822/1924. sz., 176. cs., 4–9. fol., MOL.

129. Memorandum from Daruváry to Walko. Budapest, May 18, 1924, K 69, 1924/107. t.,70.822/1924. sz., 176. cs.,12. fol., MOL.

130. Minutes of the interministerial meeting held at the Ministry of Foreign Affairs. Budapest, May 22, 1924, K 64, 10. cs., 1924/24. t., 405/1924. res. alapsz., 358/1924. res. sz., 524–530. fol., MOL.

131. Attila Kolontári, "Magyar-szovjet tárgyalások a diplomáciai és kereskedelmi kapcsolatok felvételéről (Berlin, 1924)" [Hungarian-Soviet negotiations about the resumption of diplomatic and economic relations. (Berlin, 1924)], in *Kutatási Füzetek*, no. 5 (*A*

Janus Pannonius Tudományegyetem Történelmi Doktori Programjának sorozata), ed. Mária Ormos, József Kánya, and Mónika Pilkhoffer (Pécs, 1999), 3–29.

132. Kánya's and Jungerth's notes on the first day of the negotiations in Berlin. Berlin, August 26, 1924, K 64, 10. cs, 1924/24. t., 405/1924. alapsz., 358/1924. res. sz., MOL.

133. Kánya's code telegram to Daruváry. Berlin, August 28–29, 1924, K 64, 10. cs, 1924/24. t., 405/1924. alapsz., 355/1924. res. sz., MOL.

134. Daruváry's code telegram to Kánya. Budapest, August 30, 1924, K 64, 10. cs, 1924/24. t., 405/1924. alapsz., 358/1924. res. sz., MOL.

135. Report from Masirevich to Daruváry, Berlin May 16, 1924, K 64, 10. cs, 1924/24. t., 405/1924. alapsz., 217/1924. res. sz., MOL. Notes of Waldemár Alth, a counselor at the Hungarian Legation, about the German-Soviet economic relations. Berlin, September 8, 1924, K 64, 10. cs, 1924/24. t., 405/1924. alapsz., 127–128. fol., MOL.

136. Krestinskii's report to Litvinov, Berlin, September 10, 1924, f. 04, op.11, p. 67, d. 938, l. 66–70, AVP RF.

137. Walko's telegram to Andor Wodianer, an official of the Political Division of the Ministry of Foreign Affairs, Budapest, September 9, 1924, K 64, 1924/24. t., 405/1924. alapsz., 378/1924. res. sz., 10. cs., MOL. This interpretation of the most favored nation principle by the Soviet Union allowed for the practice that if any country signed a trade agreement with the Soviet Union after Hungary, then Hungary became entitled to all of the commercial advantages granted previously to other countries.

138. The complete text of the agreement and of the confidential letters is in K 64, 1924/24. t., 405/1924. res. al. sz., 358/1924. res. sz., 10. cs., MOL.

139. Kolontári, Kolontári, "Magyar-szovjet tárgyalások," in *Kutatási Füzetek*, no. 5, ed. Ormos, Kánya, and Pilkhoffer, 25–29.

140. Report from Kánya and Jungerth to Daruváry. Berlin, Sept. 3, 1924, K 64, 1924/24. t., 405/1924. res. al. sz., 10 cs., 238–240. fol., MOL.

141. Submission of the minister of foreign affairs to the Council of Ministers. Budapest, October 10. 1924, K 64, 1924/24. t., 405/1924. res. al. sz., 10 cs., 549–558. fol., MOL.

142. *Magyar Törvénytár. 1924 évi törvénycikkek* [Hungarian Law Code.

1924 Acts], ed. Gyula Térfy (Budapest, 1925), 10.

143. *Az 1922. június hó 16-ra hírdetett Nemzetgyűlés naplója* [Minutes of the National Assembly meeting for June 16, 1922] (Budapest, 1924), 26:17–29. The provision of law granting the government a free hand in matters of international economic policy was brought to the attention of the public earlier by the semiofficial publication of the government, the *Pesti Napló*. See "Az orosz-magyar egyezmény hiteles története" [Official history of the Russian-Hungarian Agreement], *Pesti Napló*, September 24, 1924, 3.

144. Reményi, *Külkereskedelempolitika Magyarországon 1919–1924*, 230–231. It must be mentioned that the March 26, 1925, commercial agreement with Poland was ratified by the Hungarian Parliament in Act XXVI, 1925. *Magyar Törvénytár. 1925. évi törvénycikkek* [Hungarian Law Code. 1925 Acts], ed. Gyula Térfy (Budapest, 1926), 242–252.

145. Róbert Surányi, *A brit Munkáspárt és a Szovjetunió (1917–1924)* [The British Labour Party and the Soviet Union, 1917–1924] (Budapest, 1993), 194–210.

146. Jungerth's diary entry, Budapest, November 13, 1926, 972. f., 4. ő. e., 283. fol., PSzL.

147. Letter from the Manfred Weiss Company to the Rimamurány-Salgótarján Vasmű, Inc., Budapest, November 19, 1925, Z 402, 33/XLI. t., 2. cs., MOL.

148. Letter from the Manfred Weiss Company to the Minister of Finance János Bud, and to the directorate of MÁV, November 25, 1925, Z 402, 33/XLI. t., 2. cs., MOL. There was good reason for the two companies to turn to the government with such a request. In order to make the Hungarian export goods more competitive in the foreign markets, the government occasionally, and for certain items, authorized a return of the 2–3 percent transfer tax or assured a favorable transportation rate by authorizing a partial or complete return of the transportation costs. See Búzás and Nagy, *Magyarország külkereskedelme 1919–1945*, 45.

149 Memorandum from Stomoniakov to Mikoyan. Moscow, July 9, 1929, f. 04, op.11. p. 68, d. 946, l. 21. AVP RF.

150. Memorandum from Minister of Commerce Béla Kenéz to Minister of the Interior Ferenc Keresztes-Fischer, Budapest, November 5,

1931, K 149, 6/1933. t., 9015/1933. alapsz., 164.556/1931. sz., 29. d., 33 fol., MOL.

151. Stomoniakov to Mikoyan. Moscow, July 9, 1929, f. 04, op. 11, p. 68, d. 946, l. 21, AVP RF.

152. Minister of Commerce János Bud to Minister of the Interior Béla Scitovszky, Budapest, August 10, K 149, 6/1933. t., 9015/1933. alapsz., 55.565/1931. sz., 29. d., 32. fol., MOL.

153. Stomoniakov to Mikoyan, Moscow, July 9, 1929, f. 04. op. 11, p. 68, d. 946. l. 21. AVP RF.

154. Tables 1–5 were designed by me on the basis of *Magyar Statisztikai Közlemények* series. See *Magyar Statisztikai Közlemények*, vol. 75, *Magyarország 1925. és 1926. évi külkereskedelmi forgalma* [Hungary's Foreign Trade in 1925 and 1926] (Budapest, 1929), 1: 109 and 2:102; *Magyar Statisztikai Közlemények*, vol. 77, *Magyarország 1927. évi külkereskedelmi forgalma* [Hungary's Foreign Trade in 1927] (Budapest, 1929), 1:104 and 2:77; *Magyar Statisztikai Közlemények*, vol. 78, *Magyarország 1928. évi külkereskedelmi forgalma* [Hungary's Foreign Trade in 1928] (Budapest, 1930), 1:105 and 2:77; and *Magyar Statisztikai Közlemények*, vol. 80, *Magyarország 1929. évi külkereskedelmi forgalma* [Hungary's Foreign Trade in 1929] (Budapest, 1931), 98.

155. In my tables live animals (horses) are given not by volume but, on the basis of officials statistics, by number because I have no uniform rules to give the tonnage of this valuable export commodity.

Notes to Chapter Three

1. Rem A. Belousov, *Ekonomicheskaia istoriia Rossii—XX vek*, book 3, *Tiazhelye gody rosta i obnovleniia* (Moscow, 2002), 276–282.

2. Búzás and Nagy, *Magyarország külkereskedelme 1919–1945*, 137.

3. *Horthy Miklós titkos iratai* [The Secret Papers of Miklós Horthy], ed. Miklós Szinai and László Szűcs (Budapest, 1972), 124–126. The threats of the Soviet "dumping of merchandise" caused an echo in the Hungarian House of Representatives as well. Government party representative Gyula Kornis claimed in a speech on May 8, 1931, that the purpose of the Soviet dumping of merchandise was to internally undermine, revolutionize and Bolshevize the

Western states. See *Az 1927. évi január hó 25-ére hirdetett Or-szággyűlés Képviselőházának naplója* [Minutes of the Meeting of the House of Representatives of the National Assembly Held on January 25, 1927] (Budapest, 1931), 36:3.

4. Valentin M. Kudrov, *Sovetskaia ekonomika v retrospektive: opyt pereosmysleniia* (Moscow, 1997), 17 and 51–54.
5. Ibid., 15: and Werth, *Istoriia sovetskogo gosudarstva*, 220–223.
6. For the statistics see S. V. Afontsev, Ot Rossiiskoi imperii k SSSR. Struktura torgovlii so stranami Zapada," in *Ekonomicheskaia istoriia. Ezhegodnik. 2006,* ed. I. A. Petrov (Moscow, 2006), 36–37 and 40–42.
7. For details, see Kaposi, *Magyarország gazdaságtörténete,* 296–300.
8. Artúr Székely, "A magyar külkereskedelem irányainak változásai a forgalmi korlátozások éveiben (1930–1934)" [Changes in the Hungarian foreign trade during the years of traffic limitations, 1930–1934], *Közgazdasági Szemle* 78, (1935): 154–168.
9. "Kormányintézkedést sürgetnek az orosz fa beözönlése ellen" [Government action is urged against the inflow of Russian lumber], *Pesti Tőzsde,* March 13, 1930, 8.
10. "Az orosz export és a gépipar" [Russian exports and the machine industry], *Pesti Tőzsde*, September 4, 1930, 16; and "Berlini tárgyalalások a magyar-szovjet-oroszországi kereskedelmi kapcsolatok ügyében" [Negotiations in Berlin about trade relations between Hungary and Soviet Russia], *Pesti Tőzsde*, October 29, 1931, 1.
11. Sándor Kóródi, "A szovjet-oroszországi export megindítása és egyéb kiviteli célkitűzések" [Starting the exports to Soviet Russia and other export goals], *Pesti Tőzsde*, August 12, 1931, 4.
12. "Magyarország és az orosz üzlet. Beszélgetés Kóródi Sándorral, a Magyar Külkeresdelmi Intézet, Rt. vezérigazgatójával" [Hungary and business with Russia. Conversation with Sándor Kóródi the CEO of the Hungarian Foreign Trade Institute, Inc.], *Pesti Tőzsde*, March 3, 1932, 1.
13. Report of Sándor Kóródi, the CEO of the Foreign Commerce Institute to Béla Kenéz, minister of commerce, Berlin, January 4, 1932, K 149, 29. d., 1933/6. t., 9015/1933. sz., 36–41 fol., MOL.

14. Kóródi's report to Kenéz, Berlin, April 18, 1932, K 149, 29. d., 1933/6. t., 9015/1933. sz., 49–51. fol., MOL.
15. "A magyar-orosz kereskedelmi tárgyalások sikere" [The success of the Hungarian-Russian trade negotiations], *Pesti Napló*, May 19, 1932, 2.
16. Letter from András Csató to the Commissariat for Agriculture, Berlin, December 6, 1933, f. 413, op. 13, d. 518, l. 16–17, RGAE.
17. It is surprising that in the Soviet documents we find statements which are contrary to our findings and suggest balances favoring Hungary. See the telegram from Boris Rozenblum, the director of the Economic Division of the Commissariat for Foreign Affairs, to Aleksandr Bekzadian, the Soviet minister in Budapest, Moscow, December 7, 1934, f. 010, op.13, p. 81, d.1, l. 99–100, AVP RF; and Krestinskii's telegram to Bekzadian, Moscow, February 29, 1935, f. 010, op.10, p. 50, d.39, l. 12, AVP RF.
18. My reconstruction on the basis of the data of the *Magyar Statisztikai Közlemények* series. *Magyar Statisztikai Közlemények*, vol. 80, *Magyarország 1929. évi külkereskedelmi forgalma* [Hungary's 1929 Foreign Trade Activity] (Budapest, 1931), 94–95; *Magyar Statisztikai Közlemények*, vol. 81, *Magyarország 1930. évi külkereskedelmi forgalma* [Hungary's 1930 Foreign Trade Activity] (Budapest, 1931), 85; *Magyar Statisztikai Közlemények*, vol. 82, *Magyarország 1931. évi külkereskedelmi forgalma* [Hungary's 1931 Foreign Trade Activity] (Budapest, 1933), 88–89; *Magyar Statisztikai Közlemények*, vol. 84. *Magyarország 1932. évi külkereskedelmi forgalma* [Hungary's 1932 Foreign Trade Activity] (Budapest, 1933), 58; and *Statisztikai Közlemények*, vol. 85. *Magyarország 1933. évi külkereskedelmi forgalma* [Hungary's 1933 Foreign Trade Activity] (Budapest, 1934), 58.
19. Pap, "A Szovjetunió külkereskedelmi forgalma," 91.
20. "Winchkler István Berlinben tárgyalt a szovjet külkereskedelmi képviselettel" [István Winchkler has negotiated in Berlin with the Soviet Trade Mission], *Pesti Napló*, November 12, 1933, 9.
21. Notes on the discussion between Khuen-Héderváry and Ascanio Colonna, the Italian minister in Budapest, Budapest, November 13, 1933, K 63, 223. cs., 1933/24. t., 5824/1933. pol. sz., MOL.
22. "Mi van az orosz-magyar fizetési megállapodásban, melyet

Winchkler István hozott létre?" [What is in the payments agreement realized by István Winchkler?], *Pesti Tőzsde*, February 8, 1934, 2.

23. Memorandum on the Minisrty of Foreign Affairs' Foreign Trade Committee negotiations, Budapest, February 21, 1934, K 69, 756. cs., 1934–I–c. t., 162–164. fol., MOL.

24. Jungerth's report to Kánya, Moscow, March 20, 1936, K 69, 760. cs., 1936–I–3. t., 51.914/1936. sz., MOL.

25. " Orosz szovjet küldöttek tárgyalásai új orosz-magyar árue-gyezmény ügyében" [Negotiations with Russian Soviet delegates about a new Russian-Hungarian trade agreement], *Pesti Tőzsde*, July 25, 1935, 4.

26. Attila Kolontári, "A diplomácia kapcsolatok felvétele Magyar-ország és a Szovjetunió között 1934-ben" [The establishment of diplomatic relations between Hungary and the Soviet Union in 1934), *Múltunk* 49, no. 3 (2004): 120–156.

27. Jungerth, *Moszkvai napló*, 59–62.

28. See K 64, 60. cs., 1934/24. t., 32/1934. res. pol. 133-139. fol., MOL.

29. Report of Lev B. Gelfand, the secretary of the Soviet Embassy in Rome to Krestinskii, Rome, January 25, 1934, f. 05, op. 14, p. 97, d. 28, l. 32–37, AVP RF.

30. Andrei I. Pushkash, *Vneshniaia politika Vengrii. Aprel' 1927–fevral' 1934 gg.* (Moscow, 1995), 265.

31. Ibid., 266–267.

32. Jungerth, *Moszkvai napló*, 99.

33. For the original documents in French, see K 70, 337. cs., 1934–II–1. t., 36–44. fol., MOL.

34. György Réti, ed., *A Palazzo Chigi és Magyarország. Olasz diplo-máciai dokumentumok Magyarországról (a Gömbös-kormány időszakában). 1932–1936* [The Palazzo Chigi and Hungary. Italian Diplomatic Documents about Hungary in the Period of the Gömbös Government, 1932–1936] (Budapest, 2003), 131.

35. Ibid., 130.

36. Jungerth, *Moszkvai napló*, 99.

37. Memorandum on the foundation and activities of the Hungarian-Egyptian Trade Corporation, Budapest, March 4, 1933, Z 96, 66. cs., 85.t., 4367/ I. sz., MOL.

38. Bekzadian's report to Krestinskii, Budapest, January 26, 1935, f. 010, op. 10, p. 50, d. 32, l. 3–12, AVP RF.

39. Jungerth's diary entry, Budapest, April 3, 1933, 972. f., 5, ő. e., 20–25. fol., PSZL.

40. Minutes of the Politburo meeting, Moscow, March 5, 1934. f. 17, op. 3, d. 940, l. 32, RGASZPI.

41. Proposal of Krestinskii to Stalin, Moscow, March 2, 1934, f. 010, op. 13, p. 81, d. 1, l. 59, AVP RF.

42. Petrovskii's report on April 18, 1934, about his visit to Budapest, Gromyko, ed., *DVP SSSR*, 17:266–270.

43. Minutes of the Politburo meeting, Moscow, August 5, 1934, f. 17, op. 3, d. 949, l. 19, RGASPI.

44. Jungerth, *Moszkvai napló,* 104.

45. Pál Pritz, ed., *Iratok a magyar külügyi szolgálat történetéhez 1918–1945* Documents to the History of the Hungarian Foreign Service, 1918–1945] (Budapest, 1995), 452–453.

46. The Soviet press published information according to which the news about the start of diplomatic relations caused a rise in the price of the stocks on the Budapest stock exchange of the firms, like Ganz, which were interested in exporting to the Soviet Union. These firms also started a campaign asking the government to support export activities to the Soviet Union by guaranteeing credit. "Ustanovlenie normalnikh diplomaticheskikh otnoshenii mezhdu SSSR i Vengriei odobriaetsia vengerskim parlamentom," *Izvestiia*, February 12, 1934.

47. "Ganz-Jendrassik nyersolajmotor a szovjet nagy nemzetközi teherautó beszerzésén" [The Ganz-Jendrassik Diesel engine in the international Soviet truck purchases], *Pesti Tőzsde*, August 17, 1933, p. 16.

48. "Mi van az orosz-magyar fizetési megállapodásban, melyet Winchkler István hozott létre?" [What is in the Russian-Hungarian Compensation Agreement arranged by István Winchkler?], *Pesti Tőzsde*, February 8, 1934, p. 2.

49. Letter from Csató to Lengyel, Berlin, February 8, 1934, f. 413, op. 13, d. 518, l. 11–12, RGAE.

50. Lengyel's letter to Csató, Moscow, February 15, 1934, f. 413, op. 13, d. 518, l. 10, RGAE.

51. Memorandum about the negotiations of the Foreign Trade

Committee of the Ministry of Foreign Affairs, Budapest, February
21, 1934, K 69, 756. cs., 1934–I–c. dossier, 162–164. fol., MOL.

52. "V diplomaticheskom mire," *Pravda*, April 26, 1934.

53. Shtern's notes about the discussion with Jungerth, Moscow, April
28, 1934, f. 05, op. 14, p. 97, d. 28, l. 66–68, AVP RF.

54. Office memorandum of Commissar for Foreign Trade Arkadii
Rozengolts, Moscow, May 19, 1934, f. 413, op. 97, d. 518, l. 9,
RGAE.

55. Shtern's note about the discussion with Jungerth, Moscow, April
28, 1934, f. 05, op. 14, p. 97, d. 28, l. 66–68, AVP RF.

56. "Az orosz kereskedelmi delegáció tagnévsorát még e héten a kormányzó elé terjesztik jóváhagyás végett" [The membership list of
the Russian trade delegation will be submitted this week to the
regent for approval], *Pesti Tőzsde*, May 3, 1934, 7.

57. József Willerstorfer, "Oroszországból kompenzációs alapon
hozhatnánk be pamutot. Az orosz utazás részletei—Kik utaztak ki
Moszkvába?" [We Could Import Wool From Russia on a
Compensation Basis. Details of the Trip to Russia—Who Traveled
to Moscow?], *Pesti Tőzsde*, May 24, 1934, 13.

58. "Az orosz kereskedelmi delegáció," 7.

59. "V Moskvu pribyla vengerskaia torgovo-promishlennaia delegat-
sia," *Ekonomicheskaia zhizn'*, May 26, 1934, 4.

60. Bornemissza's report, Budapest, s.d. (After June 17, 1934), K 69,
756. cs., 1934–I–c. dossier, 51–105. fol., MOL. Bornemissza gave
an interview to the press about the trip to Moscow, see "Vitéz
Bornemissza Félix—oroszországi élményeiről. Milyen cikkek
kivitelére és behozatalára számíthatunk? Hajózási egyezmény
készül a Szovjettel" [Vitéz Félix Bornemissza about his experiences in Russia. What export and import items can we count on?
A navigation agreement with the Soviet Union is being prepared],
Pesti Tőzsde, August 23, 1934, 12.

61. Wettstein's report to the management of the Fantó Egyesült
Ásványolaj-ipari Rt., Budapest, July 5, 1934, Z 1202, 1. cs., 18.
t., MOL. See also "Dr. Wettstein Miklós elmondja, mit látott
Oroszországban. [Dr. Miklós Wettstein tells us what he saw in
Russia], *Pesti Tőzsde*, June 21, 1934, 7.

62. "Főleg gép, bauxit, alumínium-oxid és néhány textilcikk exportjára

számíthatunk Oroszországba" [We can count primarily on the export of machines, bauxite, aluminum oxide and a few textile items to Russia], *Pesti Tőzsde*, June 14, 1934, 7.

63. Félix Bornemissza's report.

64. "Főleg gép," 7.

65. Lorents's circular, Moscow, July 8, 1934, f. 413, op. 13, d. 518, l. 8, RGAE.

66. Rozenblum's telegram to Bekzadian, Moscow, December 7, 1934, f. 010, op. 13, p. 81, d. 1, l. 99–100, AVP RF.

67. Jungerth's report to Kánya, Moscow, December 9, 1935, K 69, 759. cs., 1935–II–f. t., 57.279/1935. sz., MOL.

68. "Dr. Wettstein Miklós elmondja," 7.

69. Jungerth's report to Kánya. Moscow, December 9, 1935.

70. Miklós Wettstein's report.

71. Bornemissza' report.

72. Miklós Wettstein's report.

73. "Franciák finanszírozzák a szovjet magyar vásárlásait" [The French are financing the Soviet's Hungarian purchases], *Magyarország*, July 29, 1934, 13.

74. "Emden áruház király finanszírozza az orosz-magyar áruforgalmat" [Department store king, Emden, finances Soviet-Hungarian trade], *Pesti Tőzsde*, September 6, 1934, 1–2. The legal precursor of Stella was the Stella Female Lingerie Confection Business, Inc. which took on the name of Stella Merchandise Trading, Inc. on June 14, 1934. The bylaws were non-specific about the proposed activities of the company. The activities included the domestic and foreign sale of a variety of agricultural and industrial products and the importation of foreign merchandise. The later history of the company reveals that the major components of its activities were the arrangement of business relations, the establishment of consignment warehouses and the assumption of representation of a companies abroad. Note on the Stella Merchandise Trading Company, Budapest, October 15, 1934, Z 450, 115. cs., 802. t., MOL.

75. János Kallós, ed., *Gazdasági, pénzügyi és tőzsdei kompasz az 1934–1935. évre* [Economic, Financial and Stock Exchange Register for 1934–1935] (Budapest, 1934), 3–4:127.

76. János Kallós, ed., *Gazdasági, pénzügyi és tőzsdei kompasz az 1935–1936. évre* [Economic, Financial and Stock Exchange Register for 1935–1936] (Budapest, 1935), 3–4:658.

77. Legation Secretary Semion Mirnii's notes on a conversation with Félix Bornemissza, Budapest, February 7, 1935, f. 010, op. 10, p. 50, d. 33. l. 31–32, AVP RF. On one occasion Bornemissza invited Mirnii for lunch at the Gellért Hotel to introduce Hoffer to him. The parliamentary representative discussed the Soviet export plans of the Office for Foreign Trade. Mirnii's notes on his discussion with Bornemissza and Hoffer, Budapest, February 21, 1935, , f. 010, op. 10, p. 50, d. 33, l. 44, AVP RF.

78. Gyula Lengyel's notes about his discussion with Aleksandr Urievich. Moscow, September 14, 1934, f. 413, op.13, d. 518, l. 7, RGAE.

79. Note of Mikhail Shaprov, the second secretary of the Soviet Legation in Budapest about his discussion with Urievich, Budapest, January 22, 1935, f. 010, op. 10, p. 50, d. 39, l. 5, AVP RF.

80. Telegram from Rozenblum to Shaprov. Moscow, February 7, 1935, f. 010, op. 10, p. 50, d. 39, l. 8, AVP RF.

81. Mirnii's notes about a conversation with Bornemissza, Budapest, February 7, 1935, f. 010, op. 10, p. 50, d. 33, l. 31–32, AVP RF.

82. Letter from Ferenc Herceg, deputy director of Hofherr-Schrantz to Ferenc Neuhaus, Budapest, March 13, 1935, Z 450, 115. cs., 802. t., MOL.

83. Report of Egon Cindric, charge d'affairs in Moscow, Moscow, September 1, 1935, K 69, 759. cs., 1935–II–b. t., 55.382/1935. sz., MOL.

84. Mirnii's report to Rozenblum, Budapest, s.d. (after September 17, 1935.) f. 010, op. 10, p. 50, d. 39. l. 51–52, AVP RF.

85. Note about the establishment and activities of the Hungarian-Egyptian Trade Corp., Budapest, March 4, 1933, Z 96, 66. cs., 85. t., 4367/I. sz., MOL.

86. Minutes of the meeting of the directors of the Hungarian-Egyptian Trade Corp., Budapest, May 16, 1935, Z 96, 66. cs., 85. t., 4367/VII. sz, MOL.

87. Report from Mirnii to Rozenblum, Budapest, August 16, 1936, f. 010, op. 11, p. 68, d. 30, l. 118–119, AVP RF,

88. Report from Mirnii to Rozenblum, Budapest, s. d. (after September 17, 1935).
89. Bekzadian's report to Krestinskii, Budapest, February 16, 1936, f. 010, op. 11, p. 68, d. 29, l. 11–29, AVP RF.
90. Report from Shaprov to the Second Western Division and to the Economic Division of the Commissariat for Foreign Affairs, Budapest, February 5–7, 1935, f. 010, op. 11, p. 68, d. 29, l. 9, AVP RF.
91. "Dr. Emden által átvett hamis váltók értéke: egymillió francia frank" [The value of the forged Soviet vouchers accepted by Dr. Emden was 1 million French francs], *Pesti Tőzsde,* December 12, 1935, 6.
92. "Hozzászólás az Urievics-ügyhöz" [Comments on the Urievich affair], *Pesti Tőzsde,* December 19, 1935, 8.
93. Mirnii's report to Rozenblum, Budapest, October 16, 1935, f. 010, op. 10, p. 50, d. 39, l. 54–55, AVP RF.
94. Fabinyi's memorandum to Kánya, Budapest, December 29, 1934, K 69, 756. cs., 1934–I–c. dossier, 50.026/1934. sz., MOL.
95. Kánya's telegram to Jungerth, Budapest, April 15, 1935, K 69, 757. cs., 1935–I–d–2. t., 52.229/1935. sz., MOL
96. Jungerth's report to Kánya, Moscow, June 14, 1935, K 69, 757. cs.,1935–I–d–2. t., 53.542/1935. sz., MOL.
97. "Orosz szovjetkiküldöttek budapesti tárgyalásai új orosz-magyar áruegyezmény ügyében" [Russian Soviet delegates' negotiations in Budapest about a new Russian-Hungarian trade agreement], *Pesti Tőzsde,* July 25, 1935, 4.
98. Memorandum from the Ministry of Commerce to the Ministry of Foreign Affairs. Budapest, August 26, 1935, K 69, 757. cs.,1935–I–d–2. t., 54853/1935. sz., MOL.
99. Letter from the United Light Bulb and Electricity, Inc. to the Ministry of Foreign Affaris, Budapest, December 3, 1935, K 69, 667. cs., 1935–II–b. t., 57.028/1935. sz., MOL.
100. Jungerth's report to Kánya, Moscow, January 11, 1936, K 69, 667. cs., 1935–II–b. t., 50.345/1936. sz., MOL.
101. Kozma's memorandum to Kánya, Budapest, December 14, 1935, K 69, 757. cs., 1935–1–d–2. t., 57.235/1935. sz., MOL.
102. Memorandum from the Ministry of Defense to Kánya, January 9, 1936, K 69, 757. cs., 1935–1–d–2. t., 50.219/1936. sz., MOL.

103. Memorandum of the Legal Division of the Ministry of Foreign Affairs on the proposal for a Hungarian-Soviet trade agreement, Budapest, February 24, 1936. K 69, 757. cs., 1935–1–d–2. t., 51.067/1936. sz., MOL.

104. Minutes of the inter-ministry meeting held at the Ministry of Foreign Affairs, Budapest, February 25, 1936. K 69, 757. cs., 1935–1–d–2. t., 51.212/1936. sz., MOL.

105. Telegram from Kánya to Jungerth, Budapest, April 11, 1936. K 69, 757. cs., 1935–1–d–2. t., 52.097/1936. sz., MOL.

106. Jungerth's report to Kánya, Budapest, May 15, 1936. K 69, 757. cs., 1935–1–d–2. t., 52.830/1936. sz., MOL.

107. MNB "Pro Memoria" on the Hungarian-Soviet negotiations. Buda-pest, June 17, 1936, K 69, 757. cs., 1935–1–d–2. t., 53.530/1936. sz., MOL.

108. Jungerth's report to Kánya, Moscow, May 27, 1936, K 69, 757. cs., 1935–1–d–2. t., 53.155/1936. sz., MOL.

109. Jungerth's report to Kánya, Moscow, April 30, 1937, K 69, 760. cs., 1937–I–3. t., 53.284/1937. sz., MOL.

110. Letter from Alfonz Weiss to Ernst Breisach, the director of Breisach, Inc., Budapest, November 30, 1925, Z 402, 2. cs., 33/XLI. t., MOL.

111. Y. A. Kumachenko, "Ispol'zovanie dunaiskogo puti v nashei vneshnei torgovle," *Vneshniaia torgovlia,* August 15, 1934, 12–13.

112. Memorandum of Bálint Vargha, technical expert, about the exports from the Diósgyőr factory of MÁVAG to the Soviet Union, Budapest, August 13, 1935, K 69, 759. cs., 1935–II–f. t., 54.933/1935. sz., MOL.

113. Memorandum from Rozenblum to Lengyel, Moscow, May 26, 1934, f. 010, op. 13, p. 81, d. 1, l. 98, AVP RF.

114. Móric Domony, "A dunai hajózás az 1934. évben" [Danubian navigation in 1934], *Pesti Tőzsde,* December 20, 1934, 18.

115. "Vitéz Bornemissza Félix—oroszországi élményeiről,"12.

116. "Nagyszabású orosz tervek a csepeli kikötővel" [Large-scale Russian plans about the Csepel port], *Magyarország,* December 15, 1934, 13.

117. Bekzadian's report to Krestinskii, Budapest, January 26, 1935, f. 010, op.10, p. 50, d. 32, l. 3–12, AVP RF.

118. Bekzadian's report to Krestinskii, Budapest, January 5, 1936, f. 010, op.11, p. 68, d. 30, l. 1–2, AVP RF.

119. Telegram from Rozenblum to Beksadian, Moscow, December 7, 1934, f. 010, op.13, p. 81, d. 1, l. 99–100, AVP RF.

120. Rozenblum's memorandum to Krestinskii, Moscow, March 9, 1936, , f. 010, op.13, p. 81, d. 30, l. 55–58, AVP RF.

121. Jungerth's report to Kánya. Moscow, April 22, 1935, K 69, 757. cs., 1935–I–d–2. sz. dossier, 38. fol., MOL.

122. Krestinskii's instructions to Mirnii, Moscow, April 7, 1936, f. 010, op.13, p. 81, l. 59–60, AVP RF.

123. Notes of Ministry of Foreign Affairs Councilor Ervin Vladár on the Hungarian-Soviet shipping negotiations, Budapest, March 27, 1936, K 69, 759. cs., II/e. t., 51.781/1936. sz., MOL.

124. Mirnii's report to Krestinskii, Budapest, April 17, 1936, f. 010, op.11, p. 68, d. 29, l. 51–56, AVP RF,

125. Notes on the first negotiating encounter on signing a shipping agreement, Moscow, April 27, 1936, f. 10, op. 11, p. 68, d. 30, l. 61–62, AVP RF.

126. Notes on the second negotiating encounter on signing a shipping agreement, Moscow May 11, 1936, f. 10, op. 11, p. 68, d. 30, l. 65–66, AVP RF.

127. Minutes of the meeting held in the Ministry of Foreign Affairs about trade going to Iran, Budapest, March 4, 1937, K 69, 667. cs., 1936–1940–III–a. t., 51.734/1937. sz., MOL.

128. Jungerth's report to Kánya, Moscow, April 30, 1937, K 69, 760. cs., I/3. dossier, 53.284/1937. sz., MOL.

129. Bekzadian's report to Krestinskii, Budapest, May 17, 1936, f. 10, op. 11, p. 68, d. 30, l. 67–68, AVP RF,

130. My reconstruction on the basis of the data of the *Magyar Statisztikai Közlemények* series. *Magyar Statisztikai Közlemények*, vol. 95, *Magyarország 1934. évi külkereskedelmi forgalma* [Hungary's 1934 Foreign Trade Activity], (Budapest, 1935), 58–59; *Magyar Statisztikai Közlemények*, vol. 98, *Magyarország 1935. évi külkereskedelmi forgalma* [Hungary's 1935 Foreign Trade Activity] (Budapest, 1936), 101; *Magyarország 1936. évi külkereskedelmi forgalma* [Hungary's 1936 Foreign Trade Activity] (Budapest, 1937), 59; *Magyar Statisztikai Közlemények,* vol. 106,

Magyarország 1937. évi külkereskedelmi forgalma [Hungary's 1937 Foreign Trade Activity] (Budapest, 1938), 47; and *Statisztikai Közlemények,* vol. 109, *Magyarország 1938. évi külkereskedelmi forgalma* [Hungary's 1938 Foreign Trade Activity] (Budapest, 1939), 47.

131. The Hungarian documents about the "rupture" of Hungarian-Soviet diplomatic relations are in *Diplomáciai iratok Magyarország külpolitikájához 1936–1945,* vol. 3, *Magyarország külpolitikája 1938–1939* [Diplomatic Documents on Hungary's Foreign Policy 1936–1945, vol. 3, Hungary's Foreign Policy, 1938–1939], ed. Magda Ádám (Budapest, 1970), 315–316, 377–379, 424–425, 432–433, 479–484, and 507–508; and *Diplomáciai iratok Magyarország külpolitikájához 1936–1945,* vol. 4, *Magyarország külpolitikája a II. világháború kitörésének időszakában 1939–1940.* [Diplomatic Documents on Hungary's Foreign Policy, 1936–1945, vol. 4, Hungarian Foreign Policy at the Time of the Outbreak of World War II, 1939–1940], ed. Gyula Juhász (Budapest, 1962), 360–361 and 539–540. The Russian documents were published by Attila Seres, "Orosz levéltári források a magyar-szovjet diplomáciai kapcsolatok történetéhez (1939)" [Russian archival sources on the history of Hungarian-Soviet diplomatic relations (1939)], *Lymbus. Magyarságtudományi Közlemények* 3, (2005): 207–249. See also Attila Kolontári, "Az egyik legstabilabb határszakasz Európában. Adalékok a szovjet-magyar kapcsolatok történetéhez 1939–1941" [One of the most stable frontiers in Europe. Addenda to the history of the Hungarian-Soviet relations 1939–1941], in *"Önkényuralom, alkotmányosság, forradalom." Előadások és tanulmányok az első orosz forradalom 100 éves évfordulója alkalmából* ["Dictatorship, Constitutionality, Revolution." Lectures and Essays on the One Hundred Year Anniversary of the First Russian Revolution] MOSZT Könyvek 1, ed. Tamás Polgár (Pécs, 2006), 118–136.

Notes to Chapter Four

1. Belousov, *Ekonomicheskaia istoriia Rossii,* bk. 3, *Tiazhelye gody rosta i obnovleniia,* 136–138.

2. Kudrov, *Sovetskaia ekonomika v retrospektive*, 127 and 54.
3. Torkunov, ed., *Ocherki istorii Ministerstva Inostrannikh Del*, vol. 2, *1917–2002 gg.*, 255.
4. Werth, *Istoriia sovetskogo gosudarstva*, 295.
5. Gabriel Gorodetsky, *Rokovoi samoobman. Stalin i napadenie Germanii na Sovetskii* Soiuz (Moscow, 2001), 40–41.
6. G. E. Mamedov, ed., *Dokumenty vneshnei politiki 1940–22 iiunia 1941* (hereafter cited as *DVP*), vol. 23, book 1, *1 ianvaria–31 oktiabria 1940 g.* (Moscow, 1995), 14–23.
7. Ibid., 260–267.
8. G. E. Mamedov, ed., *DVP*, vol 23, book 2, part 1, *1 noiabria 1940 g.–1 marta 1941 g.* (Moscow, 1998), 166–169.
9. As mentioned earlier, Romania signed a compensation agreement with the Soviet Union on February 16, 1936. For the text of the February 26, 1941, Soviet-Romanian commercial and navigation agreement, see A. A. Avdeev and M. R. Ungureanu, eds., *Sovetsko-rumynskie otnosheniia*, vol. 2, *1935–1941. Documenty i materialy* (Moscow, 2000), 443–449.
10. See f. 413, op. 13, d. 3816, l. 38–41, RGAE,
11. György Tolnai, "A Szovjetunió délkelet-európai kereskedelmi kapcsolatai" [The southeast European trade ties of the Soviet Union], *OMKE*, April 5, 1941, 3.
12. Memorandum of Rolf Krausz on the perspectives of the Hungarian-Soviet commercial relations, Budapest, November 13, 1939, K 69, 760. cs., 1939–I–7. t., 37–75. fol., MOL.
13. Búzás and Nagy, *Magyarország külkereskedelme 1919–1945*, 380.
14. "A magyar nyersanyagellátás problémái" [Problems of Hungarian raw material supplies], *OMKE*, December 9, 1939, 5.
15. The return of the Subcarpathia and of Northern Transylvania resolved the supply problems of the lumber industry. The salt mines and non-ferrous metal mines, however, were insufficient to significantly reduce the raw material supply problem.
16. Honvári, ed., *Magyarország gazdaságtörténete*, 439; Gunst, *Magyarország gazdaságtörténete*, 105; Csikós-Nagy, *A XX. század magyar gazdaságpolitikája* 100–102; and Kaposi, *Magyarország gazdaságtörténete*, 317–320.

17. Buzás-Nagy, *Magyarország külkereskedelme 1919–1945*, 380.
18. "A magyar nyersanyagellátás problémái," 5.
19. *Budapesti Közlöny,* November 25, 1939, 2.
20. *Budapesti Közlöny,* June 23, 1940, 1–7.
21. The thirty-sixth meeting of the OMKE discussed the new tasks and old injuries of commerce. *OMKE,* May 11, 1940, 9.
22. See the notice of the minutes of the 1940 annual meeting of the Országos Magyar Kereskedelmi Egyesület [National Hungarian Trade Association] (OMKE), ibid.
23. Miklós Degré and Alajos Várady-Brenner, eds., *Magyar Törvénytár, 1939. évi törvénycikkek* [Hungarian Law Code. 1939 Acts (Budapest, 1940), 69.
24. "A magyar nyersanyagellátás problémái," 5. A serious concern was also caused by the fact that the sequestration of the raw materials and their central control caused a sharp increase in prices even for the domestic raw materials. The cost of foreign raw materials was substantially increased by the navicert system and by other factors, including the considerable increase in the cost of transportation. The government wishing to prevent the difficulties of industrial production because of these factors increased the government orders within the Győr program. See Vilmos Nőtel, "A magyar ipari termelés finanszírozása" [Financing the Hungarian industrial production], pt. 2, *Közgazdasági Szemle* 84, (1941): 634.
25. Lajos Thirring, "A Szovjetunió népességének száma és összetétele" [Number and Composition of the Population of the Soviet Union], *Magyar Statisztikai Szemle,* nos. 1–6 (1945): 14–17.
26. Zoltán Szalay, "A Szovjetunió bányászata és kohászata" [Mining and Metallurgy in the Soviet Union], *Magyar Statisztikai Szemle,* nos. 1–6 (1945): 66–71.
27. For the growth statistics of the machine and metal industries, see Honvári, ed., *Magyarország gazdaságtörténete,* 439.
28. Zoltán Szőllősy, "Mezőgazdaság, állattenyésztés és erdészet a Szovjetunióban" [Agriculture, animal husbandry and forestry in the Soviet Union], *Magyar Statisztikai Szemle,* nos. 1–6 (1945): 59–61.

29. Kolontári, "Az egyik legstabilabb határszakasz," 119–121.

30 Pastor, ed., *A moszkvai követség jelentései*, 196–198; and Seres, "Orosz levéltári források," 239–240.

31. György Perényi-Lukács's notes on the inter-ministerial meeting, Budapest, November 15, 1939, K 69, 760. cs., 1939–I–12. t., 55.349/1939. sz., MOL.

32. Potemkin's submission to the Politburo, Moscow, December 30, 1939, f. 06, op. 1, p. 7, d. 60, l. 9–11, AVP RF.

33 Political diary of Deputy Commissar for Foreign Affairs Vladimir Dekanozov, Moscow, April 29, 1940, f. 077, op. 20, p. 109, d. 1, l. 37–38. AVP RF.

34. Report of Félix Bornemissza, Budapest, s.d. (after June 17, 1934), K 69, 756. cs., 1934–I–c. t, 51–105. fol., MOL.

35. Dekanozov's political diary, Moscow, June 7–8, 1940, f. 077, op. 20, p. 109, d.1, l. 49, AVP RF.

36. Report from Csató to Kristóffy, Moscow, June 21, 1940, K 69, 758. cs., 1940–I–g. t., 53.266/1940. sz., MOL.

37. Report of Oszkár Makkay, director of MÁH to Ferenc Rosty-Forgách, counselor of legation, Moscow, July 16, 1940, K 69, 758. cs., 1940–I–g. t., 59. fol., MOL.

38. Report of the textile raw materials exporting organization, Exportlen, to Commissar for Foreign Affairs Mikoyan, Moscow, September 6, 1940, f. 413, op. 13, d. 2829, l. 114, RGAE.

39. Exportles's notes on negotiations with Mór Orován, Moscow, June 29, 1940, f. 413, op. 13, d. 2821, l.1, RGAE.

40. Mamedov, ed., *DVP, ianvaria–31 oktiabria 1940 g.*, 415–416.

41. Gorodetsky, *Rokovoi samoobman*, 44–48.

42. See Kristóffy's reports of June 30, July 11 and Sept 3, 1940, in Pastor, ed., *A moszkvai követség jelentései*, 252–254, 256–257, and 258–260.

43. Csáky's circular to the heads of the affected ministries and state organizations, Budapest, July 6, 1940, K 69, 758. cs., 1940–I–h. t., 53.326/1940. sz., MOL.

44. Notes of the Ganz representative about the meeting at the Ministry of Commerce, Budapest, July 18, 1940, Z 429, 37. cs., 180. sz., MOL.

45. Minutes of the Council of Ministers meeting, Budapest, July 26,

1940, K 27, 212. d., 3633. sz., 75–77. fol., 3634. sz., 118–120. fol., MOL.

46. Telegram from Csáky to Kristóffy, Budapest, July 27, 1940, K 69, 757. cs., 1940–I–f. t., 53.692/1940. sz., MOL.

47. Report of Krivátsy-Szűcs to Minister of Justice László Radocsay, Moscow, November 8, 1940, K 69, 757. cs., 1940–I–d–1. t., 24–36. fol., MOL.

48. I could not ascertain the full name of the two Soviet economic experts.

49. Nickl's report to Csáky. Budapest, September 16, 1940, K 69, 758. cs., 1940–I–h. t., 54.400/1940. sz., MOL.

50. In the material on the Moscow negotiations, see K 69, 760. cs., 1940–I–5. t., 8–13, 24–27, 30–36. fol., MOL.

51. The text of the agreement in the original French is in K 70, 337. cs., 1934–II–1. t., 40–41. fol., MOL.

52. Report from Krivátsy-Szűcs to Radocsay, Moscow, November 8, 1940, K 69, 757. cs., 1940–I–d–1. t., 5–23. fol., MOL.

53. Notes of the first session of subcommittee no. 1, Moscow, August 9, 1940, K 69, 760. cs., 1940–I–5. t., 8–13. fol., MOL.

54. Notes on the fifth session of subcommittee no 1, Moscow, August 28, 1940, K 69, 760. cs., 1940–I–5. t., 69–72. fol., MOL.

55. Notes on the third general meeting of the Hungarian and Soviet delegations. Moscow, September 3, 1940, K 69, 760. cs., 1940–I–5. t., 83. fol., MOL.

56. The text of the agreement in Hungarian is in *Budapesti Közlöny*, September 15, 1940, 4–6. In Russian, see Mamedov, ed., *DVP, ianvaria–31 oktiabria 1940 g.*, 554–560.

57. For the text of the merchandise and compensation agreement, see K 69, 758. cs., 1940–I–h. t., 77–82. fol., MOL.

58 Report from Nickl to Csáky, Budapest, September 16, 1940, K 69, 758. cs., 1940–I–h. t., 77–82. fol., 54.400/1940. sz., MOL.

59. "Komoly kilátásokkal indul a magyar-szovjet kereskedelmi forgalom" [The Hungarian-Soviet trade starts with high hopes], *Az Ellenőr*, February 1, 1941, 1.

60. Perényi's report to Bárdossy. Moscow, February 13, 1941, K 69, 757. cs., 1941–I–d–1. t., 118–122. fol., MOL.

61. Notes on the discussions at the Office for Foreign Trade,

Budapest, November 2, 1940, K 69, 760. cs., 1940–I–12. t., 63–64. fol., MOL.

62. List of the members of the delegation going to Moscow, Budapest, November 2, 1940, K 69, 758. cs., 1940–I–h. t., 7–8. fol., MOL.

63. Report from Kristóffy to Csáky, Moscow, December 9, 1940, K 69, 758. cs., 1940–I–i., t., 1196/1940. res. sz., MOL.

64. Notes of Arzén Rankó, an official of the Foreign Commerce Office, on the status of the business negotiations in Moscow, Moscow, December 23, 1940, K 69, 760. cs., 1940–I–12. t., 70–73. fol., MOL.

65. Sharonov's report to Molotov, Budapest, October 28, 1940, f. 06, op. 2, p. 13, d. 137, l. 19–26, AVP RF.

66. Rosslav's report to the Foreign Commerce Office, Moscow, December 9, 1940, K 69, 758. cs., 1940–I–i. t., 1196/1940. res. sz., (64–68. fol.), MOL.

67. Rosslav's report to the Foreign Commerce Office, Moscow, December 29, 1940, K 69, 758. cs., 1940–I–i. t., 1196/1940. res. sz., 19–21. fol., MOL.

68. Memorandum from Exportles Opportunities and Economy Research Group to Deputy Foreign Commerce Commissar Krutikov, Moscow, March 13, 1941, f. 413, op. 13, d. 3781, l. 141–142, RGAE.

69. Perényi-Lukács's report to the Ministry of Foreign Affairs. Moscow, January 27, 1941, K 69, 757. cs., 1941–I–d–1. t., 99–100. fol., MOL.

70. For the text of the Ganz-Mashinoimport contract, see Z 429, 37. cs., 180. sz., MOL.

71. Letter from Gyula Scharbert, a director of Ganz to Foreign Commerce Office, Budapest, June 13, 1940, Z 429, 37. cs., 180. sz., MOL.

72. Notes of the directorate of Ganz on the history of building the *Magyar Vitéz* and *Magyar Tengerész* freighters, Budapest, March 6, 1942, Z 429, 37. cs., 180. sz., MOL.

73. Letter from Ganz to the Office for Foreign Trade, Budapest, June 9, 1941, Z 429, 37. cs., 180. sz., MOL.

74. Notes on the ships to be delivered to the Soviet Union, Budapest, June 24, 1941, K 69, 759. cs., 1941–I–1. t., 5–8. fol., MOL.

75. Scharbert's letter to the Office for Foreign Trade, Budapest, June 13, 1941, Z 429, 37. cs., 180. sz., MOL.

76. Nickl's notes on the interdepartmental meeting at the Ministry of Foreign Affairs, Budapest, November 27, 1940, K 69, 758. cs., 1940–I–i. t., 1144/1940. res. sz., MOL.
77. Ganz Company letter to Minister of Industry Varga, Budapest, January 21, 1941, Z 429, 37. cs., 180. sz., MOL.
78. Ganz Company letter to Rosslav, Budapest, June, 9, 1941, Z 429, 37. cs., 180. sz., MOL.
79. Notes on the seventh meeting of subcommittee no. 2, Moscow, August 26, 1940, f. 413, op.13, d. 2781, l. 13–17, RGAE.
80. Sharonov's diplomatic diary, Budapest, September 16, 1940, f. 077, op. 20, p. 109, d. 13, l. 88, AVP RF.
81. Deputy Commissar of Foreign Affairs Andrei Vyshinskii's diplomatic diary, Moscow, September 24, 1940, f. 077. op. 20, p. 109, d. 1, l. 57, AVP RF.
82. Vozhzhov's notes on his talk with Nickl, Budapest, November 23, 1940, f. 413, op. 13, d. 2772, l. 257–258, RGAE.
83. Diplomatic note from the Commissariat for Foreign Affairs to the Hungarian Legation in Moscow, Moscow, December 19, 1940, f. 077, op.18, p. 8, d. 1, l. 13, AVP RF.
84. Press communiqué on the composition of the Hungarian delegation starting for Moscow. Budapest, January 20, 1941, K 69, 758. cs., 1941–I–i. t., 50.239/1941. sz. MOL.
85. Perényi-Lukács's report to the Ministry of Foreign Affairs, Moscow, January 27, 1941, K 69, 757. cs., 1941–I–d–1. t., 99–100. fol., MOL.
86. Henceforth the names of cities in the former Poland will be rendered in their Russian version. Lavotsnie for Lawoczne, Lvov for Lwow, Sianki for Sianky and Stanislav for Stańislawow.
87. "Halló Budapest-Halló Moszkva! 10 aranyfrank a háromperces beszélgetés díja" [Hello Budapest-Hello Moscow! Ten gold francs for a three minute talk], *A Piac*, February 15, 1941, 1.
88. Perényi-Lukács's report to the Ministry of Foreign Affairs, Moscow, February 4, 1941, K 69, 757. cs., 1941–I–d–1. t., 123– 125. fol., MOL.
89. On the other two lines, Ungvár-Uzsok-Sianki and Beregszász-Kőrösmező-Stanislav, and particularly on the latter one, the direct connection with the Soviet Union could have been established only along a much longer route.

90. Minutes of the joint meeting of the Hungarian-Soviet Mixed Railway Committee, Moscow, February 8, 1941, MÁV KI, FA 17, 7515/1941. sz.

91. Perényi-Lukács's report to Minister of Foreign Affairs Bárdossy. Moscow, March 5, 1941. MOL, K 69, 758. cs., 1941–I–j. t., 50.966/1941. sz.

92. We do not have the full name of the Soviet expert.

93. For the Hungarian text of the agreement and addenda, see FA 17, 10.585/1941. sz., Magyar Államvasutak Központi Irattára [Central Archive of the Hungarian State Railways] (hereafter cited as MÁV KI).

94. "Szombattól egy gyorsvonat indul Oroszországba" [From Saturday on a fast train will start toward Russia], Magyar Nemzet, March 23, 1941, 5.

95. Pastor, ed., A moszkvai követség jelentései, 297.

96. "Nem volt utasa az első közvetlen moszkva-budapesti vonatnak" [The first direct Moscow-Budapest train had no passengers], Független Magyarország, March 24, 1941, 3.

97. Report from the MÁV administration in Miskolc to the directors of MÁV, Miskolc, March 28, 1941, FA 17, 10.585/1941. sz., MÁV KI.

98. Code telegram from Bárdossy to Kristóffy, Budapest, June 16, 1941, K 69, 758. cs., 1941–I–j. t., 52.603/1941. sz., MOL.

99. "A Szovjet-Unión keresztül való áruszállítás lehetősége" [The possibility of shipping merchandise across the Soviet Union], OMKE, March 22, 1941, 1.

100. Rosslav's report to the Ministry of Commerce, Moscow, December 29, 1940, K 69, 758. cs., 1940–I–i. t., sz. n., 19–21. fol., MOL.

101. "A Kereskedelmi Hivatal és az IBUSZ megszervezi a szállítást Oroszországon és Japánon át" [The Commerce Office and the IBUSZ arrange for the transport across Russia and Japan], Pesti Tőzsde, February 6, 1941, 5.

102. "Az oroszországi tranzitálás lehetőségei" [Transit possibilities through Russia], OMKE, August 3, 1940, 1.

103. Minutes of the fourth and fifth session of subcommittee no. 2 at the Hungarian-Soviet commercial negotiations in Moscow. Moscow, August 19, 1940, K 69, 760. cs., 1940–I–5. t., 37–41. fol., MOL.

104. Minutes of the eighth session of subcommittee no. 2 at the

Hungarian-Soviet commercial negotiations in Moscow, Moscow, August 29, 1940, K 69, 760. cs., 1940–I–5. t., 73–77. fol., MOL.

105. Notes of Arzén Rankó on Hungarian-Soviet merchandise traffic, Budapest, December 23, 1940, K 69, 760. cs., 1940–I–12. t., 70–73. fol., MOL.

106. Rosslav's report to the Foreign Commerce Office, Moscow, December 9, 1940, K 69, 758. cs., 1940–I–i. t., 1196/1940. res., 64–68. fol., MOL.

107. Rosslav's report to the Foreign Commerce Office, Moscow, December 29, 1940, , K 69, 758. cs., 1940–I–i. t., no number, 19–21. fol., MOL.

108. Report from Perényi-Lukács to the Ministry of Foreign Affairs, Moscow, January 27, 1941, K 69, 757. cs., 1941–I–d–1. t., 99–100. fol., MOL.

109. Diplomatic note from the Commissariat for Foreign Affairs to the Hungarian Legation in Moscow, Moscow, January 6, 1941, f. 077, op. 18, p. 8, d. 2, l. 1, AVP RF.

110. Report from Perényi-Lukács to the Ministry of Foreign Affairs, Moscow, February 13, 1941, K 69, 757. cs., 1941–I–d–1. t., 118–122. fol., MOL.

111. Letter from the directors of the PMKB to the directors of the Manfréd Weiss Company, Budapest, February 27, 1941, Z 402, 6. cs., 33/i–1. sz., MOL.

112. Notes of the interministry conference held at the Ministry of Foreign Affairs. Budapest, March 31, 1941, K 69, 760. cs., 1941–I–4. t., 51.394/1941. sz., MOL.

113. "A Szovjet-Unión keresztül," 1.

114. Béla Geiger, "A Szovjetunió részvétele az 1941-es Budapesti Nemzetközi Vásáron" [Participation of the Soviet Union at the 1941 Budapest International Fair], in *Tanuságtevők*, vol. 4/b, *Visszaemlékezések a magyarországi munkásmozgalom történetéből, 1933–1941* [Witnesses, vol. 4/b, Recollections from the History of the Hungarian Labor Movement, 1933–1941], ed. Katalin Petrák (Budapest, 1984), 486.

115. Report from the Soviet Trade Mission in Vienna to Deputy Commissar for Foreign Trade Moisei Frumkin, Vienna, January 14, 1925, f. 413, op. 2, d. 1991, l. 43, RGAE.

116. Minutes of the meeting of the Council of Ministers. Budapest, January 24, 1941, K 27, 221. d., 3721. sz., 41–42. fol., MOL.

117. Diplomatic note from the Hungarian Legation in Moscow to the Commissariat for Foreign Affairs, Moscow, February 1, 1941, f. 077, op. 18, p. 8, d. 2, l. 37–39, AVP RF.

118. Minutes of the Politburo meeting, Moscow, March 20, 1941, f. 17, op. 3, d. 1036, l. 28, RGASPI.

119. Bárdossy's telegram to Kristóffy, Budapest, April 18, 1941, K 74, 37. d. (Cables to Moscow, 1941), 20. fol., MOL.

120. "Das Ausland auf der Budapester Internatioalen Messe," *Pester Lloyd* (Morgenblatt), April 18, 1941, 10.

121. "Épül a vásár" [The fair is being built], *OMKE*, April 12, 1941, 6.

122. "A kormányzó nyitotta meg a Budapesti Nemzetközi Vásárt" [The regent opened the Budapest International Fair], *Magyar Nemzet*, May 3, 1941, 4.

123. In the Hungarian press the name of the Slovak minister, who was presumably of Hungarian extraction, was used in its Hungarian version as Géza Medricky. In his memoirs Medricky refers to himself under his Slovak name as Gejza. See Gejza Medrický, *Minister spomina* (Bratislava, 1994).

124. Geiger, "A Szovjetunió részvétele," in *Tanúságtevők*, vol. 4/b, *Visszaemlékezések*, ed. Petrák, 488. Béla Geiger, in Russian Bela Janovich Grigoriev, was taken to the Soviet Union as a child with his family as part of the Hungarian-Soviet prisoner of war exchange program in 1922. He worked at the Soviet Legation in Budapest as press referent and interpreter, starting in the summer of 1940.

125. Tofik M. Islamov, ed., *Transil'vanskii vopros: vengero-rumynskii territorialnyi spor i SSSR, 1940–1946: dokumenty rossiiskikh arkhivov* (Moscow, 2000), 151.

126. For instance Horthy's visit could not have been preceded by "throngs" because during his visit the fair was closed to the public. According to contemporary press reports Horthy was accompanied not only by members of his family and Bárdossy. Archduke József Ferenc's visit was most probably not on May 2 but on May 5.

127. The internal arrangements and the material displayed can best be

reconstructed from the reports in *Népszava*. See Lőrinc Kovai, "Tarka mozaikok a Nemzetközi Vásárról" [Colorful mosaics about the International Fair], *Népszava*, May 6, 1941, 7. The success of the Soviet pavilion was partly also due to the unprecedented number of visitors at the BNV in 1941. In this year there were 1.3 million visitors which was an increase of 45 percent compared to the previous year. The leadership of the BNV offered a number of inducements to attract visitors such as arranging for reduced railway fares and also having special trains provided for visitors from the Székely Counties. See "Rekorderedménnyel zárult a Vásár. A BNV zárójelentése" [The fair closed with a record attendance. Closing report of the BNV], *A Piac*, May 24, 1941, 5.

128. "A német pénzügyminiszternek nagyon tetszett a Nemzetközi Vásár" [The German minister of finance liked the fair very much], *Magyar Nemzet*, May 4, 1941, 17.

129. Geiger, "A Szovjetunió részvétele," in *Tanúságtevők*, vol. 4/b, *Visszaemlékezések*, ed. Petrák, 487–488.

130. See for example Imre Kapalyag, ed., *A Budapesti Nemzetközi Vásárok története* [The History of the Budapest International Fairs] (Budapest, 1996), picture no. 11.

131. "Milyen szemmel nézi a BNV látnivalóit a munkáslátogató?" [How does the visiting worker view the exhibits at the BNV?], *Népszava*, May 4, 1941, 11.

132. Geiger, "A Szovjetunió részvétele," in *Tanúságtevők*, vol. 4/b, *Visszaemlékezések*, ed. Petrák, 487–488.

133. Pastor, ed., *A moszkvai követség jelentései*, 314–315.

134. A reporter of *Népszava* visited the exhibit while it was being set up. According to his information parts of Soviet art films and documentaries would be shown in one of the rooms. These included such typically propaganda war movies like the one entitled *The Mannerheim Line*, showing the battles of the Red Army in Finland. Mihály Földes, "A Szovjet-Unió ipara, kereskedelme és mezőgazdasága bemutatkozik a Budapesti Nemzetközi Vásáron" [The industry, commerce and agriculture of the Soviet Union introduces itself at the BNV. *Népszava*, April 26, 1941. pp. 3–4.

135. Minutes of the Politburo meeting, September 6, 1940, f. 17, op. 3, d. 1027, l. 21, RGASPI.

136. Vozhzhov's notes on his discussion with Práger, Budapest, November 15, 1941, f. 413, op. 13, d. 2772, l. 266, RGAE. In his note written on November 18 Vozhzhov stated that after his arrival he had met with the Ganz officials on November 15 and with the MÁVAG officials on November 16. See Vozhzhov's note about his discussion with Ferenc Rosty-Forgách, the deputy chief of the Economic Policy Division of the Ministry of Foreign Affairs, Budapest, November 18, 1940, f. 413, op. 13, d. 2772, l. 262, RGAE.

137. Diplomatic note of the Hungarian Legation in Moscow to the Commissariat for Foreign Affairs, Moscow, April 19, 1941, f. 077, op. 18, p. 8, d. 1, l. 115, AVP RF.

138. Werth's note to Csáky, Budapest, March 3, 1941, K 64, 90. cs., 1941/24. t., 116/1941. res. sz., MOL.

139. The credentials issued to Ivan Stanchev by the Ministry of Foreign Affairs, Sofia, July 3, 1941, f. 176, op. 8, a. e. 1041, l. 1, Centralen darzavan archiv na Republika Bulgarija [Central State Archive of the Republic of Bulgaria] (hereafter cited as CDA).

140. Stanchov's report on the personnel of the Soviet Missions. Svilengrad, July 10, 1941, f. 176, op. 8, a. e. 1041, l. 129–130, CDA.

141. Letter from the Soviet Trade Mission in Budapest to the Manfréd Weiss Company, Budapest, April 25, 1941, Z 406, 463 cs., 9434. sz., MOL.

142. Korolev's notes for the Commissariat for Transport, Moscow, s.d. (after July 8, 1941), f. 17, op. 36, d. 202, l. 8, RGASPL.

143. "Die Finanz- und Wirtschaftpolitik der Regierung. Finanzminister Dr. Reményi-Schneller kündigt in seinem Exposé wichtige Wirtschafts- und Finanzreformen an. Verringerung des Gesamt-defizits auf 48 Millionen," *Pester Lloyd* (Morgenblatt), October 23, 1940, 1–3.

144. *Az 1939. évi június hó 10-ére hirdetett Országgyűlés Képviselő-házának naplója* [Minutes of the Meeting of the House of Representatives of the National Assembly Held on June 10, 1939] (Budapest, 1941), 7:293–294.

145. Ibid., 7:446–449.

146. Artúr Székely, "Aussenhandel der Sowjetunion und die ungarisch-

russischen Handelsabkommen," *Pester Lloyd* (Morgenblatt), October 20, 1940, 12–13.

147. Rajniss was elected to parliament in 1939 as a member of the Magyar Megújulás Párt (Hungarian Renewal Party) the extreme right-wing party of Béla Imrédy. Shortly thereafter he resigned from the party.

148. Kálmán Rátz along with Kálmán Hubay were among the founders of the Arrowcross Party. He was elected to parliament in 1939 on this party's ticket. Somewhat later he resigned from the party. He had served in parliament since 1935 and during this time obtained a doctorate in the humanities. During the early 1940s he wrote several books about Russia and was recognized as an expert.

149. *Az 1939. évi június hó 10-ére*, 287.

150. Ibid., 302–303 and 473–476. The friendly comments of the extreme right-wing parliamentary representatives about the Soviet Union were evidently due to the signing of the Non-Aggression Pact between Germany and the Soviet Union on August 23, 1939, which made the two countries allies. It was therefore improper to question the German-Soviet economic cooperation or the legitimacy and rationale of the Hungarian-Soviet economic discussions. See Balázs Sipos, "Szovjetbarát és szovjetellenes nyilas propaganda 1939–1941" [Pro-Soviet and anti-Soviet Arrowcross Party propaganda, 1939–1941], *Múltunk* 41, no. 2 (1996): 107–132.

151. Report from Kristóffy to Bárdossy, Moscow, April 30, 1941, XIX–J–1–a, 70. d., IV–178. sz. dossier, MOL.

152. My reconstruction. Source: Pap, "A Szovjetunió külkereskedelmi forgalma," 91–94.

153. Goods that can be reported only in numbers. In this instance radio vacuum tubes.

154. My construction. Source: Pap, "A Szovjetunió külkereskedelmi forgalma," p. 91. We have no data on the Hungarian share in total Soviet exports and imports. The Soviet statistics do not show Hungary because compared to the great European trade partners Hungary's share was negligible.

155. "Die Überwachung des Ausenhandels mit der Sowjetunion," *Pester Lloyd* (Morgenblatt), April 17, 1941, 8.

156. Ganz note on the case of the ships, Budapest, June 10, 1941, Z 429, 37. cs., 180. sz., MOL.

157. Minutes of the Council of Ministers meeting, Budapest, September 16, 1941, K 27, 231. d., 3814. sz., 27–30. fol., MOL.

158. Varga's letter to the directors of Ganz, Budapest, September 24, 1941, Z 429, 37. cs., 180. sz., MOL. The letter to be sent to Ganz was submitted by the minister of industry and commerce to the Council of Ministers for approval. See previous note.

159. The figures have been rounded off. The Foreign Commerce Office's statement on the balance of the Hungary-Soviet Union trade, Budapest, June 24, 1941, K 69, 759. cs., 1941–I–1. t., 5–9. fol., MOL.

160. The text of the ordinance is in *Budapesti Közlöny*, October 11, 1942, 5.

161. Ganz report to the Foreign Commerce Office, Budapest, November 10, 1942, Z 429, 37. cs., 180. sz., MOL.

162. Letter from Rosslav to Ganz, Budapest, June 30, 1943, Z 429, 37. cs., 180. sz., MOL.

SOURCES AND PROFESSIONAL LITERATURE

ARCHIVAL SOURCES

Russian Sources

Arkhiv Vneshnei Politiki Rossiiskoi Federatsii
(AVP RF)
.......................[Foreign Policy Archives of the Russian Federation]

.....Secretariat of Commissar for Foreign Affairs Georgii Chicherin (f. 04)
op. 11, p. 67, d. 938.
op. 11, p. 68, d. 946.

.....Secretariat of Commissar for Foreign Affairs Maksim Litvinov (f. 05)
op. 14, p. 97, d. 28.

.....Secretariat of Deputy Commissar for Foreign Affairs Nikolai Krestinski
(f. 010)
op. 10, p. 50, d. 32, 33, and 39.
op. 11, p. 68, d. 29 and 30.
op. 13, p. 81, d. 1.

.....Secretariat of Commissar for Foreign Affairs Viacheslav Molotov
(f. 06)
op. 1, p. 7, d. 60.
op. 2, p. 13, d. 137.
.....Hungarian Desktop. 18, p. 8, d. 1 and 2.
op. 20, p. 109, d. 1.

**Rossiiskii gosudarstvennyi arkhiv ekonomiki
(RGAE)**
...............[Russian State Archive of the Economy]

.....Commissariat for Foreign Trade (f. 413)
op. 2, d. 1803, 1991, and 2008.
op. 5, d. 1169.
op. 10, d. 194.
op. 13, d. 518, 2781, 2829, 3781, 3816, and 3829.

.....Commissariat for Transportation (f. 413)
op. 1, d. 451, l. 4.

**Gosudarstvennyi arkhiv Rossiiskoi Federatsii
(GA RF)**
...............[State Archive of the Russian Federation]

.....Supreme Concession Committee (f. 8350)
op. 1, d. 1439 and 1440.

**Rossiiskii gosudarstvennyi arkhiv sotsialno-
politicheskoi istorii (RGASPI)**
...............[Russian State Archives of Social and Political History]

.....(All-)Russian Communist Party (Bolshevik)—All-Union Communist
Party (Bolshevik), Central Committee (f. 17)
op. 3, d. 257, 940, 949, 1027, and 1036.

.....Personal Papers of Commissar for Foreign Affairs Maksim Litvinov
(f. 359)
op. 1, d. 9.

Hungarian Sources

Magyar Országos Levéltár (MOL)
...............[National Archives of Hungary]

.....Minutes of the Council of Ministers Meetings (K 27)
212. d.
221. d.
231. d.

.....Ministry of Foreign Affairs, Policy Division, Restricted Papers (K 64)
  6. cs., 1922/24. t.
 10. cs., 1924/24. t.
 60. cs., 1934/24. t.
 90. cs., 1941/24. t.

.....Ministry of Foreign Affairs, Economic Policy Division (K 69)
 85. cs., 1922/108. t.
 88. cs., 1922/109. t.
141. cs., 1923/10. t.
147. cs., 1923/10. t.
176. cs., 1924/107. t.
380. cs., 54.180/1931. sz.
381. cs., 1933/39. t.
667. cs., 1935–II–b. t.
756. cs., 1934–I–c. t.
759. cs., 1941–I–1, t., 1941–II–b. t., and 1941–II–f. t.
757. cs., 1935–I–d–2. t. and 1941–I–d. t.
758. cs., 1941–I–i. t.
760. cs., 1941–I–4. t.
789. cs., 3. sz.

.....Ministry of Foreign Affairs, Legal Division (K 70)
337. cs., 1934–II–1. t.

.....Ministry of Foreign Affairs, Code Division (K 74)
37. d.

.....Ministry of Internal Affairs, Restricted Papers (K 149)
20. d., 1933/6. t.

.....Pest Hungarian Bank of Commerce, Projects (Z 40)
9. cs., 257. sz.

.....Anglo-Hungarian Bank, Archives (Z 96)
64. cs., 83. t.
66. cs., 85. t.

.....Weiss Manfréd Steel and Metal Works, Archives (Z 402)
2. cs., 33/XLI. T., 33/XLV. t.
6. cs., 33/i–1. sz.

.....Technical Division of Ganz and Co. Electric, Machine, Wagon and Ship-building Factory (Z 429)
37. cs., 180. sz.

.....Secretariat of Hoffherr-Schrantz-Clayton-Shuttleworth Hungarian Machine Works (Z 450)
115. cs., 802. t.

.....Executive Directorate of Hungarian-Belgian Mineral Oil Company (Z1202)
1.cs., 18. t.

.....Hungarian Legation in Moscow, Reports (X–9581)
36.199. tek.

.....Ministry of Foreign Affairs, Peace Preparatory Division (XIX–J–1-a)
70. d., IV–178. sz.

Politikatörténeti és Szakszervezeti Levéltár (PSZL)
.....................[Political History and Trade Union Archives]

.....Personal Papers of Mihály Arnóthy-Jungerth (972. f.)
3. ő. e.
4. ő. e.
5. ő. e.
9. ő. e.

Hadtörténelmi Levéltár (HL
...............[Military History Archives]
.....Chief of Staff Office (1/89. f.)
B/172. tek.

Budapest Főváros Levéltára (BFL)
...............[Budapest City Archives]
.....Court of registration (VII/2. e.)
3398. d., Cg. 20788/1924. sz.

Magyar Államvasutak Központi Irattára (MÁV KI)
...............[Central Archives of Hungarian State Railways]
.....Miskolc Business Office (FA 17)
7515/1941. sz.
10.585/1941. sz.

Bulgarian Sources

Centralen darzavan archiv na Republika Bulgarija
(CDA)
...............[Central State Archive of the Republic Bulgaria]
.....Ministry of Foreign Affairs, Political Division (f. 176.)
op. 8, a. e. 1041.

PUBLISHED SOURCES

Collections of Documents

Diplomáciai iratok Magyarország külpolitikájához 1936–1945. Vol 3,
Magyarország külpolitikája 1938–1939 [Diplomatic Documents
on Hungary's Foreign Policy 1936–1945. Vol. 3, Hungary's

Foreign Policy 1938–1939]. Edited by Magda Ádám. Budapest, 1970.

Diplomáciai iratok Magyarország külpolitikájához 1936–1945. Vol. 4, *Magyarország külpolitikája a II. világháború kitörésének idősza-kában 1939–1940* [Diplomatic Documents on Hungary's Foreign Policy 1936–1945. Vol. 4, Hungary's Foreign Policy at the Period of the Outbreak of World War II 1939–1940]. Edited by Gyula Juhász. Budapest, 1962.

Dokumenty vneshnei politiki 1940–22 iiunia 1941. Vol. 23, bk. 1, *1 ianvaria–31 oktiabria 1940 g.* Edited by G. E. Mamedov. Moscow, 1995.

Dokumenty vneshnei politiki 1940–22 iiunia 1941. Vol 23, bk. 2, pt. 1, *1 noiabria 1940 g.–1 marta 1941 g.* Edited by G. E. Mamedov. Moscow, 1998. *Dokumenty vneshnei politiki SSSR.* Vol. 5, *1 ianvaria–19 noiabria 1922 g.* Edited by Andrei Gromyko. Moscow, 1961.

Dokumenty vneshnei politiki SSSR. Vol. 17, *1 anvaria– 31 dekabria 1934 g.* Edited by Andrei Gromyko. Moscow, 1971.

Horthy Miklós titkos iratai [The Secret Papers of Miklós Horthy]. Edited by Miklós Szinai and László Szücs. Budapest, 1972.

Inostrannye kontsessii v SSSR: 1920–1930 gg.: dokumenty i materialy. Edited by Maksim M. Zagorul'ko. Moscow, 2005.

Iratok az ellenforradalom történetéhez 1919–1945. Vol. 3, *Az ellenfor-radalmi rendszer gazdasági helyzete és politikája Magyarországon 1924–1926* [Documents on the History of the Counter-revolu-tion 1919–1945. Vol. 3, The Economic Situation and the Policies of the Counterrevolution 1924–1926]. Edited by Dezső Nemes and Elek Karsai. Budapest, 1959.

Iratok a magyar külügyi szolgálat történetéhez 1918–1945 [Documents on the History of the Hungarian Foreign Service 1918-1945]. Edited by Pál Pritz. Budapest, 1995.

A moszkvai magyar követség jelentései 1935–1941 [Reports of the Hun-garian Legation in Moscow 1935–1941]. Edited by Peter Pastor. Buda-pest, 1992.

A Palazzo Chigi és Magyarország. Olasz diplomáciai dokumentumok Magyarországról a Gömbös-kormány időszakában. 1932–1936 [The Palazzo Chigi and Hungary. Italian Diplomatic Documents

on Hungary in the Period of the Gömbös Government. 1932–
1936]. Edited by György Réti. Budapest, 2003.

Sovetsko-rumynskie otnosheniia. Vol. 2, *1935–1941. Documenty i materialy.* Edited by A. A. Avdeev and M. R. Ungureanu. Moscow, 2000.

*Transil'vanskii vopros: vengero-rumynskii territorial'nyi spor i SSSR,
1940–1946: dokumenty rossiiskikh arkhivov.* Edited by Tofik M.
Islamov. Moscow, 2000.

Handbooks and Reference Books

Az 1922. június hó 16-ra hirdetett Nemzetgyűlés naplója [Minutes of
the National Assembly Summoned for June 16, 1922]. Vol. 26.
Budapest, 1924.

*Az 1927. évi januar hó 25.-ére hirdetett Országgyűlés Képviselőházá-
nak naplója* [Minutes of the National Assembly House of
Representatives Summoned for January 25, 1927]. Vol. 36. Budapest, 1931.

*Az 1939. évi június hó 10.-ére hirdetett Országgyűlés Képviselőházának
naplója.* [Minutes of the National Assembly House of Representatives Summoned for June 10, 1939]. Vol. 7. Budapest, 1941.

Bélay, Vilmos and Mária Kohut, eds. *A Kereskedelemügyi Minisztériumi Levéltár (1889–1899), a Kereskedelem és Közlekedésügyi
Minisztériumi Levéltár (1935–1945). Repertórium.* (Levéltári
leltárak 12) [Ministry of Commerce Archives (1889–1899),
Ministry of Commerce and Communication Archives (1935–
1945). Repertory (Archival Collections 12)]. Budapest, 1961.

Dekrety sovetskoi vlasti. Vol 2, *17 marta–10 iiulia 1918.* g. Edited by G.
D. Obichkin. Moscow, 1959.

Gazdasági, pénzügyi és tőzsdei kompasz az 1934–1935 évre [Economic,
Financial and Stock Market Register for 1934–1935]. Vol 3–4.
Edited by János Kallós. Budapest, 1934.

Gazdasági, pénzügyi és tőzsdei kompasz az 1935–1936 évre [Econo-
mic, Financial and Stock Market Register for 1935–1936]. Vol.
3–4. Edited by János Kallós, Budapest, 1935.

Magyar Törvénytár; 1875–1876 évi törvények [Hungarian Record of
Laws, the 1875–1876 Acts]. Budapest, 1896.

Magyar Törvénytár, Az 1921. évi törvénycikkek [Hungarian Record of Laws, the 1921 Acts]. Edited by Gyula Térfy. Budapest, 1922.

Magyar Törvénytár, Az 1924. évi törvénycikkek [Hungarian Record of Laws, the 1924 Acts]. Edited by Gyula Térfy. Budapest, 1925.

Magyar Törvénytár, Az 1939. évi törvénycikkek [Hungarian Record of Laws, the 1921 Acts]. Edited by Miklós Degré and Alajos Várady-Brenner. Budapest, 1940.

Magyar Statisztikai Közlemények. Vol. 53, A Magyar Szent Korona országainak 1913. évi külkereskedelmi forgalma. [Hungarian Statistical Reports. Vol. 53, Foreign Commerce Activity of the Lands of the Hungarian Sacred Crown in 1913.]. Budapest, 1915.

Magyar Statisztikai Közlemények. Vol. 75, Magyarország 1925 és 1926. évi külkereskedelmi forgalma [Hungarian Statistical Reports. Vol. 75, Hungary's foreign commerce activity in 1925 and 1926]. Budapest, 1929.

Magyar Statisztikai Közlemények. Vol. 77, Magyarország 1927. évi külkereskedelmi forgalma [Hungarian Statistical Reports. Vol. 77, Hungary's Foreign Commerce Activity in 1925 and 1926]. Budapest, 1929.

Magyar Statisztikai Közlemények. Vol. 75, Magyarország 1928. évi külkereskedelmi forgalma [Hungarian Statistical Reports. Vol. 75, Hungary's Foreign Commerce Activity in 1928]. Budapest, 1930.

Magyar Statisztikai Közlemények. Vol. 80, Magyarország 1929. évi külkereskedelmi forgalma [Hungarian Statistical Reports. Vol. 80, Hungary's Foreign Commerce Activity in 1929]. Budapest, 1931.

Magyar Statisztikai Közlemények. Vol. 81, Magyarország 1930. évi külkereskedelmi forgalma [Hungarian Statistical Reports. Vol. 81, Hungary's Foreign Commerce Activity in 1930). Budapest, 1931.

Magyar Statisztikai Közlemények. Vol. 82, Magyarország 1931. évi külkereskedelmi forgalma [Hungarian Statistical Reports. Vol. 82, Hungary's Foreign Commerce Activity in 1931]. Budapest, 1933.

Magyar Statisztikai Közlemények. Vol. 84, Magyarország 1932. évi külkereskedelmi forgalma [Hungarian Statistical Reports. Vol. 84, Hungary's Foreign Commerce Activity in 1932), Budapest, 1933.

Magyar Statisztikai Közlemények. Vol. 85, Magyarország 1933. évi külkereskedelmi forgalma [Hungarian Statistical Reports. Vol. 85, Hungary's Foreign Commerce Activity in 1933]. Budapest, 1934.

Magyar Statisztikai Közlemények. Vol. 95, *Magyarország 1934. évi külkereskedelmi forgalma* [Hungarian Statistical Reports. Vol. 95, Hungary's foreign commerce activity in 1934]. Budapest, 1935.
Magyar Statisztikai Közlemények. Vol. 98, *Magyarország 1935. évi külkereskedelmi forgalma* [Hungarian Statistical Reports. Vol. 98, Hungary's Foreign Commerce Activity in 1935]. Budapest, 1936.
Magyar Statisztikai Közlemények. Vol. 101, *Magyarország 1936. évi külkereskedelmi forgalma* [Hungarian Statistical Reports, Vol. 101, Hungary's foreign commerce activity in 1936]. Budapest, 1937.
Magyar Statisztikai Közlemények. Vol. 106, *Magyarország 1937. évi külkereskedelmi forgalma* [Hungarian Statistical Reports. Vol. 106, Hungary's Foreign Commerce Activity in 1937]. Budapest, 1938.
Magyar Statisztikai Közlemények. Vol. 109, *Magyarország 1938. évi külkereskedelmi forgalma* [Hungarian Statistical Reports. Vol. 109, Hungary's Foreign Commerce Activity in 1938]. Budapest, 1939.
Nagy Magyar Compass (Azelőtt Mihók-féle). 1922–1924. Vol. 49, pt. 2, *(Az 1925-ik évre)* [The Great Hungarian Annals (Formerly à la Mihók). 1922–1924. Vol. 49, pt. 2, (For year 1925). Published by Sándor Galánthai Nagy. Budapest 1925.
Vneshniaia torgovlia SSSR za 1918–1940 gg.: Statisticheskii obzor. Edited by A. D. Chistov. Moscow, 1960.
Vneshniaia torgovlia SSSR za 20 let. Statisticheskii spravochnik. Edited by Sergei N. Bakulin and Dmitrii D. Mishustin. Moscow, 1939.

MEMOIRS

Béla Geiger, "A Szovjetunió részvétele az 1941-es Budapesti Nemzetközi Vásáron" [Participation of the Soviet Union at the Budapest International Fair]. In *Tanúságtevők.* Vol. 4/b, *Visszaemlékezések a magyarországi munkásmozgalom történetéből 1933–1941* [Witnesses. Vol. 4/b, Recollections from the History of the Hungarian Labor Movement 1933–1941]. Edited by Katalin Petrák. Budapest, 1984.
Gusztáv Gratz, *Magyarország a két háború között* [Hungary between the Two Wars]. Budapest, 2001.
Mihály Arnóthy-Jungerth, *Moszkvai napló* [Moscow Diary]. Edited Péter Sipos and László Szücs. Budapest, 1989.

MONOGRAPHS

Belousov, Rem A. *Ekonomicheskaia istoriia Rossii—XX vek*, bk. 2, *Cherez revoliutsiiu k NEPu*. Moscow, 2000.

Belousov, Rem A. *Ekonomicheskaia istoriia Rossii*, bk. 3, *Tiazhelye gody rosta i obnovleniia*. Moscow, 2002.

Buday, László. *Magyarország küzdelmes évei* [Hungary's Years of Struggle]. Budapest, 1923.

Búzás, József and András Nagy. *Magyarország külkereskedelme 1919–1945* (Hungary's Foreign Trade 1919–1945). Budapest, 1961.

Csikós-Nagy, Béla. *A XX. század magyar gazdaságpolitikája. Tanulságok az ezredforduló küszöbén* [Hungary's Twentieth Century Econo-mic Policy. Lessons at the Threshold of the New Millennium]. Buda-pest, 1996.

Gimpel'son, Efim G. *NEP i sovetskaia politicheskaia sistema: 20-e gody*. Moscow, 2000.

Gorodetsky, Gabriel. *Rokovoi samoobman. Stalin i napadenie Germanii na Sovetskii Soiuz*. Moscow, 2001.

Gunst, Péter. *Magyarország gazdaságtörténete (1914–1989)* [Hungary's economic history 1914–1989]. Budapest, 1996.

Hegedűs, István, *Az egykéz* [The One Hand]. Budapest, 1938.

Honvári, János, ed. *Magyarország gazdaságtörténete a honfoglalástól a 20. század közepéig* [Hungary's Economic History from the Conquest to the Middle of the Twentieth Century]. Budapest, 1995.

Juhász, Gyula. *Magyarország külpolitikája 1919–1944* [Hungary's Foreign Policy 1919–1944]. Budapest, 1988.

Kaposi, Zoltán. *Magyarország gazdaságtörténete* [The Economic History of Hungary]. Budapest, 2002.

Khlevniuk, Oleg V. *Politbiuro: mekhanizmy politicheskoi vlasti v 1930-e gody*. Moscow, 1996.

Khromov, Semen S., ed. *Inostrannye kontsessii v SSSR: istoricheskii ocherk, dokumenty*. Moscow, 2006.

Kudrov, Valentin M. *Sovetskaia ekonomika v retrospektive: opyt pereosmysleniia*. Moscow, 1997.

Pushkash, Andrei I. *Vneshniaia politika Vengrii. Aprel' 1927–fevral' 1934 gg.* Moscow, 1995.

Ránki, György. *Gazdaság és külpolitika. A nagyhatalmak harca a dél-kelet-európai gazdasági hegemóniáért. 1919–1939* [Economiy and Foreign Policy. The Fight of the Great Powers for Economic Hegemony in Southeastern Europe, 1919–1939]. Budapest, 1981.

Reményi, Lajos. *Külkereskedelempolitika Magyarországon 1919– 1924.* Gazdaságtörténeti értekezések. 5 [Foreign Trade Policy in Hungary 1919–1924. Economic History Dissertations 5]. Budapest, 1969.

Shishkin, Valerii A. *Stanovlenie vneshnei politiki poslerevoliutsionnoi Rossii (1917–1930 gody) i kapitalisticheskii mir: ot revoliut-sionnogo "zapadnichestva" k "natsional-bol'shevizmu bol'shevizmu": ocherk istorii.* St. Petersburg, 2002.

Surányi, Róbert. *A brit Munkáspárt és a Szovjetunió (1917–1924)* [The British Labour Party and the Soviet Union (1917–1924)]. Budapest, 1993.

Torkunov, Anatolii V., ed., *Ocherki istorii Min*

Werth, Nicolas. *Istoriia sovetskogo gosudarstva, 1900–1991.* Moscow, 2003.

Zhiromskaia, V. B., ed. *Naselenie Rossii v XX veke: istoricheskie ocherki.* Moscow, 2000.

ESSAYS

Ádám, Magda. "The Genova Conference and the Little Entente." In *Genoa, Rapallo and European reconstruction in 1922,* edited by Carole Fink, Axel Frohn, and Jurgen Heideking, 187–199. Cambridge, 1991.

Afontsev, S. V. "Ot Rossiskoi imperii k SSSR. Struktura torgovlii so stranami Zapada." In *Ekonomicheskaia istoriia. Ezhegodnik. 2006,* edited by I. A. Petrov, 32–60. Moscow, 2006.

Bekker, Zsuzsa and Mária Hild, "Közgazdaságtan a két világháború között" [Economics between the two World Wars]. In *Magyar közgazdasági gondolkodás (a közgazdasági irodalom kezdeteitől a II. világháborúig). Gazdaságelméleti olvasmányok 2* [Hungarian Economic Thought (from the Beginning of the Economic Literature to World War II). Readings in Economic Theory 2], edited by Zsuzsa Bekker, 413–541. Budapest, 2002.

Bokarev, Y. P. "Rossiiskaia ekonomika v mirovoi ekonomicheskoi sisteme (konets XIX–30–e gg. XX v.)." in *Ekonomicheskaia istoriia Rossii XIX–XX vv.: sovremennyi vzgliad,* edited by Vladimir A. Vinogradov, 433–457. Moscow, 2001.

Búzás, József. "A szovjet-magyar kereskedelmi kapcsolatok történetéhez 1919–1938" [On the History of the Soviet-Hungarian Trade Relations, 1919–1938]. *Századok* 89, nos. 4–5. (1955): 588–633.

Dolmányos, István. "A magyar-szovjet diplomáciai kapcsolatok egy napló tükrében (1920–1939)" [Hungarian-Soviet diplomatic relationships as reflected in the mirror of a diary, 1920–1939]. *Valóság* 9, no. 1 (1966): 73–85.

Fink, Carole. "NEP vo vneshnei politike. Genuezskaia konferentsia i rapallskii dogovor." In *Sovetskaia vneshniaia politika v retrospective, 1917–1991,* edited by Aleksandr O. Chubar'ian, 60–69. Moscow, 1993.

Gellért, Andor. "Magyar diplomaták Moszkvában. A magyar-szovjet viszony a moszkvai magyar királyi követség titkos jelentései tükrében" [Hungarian diplomats in Moscow. Hungarian-Soviet Relations as reflected by the secret reports of the Royal Hungarian Legation in Moscow]. *Új Látóhatár* 26, no.1 (1975): 17–37.

Kolontári, Attila. "Magyar-szovjet tárgyalások a diplomáciai és kereskedelmi kapcsolatok felvételéről (Berlin, 1924)" [Hungarian-Soviet negotiations about the resumption of diplomatic and economic relations. (Berlin, 1924)]. In *Kutatási Füzetek, no. 5 (A Janus Pannonius Tudományegyetem Történelmi Doktori Programjának sorozata),* edited by Mária Ormos, József Kánya, and Mónika Pilkhoffer, 3–29. Pécs, 1999.

Kolontári, Attila. "A magyar-szovjet viszony alakulása 1925 és 1934 között" [Evolution of Hungarian-Soviet Relations between 1925 and 1934]. In *A Pécsi Tudományegyetem Illyés Gyula Főiskolai Kara Társadalomtudományi Tanszékének Közleményei* [Publications of the Illyés Gyula College Faculty's Sociology Department at the University of Pécs], edited by Attila Kolontári, 5:66–113. Szekszárd, 2002.

Kolontári, Attila. "A diplomáciai kapcsolatok felvétele Magyarország és a Szovjetunió között 1934-ben" [The establishment of diplomatic relations between Hungary and the Soviet Union in 1934]. *Múltunk* 49, no. 3 (2004): 120–156.

Kolontári, Attila. "A Szovjetunió és az első bécsi döntés" [The Soviet Union and the First Vienna Award]. *Limes* 20, no. 2 (2007): 21–36.

Kolontári, Attila. "Az egyik legstabilabb határszakasz Európában. Adalékok a szovjet-magyar kapcsolatok történetéhez 1939–1941" [One of the most stable frontiers in Europe. Addenda to the history of of the Hungarian-Soviet relationships 1939–1941]. In *"Önkényuralom, alkotmányosság, forradalom." Előadások és tanulmányok az első orosz forradalom 100 éves évfordulója alkalmából.* MOSZT Könyvek 1 ["Dictatorship, Constitutionality, Revolution." Lectures and Essays on the One Hundredth Anniversary of the First Russian Revolution. MOSZT Books 1], edited by Tamás Polgár, 118–136. Pécs, 2006.

Kövér, György. "A Szovjetunió és Közép-Kelet-Európa. Gazdasági érintkezés a két világháború között" [The Soviet Union and east central Europe. Economic contacts between the two World Wars]. *Történelmi Szemle* 29, nos. 3–4 (1986): 481–489.

Kövér, György. "Egy magánbankár a XX. században—Krausz Simon" [A Private banker in the twentieth century—Simon Krausz]. *Valóság* 30, no. 9 (1987): 56–62.

Mozokhin, O. B. and V. P. Iampolski. "O privlechenii inostrannogo kapitala v ekonomiku SSSR. 1920-e gg." *Istoricheskii arkhiv*, 2002, no. 1:101–115.

N. Czaga, Viktória. "A cégbíróságról és a cégbírósági irattárról" [On the Court of Registration and on the Court of Registration Archives]. *Üzemtörténeti Értesítő* 10, no. 10 (1991): 72–83.

Nőtel, Vilmos. "A magyar ipari termelés finanszírozása" [Financing Hungarian Industrial Production]. Pt. 2. *Közgazdasági Szemle* 84 (1941): 628–654.

Pap, László. "A Szovjetunió külkereskedelmi forgalma" [The Foreign Trade of the Soviet Union]. *Magyar Statisztikai Szemle* 12, nos. 1–6 (1945): 80–95.

Peikovska, Penka. "Bâlgarskijat dnevnik na Mihály Jungerth-Arnóthy, ungarski p'lnomoshchen ministr v Sofija prez 1939–1944" [Bulgarian log of Mihály Jungerth-Arnóthy, Hungarian plenipotentiary minister in 1939–1944]. *Izvestija na dârzhavnite arkhivi* 63 (1992): 87–139.

Petrov, Iurii. A. "Rossiiskaia ekonomika v nachale XX v." In *Rossiia v nachale XX veka*, edited by Andrei N. Sakharov et al., 168–223. Moscow, 2002.

Pogány, Ágnes. "Bankárok és üzletfelek. A Magyar Általános Hitelbank és vállalati ügyfelei a két világháború között" [Bankers and clients. The Hungarian General Bank of Credit and its corporate clients between the two World Wars]. *Replika* 8, no. 3. (1997): 55– 66.

Pritz, Pál. "A magyar külügyi szolgálat 1944-ben a német megszállástól október 15-ig" [The Hungarian Foreign Service in 1944 from the German Occupation to October 15]. *Múltunk* 44, no. 4 (1999): 120–137.

Seres, Attila. "Magyar-szovjet titkos tárgyalások Genovában, 1922-ben. Bánffy Miklós magyar külügyminiszter feljegyzései" [Secret Hungarian-Soviet negotiations in Genoa, in 1922. The Hungarian Minister of Foreign Affairs Miklós Bánffy's notes]. *Fons* 8, no. 3 (2001): 397–411.

Seres, Attila. "Orosz levéltári források a magyar-szovjet diplomáciai kapcsolatok történetéhez (1939)" [Russian archival sources on the history of the Hungarian-Soviet Diplomatic Relations]. *Lymbus. Magyarságtudományi Forrásközlemények* 3 (2005): 207–249.

Seres, Attila. "Orosz levéltári források a magyar-szovjet diplomáciai kapcsolatok felvételéről (1934)" [Russian Archival Sources on the establishment of the Hungarian-Soviet Diplomatic Relationships]. *Világtörténet* 30, nos. 1–2 (2008): 69–92.

Seres, Attila. "Magyar külkereskedelmi politika és a szovjet piac az 1920-as években" [Hungarian Foreign Trade Policy and the Soviet Market in the 1920s]. *Történelmi Szemle* 50, no. 3 (2008): 407–433.

Seres, Attila. "Magyar-szovjet kereskedelmi kapcsolatok 1939–1941. Adalékok Magyarország hadba lépés előtti külgazdasági mozgásterének vizsgálatához" [Hungarian-Soviet trade relations 1939–1941. Addenda for the study of Hungary's economic moves abroad prior to its entry into war). Pts. 1 and 2, *Történelmi Szemle* 49, no. 3 (2007): 403–427; 50, no. 1 (2008): 73–94.

Seres, Attila. "Koncessziós vállalatok a Szovjetunióban a két világháború között" [Concession enterprises in the Soviet Union between the two World Wars]. *Világtörténet* 29, nos. 3–4 (2007): 30–46.

Seres, Attila. "A budapesti szovjet követség jelentései 1934–1935" [Reports from the Soviet Legation in Budapest, 1934–1935]. *Lymbus. Magyarságtudományi Forrásközlemények* 5 (2007): 225–292.

Seres, Attila. "A szovjet piac 'meghódítása' és a magyar tőke Trianon után. Iratok a szovjet-magyar vegyes kereskedelmi társaság történetéhez (1923)" [The conquest of the Soviet market and Hungarian capital after Trianon. Documents for the history of the Soviet-Hungarian Joint Trade Enterprise (1923)]. *Századok* 140, no. 1 (2006): 79–125.

Sipos, Balázs. "Szovjetbarát és szovjetellenes nyilas propaganda 1939–1941" (Pro-Soviet and anti-Soviet Arrowcross Party propaganda 1939–1941) *Múltunk* 41, no. 2 (1996): 107–132.

Szalay, Zoltán. "A Szovjetunió bányászata és kohászata" [Mining and Metalurgy in the Soviet Union]. *Magyar Statisztikai Szemle* 12, nos. 1–6 (1945): 62–75.

Székely, Artúr. "A magyar külkereskedelem irányainak változásai a forgalmi korlátozások éveiben, 1930–1934" (Changes in the Hungarian foreign trade during the years of traffic limitations, 1930–1934). *Közgazdasági Szemle* 78 (1935): 154–168.

Seniavskii, A. S. "Novaia ekonomicheskaia politika. Sovremennie podkhodi i perspektivy izucheniia." In *NEP. Ekonomicheskie, politicheskie i sotsiokul'turnye aspekty,* 5–25. Moscow, 2006.

Szőllősy, Zoltán. "Mezőgazdaság, állattenyésztés és erdészet a Szovjetunióban" [Agriculture, animal husbandry and forestry in the Soviet Union] *Magyar Statisztikai Szemle* 12, nos. 1–6 (1945): 50–61.

Thirring, Lajos. "A Szovjeunió népességének száma és összetétele" [The number and composition of the population of the Soviet Union]. *Magyar Statisztikai Szemle* 12, nos. 1–6 (1945): 12–28.

Varga, Éva Mária. "Hungarica-kutatás az oroszországi levéltárakban" [Hungary-related research in the Russian archives]. *Levéltári Szemle* 53, no. 4 (2003): 3–18.

Vatlin, Aleksandr Y. "Vneshniaia politika i Komintern." In *Rossiia nepovskaia,* edited by Sergei A. Pavliuchenkov, 331–375. Moscow, 2002.

Zeidler, Miklós. "Társadalom és gazdaság Trianon után" [Society and economy after Trianon]. *Limes* 15, no. 2 (2002): 11–18.

DAILY AND WEEKLY PAPERS

Soviet daily and weekly papers
Ekonomicheskaia Zhizn', *Izvestiia*, *Pravda*, *Vneshniaia torgovlia*

Hungarian daily and weekly papers
Az Ellenőr, A Piac, Budapesti Hírlap, Budapest Közlöny, Független Magyarország, Jövő, Külkereskedelmi Hírek, Magyar Gyáripar, Magyar Nemzet, Magyarország, Magyarság, Népszava, OMKE, Pesti Napló, Pesti Tőzsde, Pester Lloyd, Az Újság.

ECONOMIC RELATIONS
IN PICTURES

Members of the Hungarian trade delegation after their arrival at Kiev Station
Moscow, May 25, 1934
Rossiiski gosudarstvenyi arkhiv kino-fotodokumentov (RGAKFD)
[The Russian State Archives of Film and Photo Documentation]

Mihály Arnóthy-Jungerth, Hungarian minister in Moscow, at the reception of the Hungarian trade delegation at Kiev Station
Moscow, May 25, 1934
(RGAKFD)

The members of the Hungarian trade delegation in front of Hotel Astoria
Leningrad, June 10, 1934
Magyar Nemzeti Múzeum (MNM) [Hungarian National Museum] Photo Collection

Aleksandr Bekzadian, Soviet minister, on his arrival in Budapest
On the right: Semion Mirnii, first secretary of legation, on the left: Mikhail Shaprov, second secretary
Budapest, December 19, 1934
(MNM Photo Collection)

Aleksandr Bekzadian and his two secretaries of
the legation in the Parliament Building
Budapest, January 3, 1935
(MNM Photo Collection)

Aleksandr Bekzadian, Soviet minister and his
wife at the entrance to the Mátyás Church
Budapest, August 22, 1935
(MNM Photo Collection)

Regent Miklós Horthy and
Prime Minister László
Bárdossy in front of the
Soviet Pavilon
Budapest International Fair
(BNV), May, 2, 1941
(MNM Photo Collection)

Inner portal of the Soviet
pavilion.
BNV, May 2–12, 1941.
Photo by József Olbort
(MNM Photo Collection)

Interior of the Soviet pavilion. Decorative
porcelain dish with Stalin's portrait
BNV, May 2–12, 1941
(MNM Photo Collection)

Interior of the Soviet pavilion
BNV, May 2–12, 1941
Photo by Tamás Fehér
(MNM Photo Collection)

Interior of the Soviet pavilion. The writer, Zsigmond Móricz, in front of the model of the Lenin statue
BNV, May 2–12, 1941 (MNM Photo Collection)

MAPS

1. The Regions of Historic Hungary

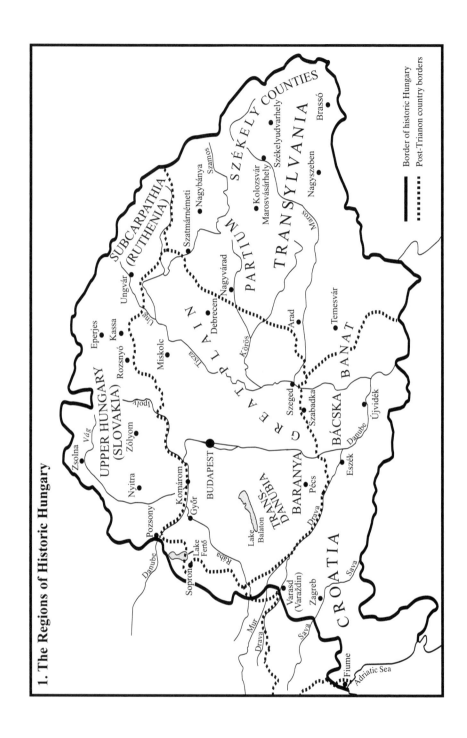

SZÉKELY COUNTIES

SUBCARPATHIA (RUTHENIA)

TRANSYLVANIA

PARTIUM

Brassó
Székelyudvarhely
Marosvásárhely
Kolozsvár
Nagyszeben

Nagybánya
Szamos
Szatmárnémeti
Ungvár
Ung
Nagyvárad
Debrecen
Arad
Körös
Temesvár
Maros

BANAT
GREAT PLAIN

Eperjes
Kassa
Rozsnyó
Miskolc
Tisza
Szeged
Szabadka
Újvidék

UPPER HUNGARY (SLOVAKIA)
Zólyom
Ipoly
BÁCSKA
Danube

Vág
Zsolna
Nyitra
Komárom
BUDAPEST
TRANS-DANUBIA
BARANYA
Pécs
Eszék
Győr
Pozsony
Danube
Lake Fertő
Rába
Lake Balaton
Dráva
Drava
Sopron
CROATIA
Sava
Varasd (Varaždin)
Zagreb
Mur
Drava
Sava

Fiume
Adriatic Sea

Border of historic Hungary
Post-Trianon country borders

2. Recovered Hungarian Territories (1938–1941)

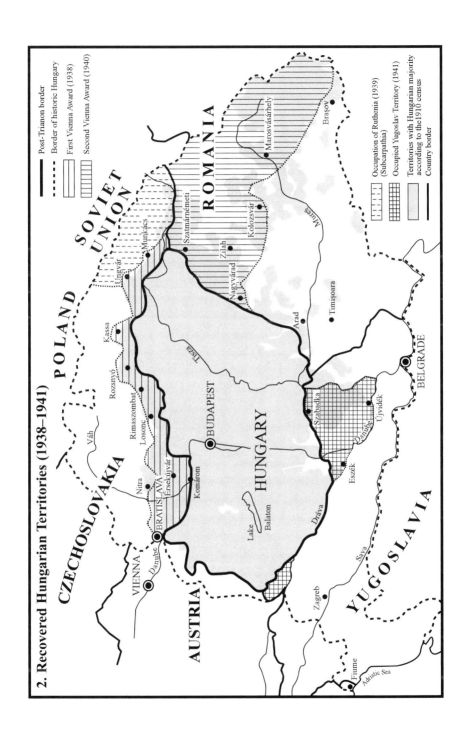

Post-Trianon border
Border of historic Hungary
First Vienna Award (1938)
Second Vienna Award (1940)

Occupation of Ruthenia (1939) (Subcarpathia)
Occupied Yugoslav Territory (1941)
Territories with Hungarian majority according to the 1910 census
Country border

POLAND

SOVIET UNION

CZECHOSLOVAKIA

VIENNA

AUSTRIA

Danube
Váh
Nitra
BRATISLAVA
Érsekújvár
Komárom
Rimaszombat
Losonc
Rozsnyó
Kassa
Ungvár
Munkács

HUNGARY

BUDAPEST

Lake Balaton

Tisza

Tisza

ROMANIA

Szatmárnémeti
Zilah
Nagyvárad
Kolozsvár
Marosvásárhely
Brașov
Arad
Mureș
Timișoara

Dráva

Eszék
Újvidék
Szabadka
Danube

BELGRADE

YUGOSLAVIA

Zagreb
Sava

Fiume
Adriatic Sea

INDEX

ABOUT THE AUTHOR

Attila Seres is the deputy director of the Hungarian Cultural, Scientific and Information Center in Moscow. He received his PhD in 2006 from Eötvös Loránd University in Budapest. Before taking his post in Russia, he was research associate at the Institute of History of the Hungarian Academy of Sciences from 2003 to 2011. He is the author of a monograph and of numerous articles on Hungarian-Russian and Hungarian-Romanian relations.

BOOKS PUBLISHED BY THE CENTER FOR HUNGARIAN STUDIES AND PUBLICATIONS

CHSP Hungarian Authors Series:

No. 1. *False Tsars*. Gyula Szvák. 2000.

No. 2. *Book of the Sun*. Marcell Jankovics. 2001.

No. 3. *The Dismantling of Historic Hungary: The Peace Treaty of Trianon, 1920*. Ignác Romsics. 2002.

No. 4. *The Soviet and Hungarian Holocausts: A Comparative Essay*. Tamás Krausz. 2006.

No. 5. *The Place of Russia in Europe and Asia*. Edited by Gyula Szvák. 2010.

CHSP Hungarian Studies Series:

No. 1. *Emperor Francis Joseph, King of the Hungarians*. András Gerő. 2001.

No. 2. *Global Monetary Regime and National Central Banking. The Case of Hungary, 1921–1929*. György Péteri. 2002.

No. 3. *Hungarian-Italian Relations in the Shadow of Hitler's Germany, 1933–1940*. György Réti. 2003.

No. 4. *The War Crimes Trial of Hungarian Prime Minister László Bárdossy.* Pál Pritz. 2004.

No. 5. *Identity and the Urban Experience: Fin-de-Siècle Budapest.* Gábor Gyáni. 2004.

No. 6. *Picturing Austria-Hungary. The British Perception of the Habsburg Monarchy, 1865–1870.* Tibor Frank. 2005.

No. 7. *Anarchism in Hungary: Theory, History, Legacies.* András Bozóki and Miklós Sükösd. 2006.

No. 8. *Myth and Remembrance. The Dissolution of the Habsburg Empire in the Memoir Literature of the Austro-Hungarian Political Elite.* Gergely Romsics. 2006.

No. 9. *Imagined History. Chapters from Nineteenth and Twentieth Century Hungarian Symbolic Politics.* András Gerő. 2006.

No. 10. *Pál Teleki (1879–1941). A Biography.* Balázs Ablonczy. 2006.

No. 11. *The Hungarian Revolution of 1956. Myths and Realities.* László Eörsi. 2006.

No. 12. *The Jewish Criterion in Hungary.* András Gerő. 2007.

No. 13. *Remember Hungary 1956. Essays on the Hungarian Revolution and War of Independence in American Memory.* Tibor Glant. 2007.

No. 14. *Reflections on Twentieth Century Hungary: A Hungarian Magnate's View.* Baron Móric Kornfeld. 2007.

No. 15. *Ideas on Territorial Revision in Hungary 1920–1945.* Miklós Zeidler. 2007.

No. 16. *Hungarian Illusionism*. András Gerő. 2008.

No. 17. *Romanians in Historic Hungary*. Ambrus Miskolczy. 2008.

No. 18. *The Kingdom of Hungary and the Habsburg Monarchy in the Sixteenth Century*. Géza Pálffy. 2009.

No. 19. *A Possible and Desirable Pension System*. József Banyár and József Mészáros. 2009.

No. 20. *The Austro-Hungarian Monarchy Revisited*. Edited by András Gerő. 2009.

No. 21. *Public Space in Budapest. The History of Kossuth Square*. András Gerő. 2009.

No. 22. *The Council for Foreign Ministers and the Hungarian Peace Treaty*. Mihály Fülöp. 2010.

No. 23. *Neither Woman Nor Jew. The Confluence of Prejudices in the Monarchy at the Turn of the Century*. András Gerő. 2010.

No. 24. *Social History of Fine Art in Hungary, 1867–1918*. Erika Szívós. 2011.

No. 25. *Risky Region: Memoirs of a Hungarian Righteous Gentile*. Eugene De Thassy. 2012.

No. 26. *Essays on World War I*. Edited by Peter Pastor and Graydon A. Tunstall. 2012.

No. 27. *Hungarian-Soviet Economic Relations, 1920–1941*. Attila Seres. 2012.